With be[illegible] regards,

Richard

WORLD INDUSTRY STUDIES 8

Microelectronics

An Industry in Transition

WORLD INDUSTRY STUDIES

Edited by Professor Ingo Walter,
Graduate School of Business Administration,
New York University

1 COLLAPSE AND SURVIVAL: INDUSTRY STRATEGIES IN A CHANGING WORLD
Robert H. Ballance and Stuart W. Sinclair

2 THE GLOBAL TEXTILE INDUSTRY
Brian Toyne, Jeffrey S. Arpan, Andy H. Barnett, David A. Ricks and Terence A. Shimp

3 BLUE GOLD: THE POLITICAL ECONOMY OF NATURAL GAS
J. D. Davis

4 POLITICS VS ECONOMICS IN WORLD STEEL TRADE
Kent Jones

5 ELECTRONICS AND INDUSTRIAL POLICY
The case of computer controlled lathes
Staffan Jacobsson

6 THE WORLD MINING INDUSTRY
Investment strategy and public policy
Raymond F. Mikesell and John W. Whitney

7 THE GLOBAL CONSTRUCTION INDUSTRY
Edited by W. Paul Strassmann and Jill Wells

8 MICROELECTRONICS
An Industry in Transition
Richard N. Langlois, Thomas A. Pugel, Carmela S. Haklisch, Richard R. Nelson, and William G. Egelhoff

Microelectronics

An Industry in Transition

Richard N. Langlois, Thomas A. Pugel,
Carmela S. Haklisch, Richard R. Nelson, and
William G. Egelhoff

Foreword by Pierre Aigrain

CENTER FOR SCIENCE AND TECHNOLOGY POLICY,
RENSSELAER POLYTECHNIC INSTITUTE, NEW YORK

Boston
UNWIN HYMAN
London Sydney Wellington

Unwin Hyman Inc.
8 Winchester Place, Winchester, Mass. 01890, USA

Published by the Academic Division of
Unwin Hyman Ltd
15/17 Broadwick Street, London W1V 1FP, UK

Allen & Unwin (Australia) Ltd,
8 Napier Street, North Sydney, NSW 2060, Australia

Allen & Unwin (New Zealand) Ltd in association with the
Port Nicholson Press Ltd,
60 Cambridge Terrace, Wellington, New Zealand

First published in 1988

Library of Congress Cataloging in Publication Data

Microelectronics: an industry in transition /
Richard N. Langlois . . . [et al].
p. cm.
Bibliography: p.
Includes index.
ISBN 0-04-338119-7
1. Microelectronics industry. 2. International trade.
3. Competition, International.
I. Langlois, Richard N.
HD9696.A2M48 1988 88-15685
338.4'76213817--dc19 CIP

British Library Cataloguing in Publication Data

Langlois, Richard N.
Microelectronics: an industry in transition.
— (World industry series).
1. Microelectronics industries
I. Title II. Series
338.4'76213817
ISBN 0-04-338119-7

Disk manipulation and typesetting in 10 on 11 point Times
by Computape (Pickering) Ltd, North Yorkshire
and printed in Great Britain by
Billing and Sons, London and Worcester

Contents

Foreword

Pierre Aigrain

This book fills an important gap in our understanding of the semiconductor industry. No previous study is in any way comparable in its thoroughness. Numerous partial studies are, of course, available, and no doubt they can be useful to specific fields; but it was clearly necessary to have in a single volume a discussion of what the semiconductor industry is; what its peculiarities are; and what its evolution has been over the relatively short time (one generation) since it first appeared.

The picture that emerges from this study is one of an industry that is in many ways unique. First of all, the semiconductor industry is perceived by many companies and governments as a strategic industry – and this is certainly true to a large extent. Its products are components used by an increasing number of other industrial sectors, not only in the field of information and telecommunications but also in everything from automobiles to toys. As a result, everyone keeps asking the same question: can we be fully dependent on some distant, possibly unreliable, producer? Might not some government action in another country cut this essential lifeline for one reason or another? This sense of the strategic importance of the semiconductor industry is heightened by the fact that the industry applies technologies that are in many ways the most advanced of any sector. The industry fabricates devices with the complexity of a million-transistor structure. Its components require a dimensional accuracy where critical lines are in the submicron range and where multiple levels have to be piled up with an accuracy that is only a small fraction of the already tiny line size. All this cannot but suggest that these technologies may some day become essential for things other than semiconductors.

On the one hand, this strategic worry has often led to the survival of operations that would not otherwise be profitable – operations supported as a kind of insurance with money from other parts of the company or from the government. On the other hand, there remains strong economic pressure for concentration of operations in fewer producing units. These two imperatives obviously work in opposite directions. Where does this pressure for concentration come from? Besides the usual advantages of economies of scale, the semiconductor industry partakes of a very specific phenomenon – excellently described in this book – called the learning curve. At the risk of stealing the thunder of the authors, let me describe this effect briefly. Maintaining a high production yield in such a difficult technology requires that everybody on the production line – not just the research engineers – constantly accumulate an enormous amount of experience. This accumulation of experience is related to production: the greater the quantity you produce of a given component, the higher the production yield, the lower the cost, and the more competitive you are. The history of the semiconductor industry is to a large extent the history of a constant battle between these two phenomena – between the strategic value of semiconductor production and the learning curve.

Of course, several other factors also come into play. Let me name just two. The semiconductor industry is probably the only industrial sector that is both capital intensive and R&D intensive. Smokestack industries are well known to be capital intensive, but they spend little on R&D. Pharmaceutical industries are R&D intensive, but their capital requirements are moderate compared with the added value of the product. The semiconductor industry is becoming more capital intensive every day. Consider, for example, the increasing cost of testing-machines, which have a hard time keeping up with the increasing performance levels of the components they have to test. And when the density and performance of components double every few years, an enormous amount of research money has to be constantly poured into R&D.

In addition, there is the well-known problem of business cycles. Every four or five years or so there is a recession in the semiconductor market. There are mild recessions – a simple slowdown in the growth rate – but these are sufficient to cause serious excess production capacity. There are also deep recessions like the one in 1985, when growth not merely slowed but actually turned negative. These cycles have to do, of course, with the stocking–destocking phenomenon, which tends to amplify any fluctuation in the business of the user industries. Indeed, semiconductor components have a long shelf-life – practically indefinite in comparison with the rate of obsolescence. Furthermore, semiconductors are cheap not only because of competition among producers but because they typically account for only a small part of the cost of the finished product. Economists have long recognized that such a situation must inevitably lead to the kind of relaxation oscillations observed in the semiconductor industry. Mortality is high among semiconductor firms during these recessions, and it would be higher still were it not for the support of governments or other company divisions.

It may be that, as technology becomes more and more important in various aspects of industrial life, other sectors may eventually acquire some of the traits of the semiconductor industry. (It isn't obvious any industry would want to take on these characteristics, but they may have to do so.) By reading this book now, these sectors can learn a lot about their present role as users of semiconductor products – and probably also something about their future.

Acknowledgements

This report is an overall summary of a program on "Microelectronics: An Industry in Transition" undertaken by the Center for Science and Technology Policy under the direction of Herbert I. Fusfeld. The program was supported in part by the Center's Corporate Membership Fund and by grants from the National Science Foundation, the North American Philips Corporation, and IBM. We are grateful for the support and encouragement of these organizations.

This report is the work of several people. Richard N. Langlois had overall editing and management responsiblity. He contributed to and edited all the chapters, and is sole author of Chapters 1 and 8. He would like to thank Herbert Fusfeld, Lois Peters, and Polly Allen for helpful comments. Thomas A. Pugel contributed much of the background material on the semiconductor industry as well as material on corporate strategy. His contributions appear in Chapters 2, 3, 4, 5, and 6. Carmela S. Haklisch contributed the material on international interfirm agreements in Chapter 5 and on cooperative research arrangements in Chapter 7. William G. Egelhoff contributed the comparison between American and Japanese corporate strategies in Chapter 6. Richard R. Nelson contributed the analysis of public policies in Chapter 7 and lent overall intellectual guidance to the project. William H. McNeill of GTE contributed technical material to Chapter 2, and Pierre Pouletty provided research assistance for Chapters 5 and 7.

The authors would like to thank Dr. Lee L. Davenport and the other members of the Center's Advisory Board for help and advice along the way. The views in this study remain those of the authors, however, and are not necessarily those of the Center's Advisory Board or sponsors. The authors would also like to thank William J. McClean of the Integrated Circuit Engineering Corporation for permission to reprint data from his company's *Status* reports.

List of Contributors

Pierre Aigrain is currently Scientific Advisor to the President of the Thomson Group and has been active in developing the ESPRIT program.

William G. Egelhoff is Visiting Research Professor at the Center for Science and Technology Policy, School of Management, Rensselaer Polytechnic Institute.

Carmela S. Haklisch is Senior Policy Research Analyst at the Center for Science and Technology Policy, School of Management, Rensselaer Polytechnic Institute.

Richard N. Langlois is Associate Professor of Economics at the University of Connecticut, Storrs.

Richard R. Nelson is Henry Luce Professor in the School of International and Public Affairs, Columbia University.

Thomas A. Pugel is Associate Professor of Economics and International Business in the Graduate School of Business Administration, New York University.

Microelectronics

An Industry in Transition

1

Introduction and Executive Summary

By the late 1970s, it was clear that fundamental forces were changing the worldwide semiconductor industry. The strong American technical base in this field, nourished first by defense procurement and later by an expanding computer industry, had given the United States market leadership in a wide range of electronics products and systems for consumers, for industry, and, not incidentally, for defense. It was thus both surprising and somewhat shocking – however naive that seems today – to realize that most common consumer electronics products were being supplied in great part by Japan, that innovations in many new products were being introduced by Japan (e.g., the ubiquitous Walkman), and that Japanese companies were moving rapidly into advanced semiconductor components.

The market penetration of Japanese firms was disturbing enough to the established industry and to the trade balance in high-technology products. Potentially more serious for long-term economic growth and for national security was the apparent threat to the American capacity to generate continuing advances in microelectronics – advances critical to industrial strength and military systems. Not surprisingly, these disturbing trends called forth a flurry of policy proposals. The proposals varied in sophistication and intentions; but most if not all of them were united in seeing the problem as a battle between a well-defined Japanese industry and a well-defined American industry competing in international trade.

The Center for Science and Technology Policy became interested in these issues by the early 1980s. The first step was to come to some understanding of the shape of the American industry and the nature of the problems it faced. In 1981, a visiting fellow from Philips, Nico Hazewindus, completed a background study of the American microelectronics industry (Hazewindus, 1982). In 1983, the Center devoted a spring-semester seminar series to the topic of microelectronics, calling on speakers from industry, government, and academe. Both of these experiences convinced us that something had been missing from the policy debate. It became increasingly clear as we studied the industry that understanding the nature and role of interdependence among semiconductor firms – especially the international aspects of that interdependence – would be an essential prerequisite to intelligent discussion of the microelectronics industry. With this in mind, the Center set out in 1984 to document and analyze the growing internationalization of the industry.

Two products of this effort have already emerged. Haklisch (1986) looks at the evolution of technical alliances in the industry, while Egelhoff (1986) provides a careful and original study of corporate strategy in American, Japanese, and European firms, with some emphasis on the strategic rationale for technical alliances and other co-operative arrangements.

As this report goes to press, the worldwide microelectronics industry is even more in the headlines than usual. In the United States, long-simmering worries about the competitiveness of the American semiconductor industry have suddenly come to the boil. Congress is writing trade legislation inspired by and aimed at microelectronics, and the Executive Branch has chimed in its sympathies, along with its disapproval of the proposed Japanese acquisition of an American-grown merchant semiconductor firm. At the same time, bookshelves are becoming weighted down with studies trumpeting the demise of American technological leadership – and sometimes the American semiconductor industry *tout court* – and calling for swift action of various sorts. The Defense Science Board, in concert with the Semiconductor Industry Association (SIA), has led the way, calling for a massive federal program of co-operative research and the formation of a co-operative manufacturing facility aimed at boosting American capabilities in process technology.

A time of ferment is seldom a time for thought; but it is usually a time when clear-headed reasoning is most needed. It is in the latter spirit that we offer this report. This is not a pronouncement of doom. It is not even a book of specific recommendations. Rather, it is an attempt to step back and survey some controversial issues from a relatively detached perspective.

The present study is the culmination not only of this examination of interdependence and internationalization; it is also in many ways the culmination of the Center's research in microelectronics over the past seven or so years. It attempts not only to integrate a number of previous Center studies but also to provide a detailed look at the worldwide microelectronics industry in all its aspects – technological, economic, strategic, and institutional. The study goes beyond organizing and presenting the facts: it also provides some new perpectives, opinions, and analyses that we hope will be useful in today's policy debate. If this report does nothing else, it should convince its readers that the model of a battle between distinct and well-defined "national" industries is an inappropriately unsophisticated one in the case of microelectronics. Although interdependence was our focus, we found it impossible not to stray into the issue of international competitiveness. Indeed, we would maintain that it is impossible to come to terms with competitiveness without first recognizing and appreciating the international interrelatedness of the industry. Along the way, we also developed some additional perspectives on the issue of competitiveness.

The policy recommendations in this report are broad and largely cautionary ones. The future of the microelectronics industry is uncertain, far more uncertain than many of the participants in today's debates pretend. Our goal here is to warn the reader that, as Chapter 7 puts it, there are rocks in the path ahead – rocks not only for the industry but for policymakers as well. Many of the proposals floating about today, not to mention many of the programs around the world already in place, have not been terribly well thought out. Many are based on more-or-less naive versions of the "Japanese model," attempts to emulate in some fashion the structures and policies that have made Japanese firms so successful. But the lessons of Japan are complex ones and the crucial differences in the American (or European) context introduce hurdles to making use of lessons correctly taken.

Our goal, then, is not to take on particular proposals, although we do offer some more-or-less specific comments at times. Rather, we see a need for broadening the context of debate, for offering new ideas to ponder. In short, we hope this report comes to be viewed as the thinking person's book on microelectronics.

This report has three main objectives:

(1) To present a comprehensive picture of the worldwide microelectronics industry – technology, economic structure, international trade, co-operative agreements, corporate strategy, and government policy.
(2) To document and analyze the growing interdependence within and internationalization of this industry.
(3) To offer a reasoned appraisal of the major factors affecting international competitiveness in microelectronics.

Beyond this, we hope the book will be useful in other ways. In addition to analysis, we also provide data about the industry – some, especially in the area of technical agreements, not available elsewhere. Indeed, the report can be approached on several levels. Here is a brief reader's guide.

The first few chapters concentrate on painting a picture of the industry. Chapter 2 discusses the technology of semiconductors; such a discussion is useful for understanding what goes on in this technology-driven industry, but the chapter may profitably be skipped or skimmed by the technically knowledgeable. Chapters 3 and 4 provide information about the economic structure and international trade pattern of the industry. These chapters may serve as a general resource as well as a background education. Readers should note, however, that any attempt to chart patterns and trends in the semiconductor industry is hampered by the lack of a single comprehensive set of data. There are also serious problems of definition. Some data refer to all semiconductors, while others include only integrated circuits. Some data include only market sales, while others attempt to include nonmarketed semiconductor production, both that used in-house by vertically integrated merchant firms and that of the purely captive producers such as IBM. Also, national data must be defined carefully with respect to the activities of foreign subsidiaries of multinational semiconductor firms. For instance, many American-based firms have European subsidiaries producing semiconductors and operate offshore assembly subsidiaries in developing countries. At the same time, several European firms have acquired American firms, but the operations of these subsidiaries remain sufficiently independent that they might still be considered American. Because of these and other problems of definition, government sources of data on semiconductors are less useful than in most other manufacturing industries. A number of private sources of data exist, but these estimates often are somewhat conflicting.

In the face of such difficulties, this report attempts to present authoritative data, and to define the limits of the data as carefully as possible. We believe the patterns and trends identified to be accurate, although individual pieces of data are often estimates undoubtedly subject to some error. A final caveat is that comparisons across countries usually require translation of data measured in national currencies into a common currency unit using exchange rates, and these exchange rates may not, at any point in time, represent long-run equilibrium values.

Readers interested specifically in the theme of international interdependence can turn to Chapter 5 for the details. The implications of this interdependence are spun out, in various ways, in Chapters 6, 7, and 8.

Chapter 6 is a treatise on corporate strategy in the microelectronics industry. It provides theoretical spectacles for looking at strategy in the industry. And it presents a careful – and somewhat novel – comparison of American and Japanese strategy.

Chapter 7 surveys contemporary government policies towards microelectronics, with a detailed look at the newest in policy wrinkles: government-sponsored co-operative-research arrangements. Chapter 7 also meditates on the problems of government policy for microelectronics and points out some of the difficulties of current proposals.

Chapter 8 attempts to summarize what went before and to offer some overall conclusions and perspectives. It is intended in part to be a stand-alone representative of the whole report.

Executive summary

The principal conclusions of the report revolve around two themes – interdependence and competition.

- Technological interdependence among firms in the microelectronics industry is a worldwide phenomenon of considerable, and growing, importance.
- This interdependence takes many forms: foreign direct investment; acquisitions; joint ventures; licensing and cross-licensing; and co-operative research.
- The flows of technology in this system are increasingly bidirectional; for the most part, firms in the USA, Japan, and Europe are exchanging capabilities of comparable sophistication.
- This bi-directionality signals a considerable degree of convergence among the three regions in their levels of technical sophistication in microelectronics. Europe and, especially, Japan have joined the United States at the technological frontier.
- The international interdependence of the microelectronics industry creates serious difficulties for policies attempting to aid national or regional firms. It even begins to blur the very concept of the nationality of a firm.
- This problem is particularly acute where interests of national defense overlap with those of international competitiveness. The desire for national autarky in microelectronics technology

is at odds not only with the fact of international interdependence but often also with the imperatives of international competitiveness.

- International interdependence also calls into question the value of government-sponsored research consortia as prime engines of national or regional competitiveness. Although these arrangements may prove valuable for many reasons, they are vulnerable as competitive weapons to the extent that the advantages they create inevitably diffuse to competitors through the web of international connection.
- Another implication of internationalization is the tendency for market structures, corporate strategies, government policies, and social institutions to converge and grow similar along some dimensions. This trend is by no means complete, however, and many of the differences in structure, strategy, and policy in the three regions can be explained by the different historical paths the industries in those regions took to achieve the technological frontier.
- It is thus crucial to distinguish features of a region's industry that are (or were) adapted to *achieving* the technological frontier from those features adapted to prospering *at* the frontier. In particular, the many policy proposals in the United States that implicitly seek to imitate the "Japanese model" may be emulating policies and structures Japan is increasingly abandoning now that its firms have achieved the frontier.
- The American microelectronics industry remains the most diverse in the size, level of integration, and strategic orientation of its firms. In general, the strengths of American firms lie in product development, innovativeness, and customer orientation. As a rule, these firms compete by attempting to find unique product or market advantages – to find strategies better than those of competitors.
- The Japanese microelectronics industry is dominated by about ten large, vertically integrated systems firms with fundamentally similar strategic orientations. The strengths of Japanese firms lie in process technology and low-cost manufacture of more-or-less standardized products. As a rule, Japanese firms compete not by seeking superior strategies but by trying to implement a common strategy more successfully than competitors.
- The competitive battle between the US and Japan thus shapes up as a tussle between firms with fundamentally different attitudes toward competition. Each side sees the other as "not playing by the rules."

- Like the Japanese, the European microelectronics industry is dominated by large, vertically integrated systems firms. But, like the American, it is more oriented to product than to process. The relative lack of success of the European industry may signal the worst of both worlds: a lack of Japanese manufacturing capability not balanced by American-style innovativeness in product development. The structure of European industry may, however, leave it in a good position to imitate the Japanese approach if it can.
- The acute problems of competitiveness that have now reached a boiling point in the United States are partly traceable to macroeconomic causes, principally the strength of the dollar through mid-1985. This in turn is partly the fault of the American budget deficit and of the defense spending that is largely responsible for that deficit.
- There remain, however, serious questions about American competitiveness at the microeconomic level. Whether the American industry can succeed in the future will depend on the shape the market takes and the ability of American firms as a whole to adapt to whatever market develops.
- The structure of the Japanese industry is adapted to relatively "mature" markets in which high-volume, low-cost production of standardized devices is important. If the market evolves more in this direction, American industry will have serious problems keeping up.
- If, however, the market evolves in new directions or in directions favoring product innovation over low-cost production (perhaps because of the increased importance of application-specific integrated circuits), American industry may actually be at an advantage.
- It is important to recognize that the shape of the future is partly endogenous – it depends on the choices we make today. Policies that attempt to remake American industry in the perceived image of Japan may have the effect of bringing about precisely the kind of market in which the Japanese will have the advantage. By contrast, policies that seek to build on the existing strengths of American industry may help create a climate more favorable to American firms.

2

Interdependence: The Technological Dimension

A semiconductor, as the name implies, is a material whose properties of electrical conduction lie somewhere between those of a metal and those of an insulator. Devices using such materials – semiconductor devices – are able to amplify or switch electronic signals. It is this marvelous ability that has given rise to modern microelectronics technology.

In order to understand the structure and evolution of the microelectronics industry, we need to look more closely at that underlying technology. This chapter takes on the task. It recounts briefly the history of semiconductor technology, surveys the present-day technological landscape, and discusses the directions that microelectronics technology may take in the near future. This chapter also tries to suggest how technology helps shape the structure of interdependence in the industry and how trends in technology are likely to affect that structure.

We do not intend here to present a complete technical treatise on semiconductors. However, emerging strategies in the microelectronics industry are often driven in significant part by the structure of technology and by the pattern of technical change. This chapter tries to present enough background on the relevant technologies to enable the non-expert reader to appreciate their impact on the economics, strategy, and organization of the semiconductor industry.

The Origins of Microelectronics Technology

Although several discoveries before World War II incorporated semiconductor technology, the event that effectively launched the modern semiconductor industry was the fabrication of the first successful transistor at Bell Laboratories in 1948.[1]

In essence, a transistor is a device in which one current controls another. As a result, one can use transistors to amplify a signal or to switch signals. (This is in contrast to the other major type of semiconductor device – the diode – whose function is to rectify current, that is, to allow it to pass in only one direction.) A device that amplifies current is called a linear device because its output is more or less proportional to its input. A device that switches signals is called a digital device; rather than smoothly amplifying a signal, a digital device turns the flow of current on or off in response to a signal. Because of this all-or-nothing – one or zero – quality, digital devices are able to perform logical operations within a computer.

The transistor's ability to control current comes from the peculiar properties of semiconductors. Unlike conductors, semiconductors possess no natural free charges; but, unlike insulators, they can produce such charges with an application of a current. One way to create a semiconducting material is to "dope" a poorly conducting material by carefully introducing impurities. This doping can take two forms: negative doping, which results in a surfeit of electrons; and positive doping, which produces a deficit of electrons (or an excess of "holes"). The former results in an n-type semiconductor; the latter in a p-type. The transistor effect – the ability to amplify a signal – requires both kinds of semiconductor materials.

William Shockley, one of the three principal inventors of the device, had been working since the 1930s on a design for what is now called a field-effect transistor (FET). In attempting to understand why Shockley's prototype failed, his colleagues Walter H. Brattain and John Bardeen accidentally produced the first working transistor – a so-called point-contact design. Their work led Shockley to design a third type of transistor – the "junction" or "bipolar" transistor – which was to become the dominant design of the early years of the semiconductor era.

A bipolar transistor works by layering together p-type and n-type material to create either a pnp or an npn sandwich. (See Figure 1.) A current applied to the center region controls the flow of current through the sandwich. In an FET, by contrast, there is no physical connection between the opposite-polarity regions. A "gate" of one material (p-type, let us say) sits above the path of a current flowing between two regions of the other type (n-type, in this case); a current applied to the gate creates an electric field that controls the

[1] For a comprehensive account of the history of innovation in the semiconductor industry, see Braun and Macdonald (1978).

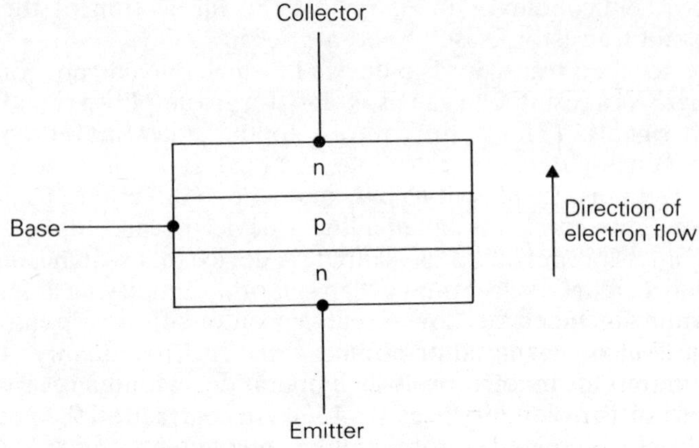

Figure 1 *Structure of a Bipolar Transistor*

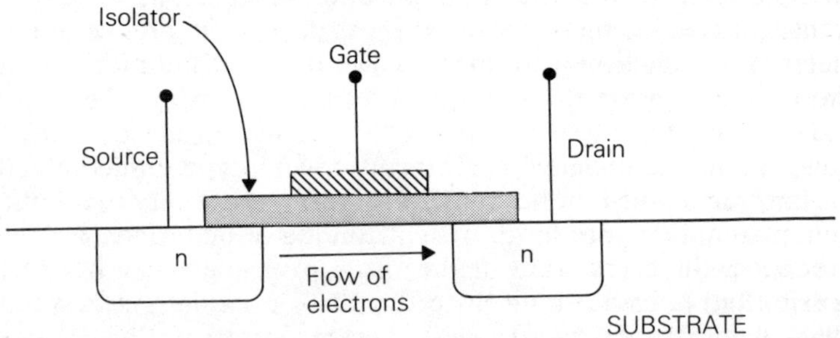

Figure 2 *Structure of a Field-effect Transistor*

flow beneath. (See Figure 2.) The most common type of FET is called a metal-oxide semiconductor (MOS) device.

By 1951, American Telephone and Telegraph Company (AT&T), owner of Bell Laboratories, was producing junction transistors through its Western Electric subsidiary. Shockley had produced a working version of the FET transistor by that time, but bipolar transistors held the early economic advantage. The base material for these first transistors was germanium. In 1954 Texas Instruments introduced the silicon transistor, which has noise, temperature, and frequency-range characteristics superior to those of germanium. Production of silicon transistors overtook that of germanium ones by the mid 1960s.

Throughout the 1950s, however, the most important innovations were process innovations, especially in the areas of materials purification, crystal growth and doping techniques. The principal

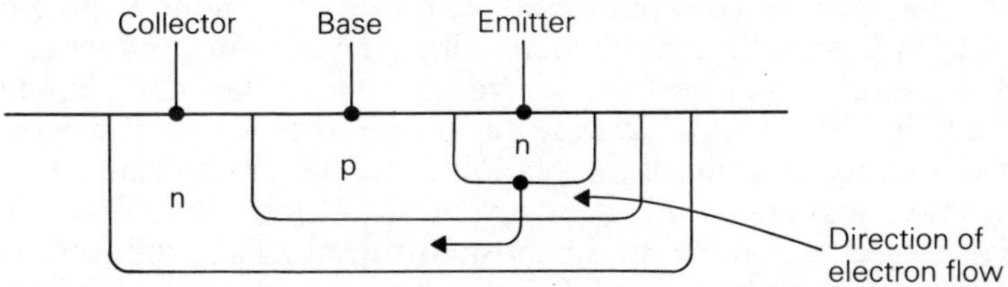

Figure 3 *Structure of a Planar Transistor*

innovators included Bell Labs, several established electronics firms such as Philco, and new entrants like Texas Instruments. One of the most important innovations was Fairchild Semiconductor's development of the planar process in 1958. In the planar process, the "sandwich" is created on a single layer or substrate. (See Figure 3.) One selectively dopes the substrate by diffusing impurities in gaseous form into some regions while masking other areas. A transistor created by this method is essentially flat, and its internal electrical connections can be made cheaply by techniques similar to those used in doping.

The semiconductors produced during the 1950s were what are now called discrete devices. That is, each transistor has its own package and must be connected to other transistors and components on a circuit board. The planar process not only made the production of discrete devices less expensive, it also opened up the possibility of fabricating entire circuits on a single substrate. In 1958–9, researchers at Texas Instruments and Fairchild independently but simultaneously achieved just such a breakthrough – the monolithic integrated circuit (IC). This development brought to a close the era of discrete devices and opened up the modern era of integrated circuits.[2]

The monolithic IC is a single semiconductor, often called a "chip," containing more than one element, that is, more than one area functioning as a transistor or diode. The first ICs were bipolar, but the MOS IC followed quickly in 1962. The MOS ICs are of several types: NMOS, in which current flows through channels having a predominantly negative charge; PMOS, in which the channels have a predominantly positive charge; and CMOS, or complementary MOS, combining n-channel and p-channel transistors on a single chip. In

[2] Although discrete semiconductors are generally a mature technology, advances continue to be made in certain areas of the technology. Light-emitting diodes (LED) achieved a rapid growth rate of sales in the late 1970s, and transistors with specialized uses, such as high-power applications, are another area of continued technological and sales advances.

general, MOS technology permits lower power consumption, greater density in the packing of elements, higher yields in production – and therefore lower cost per active element – than does bipolar technology. Bipolar ICs have the advantage in processing speed.[3]

The density or scale of integration of ICs has risen dramatically and rather regularly since their invention. In fact, the number of active elements per chip in the most advanced chips produced has approximately doubled each year since then.[4] The density of circuitry on a chip is generally described by the "scale" of integration that chip represents. Small-scale integration (SSI) refers to ICs with fewer than 100 active elements. Medium-scale integration (MSI) refers to ICs with between 100 and 999 active elements. Large-scale integration (LSI) refers to ICs with between 1000 and 99,999 elements or the equivalent in memory capacity. Very large-scale integration (VLSI) refers to ICs with between 100,000 and 999,999 active elements or the equivalent in memory capacity. Integrated circuits with one million or more active elements will receive another designation, probably ultra-large-scale integration (USLI). As shares of the value of the worldwide merchant IC market in 1984, SSI accounted for 5 per cent, MSI for 21 per cent, LSI for 36 per cent, and VLSI for 38 per cent, according to the Integrated Circuit Engineering Corporation (1985).

Bipolar logic technology evolved rather rapidly after 1960. In 1964, Sylvania developed transistor-transistor logic (TTL). Texas Instruments' family of bipolar TTL came to dominate the computer market, based in part on that company's emphasis on increasing complexity. In 1970, Texas Instruments developed Schottky TTL, offering faster switching speeds, in response to competition from emitter-couple logic (ECL). In 1973, Texas Instruments introduced low-power Schottky TTL in response to competition from the evolving MOS technology. Recent advances include Fairchild Advanced Schottky TTL (FAST), promoted by Fairchild and Signetics, and advanced low-power Schottky and advanced Schottky (ALS/AS), promoted by Texas Instruments and National Semiconductor.

Major MOS innovations include PMOS by Fairchild in 1962; NMOS by RCA, KMC, Siliconix, and TRW in 1963, and CMOS by RCA in 1969. Innovations to enhance the speed of CMOS and lower production costs began to appear in the late 1970s and continue.

The two major MOS product areas are microprocessors and

[3] Such comparisons are generalizations, and these characteristics can vary according to the particular configurations compared.

[4] This phenomenon is often called Moore's law after Gordon Moore of Intel. See Moore (1979).

Dynamic Random-Access Memories (DRAMs). A microprocessor is a logic circuit that includes most or all of the central processing functions of a computer on a single chip. One important feature of a microprocessor is the number of pieces – or "bits" – of information it can process at a time. Intel introduced the 4-bit microprocessor in 1971 and the 8-bit microprocessor in 1972. General Instruments introduced the 16-bit microprocessor in 1974. The 32-bit microprocessor appeared in the early 1980s, and a large number of firms have introduced or are preparing versions of this product.

A DRAM is a particular kind of memory circuit. (In contrast to a static RAM, a DRAM requires that stored data be continually refreshed.) The storage capacity of a memory device is measured in thousand-bit units called kilobits (or "K"). Intel and Advanced Memory Systems introduced the 1K DRAM late in 1970, and the Intel design became the market standard. Four American firms began production of the 4K DRAM late in 1973, including Intel, Texas Instruments, and Mostek. The Mostek design became the industry standard. The 16K DRAM appeared in 1976, with Intel, Mostek, and Texas Instruments again leading the entry. Fujitsu was the first to the commercial market with a 64K DRAM in 1978, although IBM was apparently already producing this product for in-house use by that time. The Fujitsu design was not accepted by the market, however; instead, a number of producers achieved large volumes with somewhat different designs. It does not seem possible any longer to identify an unofficial industry standard for this product. Indeed, a large number of firms are expected to offer distinctive designs of the 256K DRAM.

Microelectronics: The Production Process

The production process for semiconductors, especially for ICs, is often described as one of the most complicated high-volume processes in all industry. In addition to the manufacture of the crystalline wafers that are the raw material for semiconductors, there are four basic stages of IC production: the design and generation of photomasks, wafer fabrication, assembly and final testing. Within each stage various techniques may be used, depending in part on the device produced. The description of the process that follows is based upon a typical method of manufacturing silicon MOS ICs.[5]

The division of semiconductor production into four stages is

[5] This description draws upon Webbink (1977), U. S. Department of Commerce (1979), and Office of Technology Assessment (1983).

important because each stage can be – and usually is – physically divorced from the others without any significant increase in total costs. Indeed, one or more of the stages can be subcontracted out.

The manufacture of the raw silicon wafer begins with the growth of a crystal of high-purity silicon. The crystal is then ground to a uniform diameter and sawed into thin slices. Each slice – a silicon wafer – is polished and cleaned. The economies of scale in producing silicon wafers are great enough that most American semiconductor companies purchase their wafers from chemical companies such as Monsanto and Wacker. Only the largest American semiconductor companies are integrated backward to produce some of their own wafers.

Once the raw wafers are in hand, the first stage of the production of the ICS is the design and generation of photomasks. The initial design work is often thought of as part of the R&D function, and it often takes places at special "design centers" geographically distant from the main production facilities.

The output of this stage is a set of patterns containing the device design. Each pattern begins as a master drawing, frequently generated by computer-controlled equipment. Special cameras are used to reduce this pattern to an image on a glass plate less than one-hundredth its original size. A master photomask is then produced. Lines on these patterns are extremely thin, and defects in pattern definition are a major cause of chip failure. But measurement of these errors is not practical with currently available instruments, so manufacturers usually adopt a trial-and-error approach.

The second stage of the production process – wafer fabrication – involves a series of steps. The wafer is heated, and an additional layer of silicon is grown on to the wafer. This new layer is impregnated with a carefully controlled amount of an impurity, called a dopant, that gives the wafer its electrical properties. The semiconductor devices are formed in this layer. The wafer is then heated in another furnace and exposed to oxygen to form a layer of silicon dioxide, an electrical insulator. A thin layer of photoresist, a light-sensitive chemical, is spread over the wafer. Through lithographic processing techniques the photomask pattern is photographed onto the wafer. After the entire wafer has been processed, the unexposed part of the photoresist is dissolved.

The wafer is then etched in acid to remove the silicon dioxide not protected by the remaining exposed photoresist, which is then also removed. The wafer is heated, and a gaseous dopant (for instance, phosphorus) is allowed to diffuse into the silicon not protected by the remaining pattern of silicon dioxide.

The precision required in this lithographic process depends upon the line widths used in the production of the ICs. Line widths of 20 micrometers (or microns) were typical in the early 1970s. As integration scale has risen, line widths have been reduced to 2 to 4 micrometers in the early and mid-1980s. With advances in processing techniques, line widths can continue to fall until the ultimate limit of perhaps 0.01 to 0.1 micrometers is achieved. Such declines in line width will require processing techniques such as electron-beam lithography (already in limited use), X-ray lithography, or ion-beam lithography.

The steps to produce the pattern on the wafer are usually repeated two to seven times. A crucial requirement is that the pattern of the new photomask be aligned precisely with the pattern already on the wafer. Once the repetitions are completed, a thin coat of metal, often aluminum or gold, is evaporated over the wafer. The metal is then covered with a photoresist, exposed, and etched to form a pattern of electrically conducting material. This metal pattern is in effect the wiring network for the chip, providing surfaces for outside connections and, in ICs, internal connections among regions of the device.

Throughout the wafer-fabrication process, workers inspect the devices visually to eliminate wafers that are obviously defective. Often the wafer has a test area designed to permit such inspections. Once the metal contacts are in place, however, electrical testing becomes possible. This probe-testing is quick and highly automated, usually involving computer-controlled equipment. Defective devices are marked for disposal without further processing.

The final step in wafer fabrication is scribing the wafer into its individual chips, although this step may also be performed as part of the assembly stage.

The third production stage involves assembling the chips into usable packaged devices. Assembly involves mounting each chip on to a base and connecting the contacts on the chip to the external connections of the base using a fine metal wire, often gold. The assembled device is then sealed in a protective package, usually plastic but sometimes metal or ceramic. Workers also inspect visually at this stage and discard those devices with poor bonding.

The fourth production step is the final electrical testing of the semiconductor devices. The complexity of testing of ICs requires the use of computer-controlled equipment. Often devices are sorted by performance characteristics and sold accordingly.

No matter how carefully the production process is performed, some of the chips will prove to be defective. The ratio of usable chips to the maximum possible is called the yield. The yield is the most important factor in determining the unit manufacturing cost of the ICs that are marketable. It depends on many factors, including die size, number of mask steps, wafer size, feature size, materials purity and clean-air control; but "experience" in production is perhaps the single most important factor. A general rule used in the industry is that cumulative unit cost on average falls by about 30 per cent as cumulative production volume doubles, a relationship often called the "experience curve" or "learning curve." Thus, marginal cost is below unit cost. Firms often use "forward pricing" or "penetration pricing" – pricing below average cost – in order to build volume and market share and continue to achieve learning economies.

For new devices, yields are often below 10 per cent, mostly because of problems and low yields in the wafer-fabrication process. As manufacturers learn and acquire experience, they adopt better techniques and technology. Yields on mature devices are often 60 to 90 per cent. Learning economies do not generally arise from improvements in the skill wielded by production workers themselves; rather, yields are improved by engineers and technicians experimenting with such aspects of fabrication as temperatures, time, dopant concentrations, equipment, and scheduling. Yield improvements also result from modifications of devices by circuit designers.

A key feature of learning economies is that they are at best partially transferable among plants – even plants of the same company – and successful transfer usually requires technical assistance. Therefore, within a company, plants involved in wafer fabrication are often specialized by process or product. The learning associated with one type of fabrication is not readily transferable to another type, so there is no advantage to performing both operations in the same location. Because of learning advantages, however, there are usually few plants producing any one device. Significant learning economies or scale economies do not attach to the assembly phase, so multiple assembly sites are often used. Assembly has been the most labor-intensive of the production stages, motivating many companies to use assembly facilities in low-wage countries – so-called offshore assembly. The assembly stage is becoming increasingly automated, however, which will likely begin to militate against this practice. (See Chapter 4.)

Microelectronics: Technology and Technological Trends

Devices

As suggested earlier, there are two types of transistors used in modern semiconductor chips: bipolar (or junction) transistors and field-effect transistors (FETs), especially metal-oxide semiconductor (MOS) FETs. The former type dominated production in the early years of the integrated-circuit era, but the latter have now become dominant. In 1970, bipolar ICs accounted for 90 per cent of worldwide merchant IC sales.[6] In 1986, bipolar ICs had declined to 45 per cent of the market and MOS ICs had risen to 55 per cent. The Integrated Circuit Engineering Corporation (1987) forecasts a continuation of this trend to 1991, when, they predict, bipolar ICs will capture 32 per cent of the market and MOS ICs 68 per cent.[7] (The latter figure includes 2 per cent gallium arsenide (GaAs) ICs, which use a technology very similar to MOS. More on this shortly.)

In 1986, 51 per cent of the worldwide MOS IC market was NMOS; 2 per cent PMOS; 47 per cent CMOS; and less than 1 per cent GaAs. The Integrated Circuit Engineering Corporation (1987) predicts a continuing major shift toward CMOS ICs by 1991, with the shares being 18 per cent, less than 1 per cent, 79 per cent, and 3 per cent, respectively.

As the adjective "complementary" suggests, CMOS devices employ both positive and negative semiconductors on the same chip. This takes up considerable space on the chip and increases the number of process steps required. But the corresponding advantages include lower power consumption, greater ease in implementing both analog and digital functions on the same chip, and greater immunity or resistance to noise and radiation damage, properties of great concern in defense applications. Initially, CMOS ICs were slower in speed and higher in cost than NMOS ICs; but, beginning in the late 1970s, the gaps began to close, and they should soon decline to insignificance.

Bipolar transistors are capable of switching very large currents. They are also extremely fast in the right kind of circuit. These advantages are bought, however, at the expense of power consumption. It is this disadvantage that has led in large part to the

[6] "Merchant" sales refers to sales by semiconductor firms who sell their chips to others rather than producing principally for their own use. Merchant firms are distinguished from "captive" suppliers of semiconductors – like IBM or AT&T – who do produce semiconductors principally for internal use. See Chapter 3 below. Data are more difficult to obtain for captive suppliers, but these firms have also moved away from bipolar devices over the last decade.

[7] Unless otherwise noted, data cited in this section are from 1987 or earlier annual editions of this source.

decline of bipolar devices. But CMOS devices are constantly increasing in speed as miniaturization continues, and the power consumption of CMOS devices goes up as speed increases – thereby wiping out their principal advantage. This has led some analysts to suggest that bipolar transistors may make a comeback in the longer term, especially for high-speed circuits.

Product types

As suggested earlier, all ICs – whether bipolar or MOS – fall into one of two categories: linear or digital.

In 1986, bipolar linear ICs, used mainly in consumer-product applications, accounted for 53 per cent of the worldwide merchant bipolar IC market; digital bipolar ICs, used mainly for logic, accounted for 47 per cent. CMOS ICs are expected to offer increasing competition to bipolar linear ICs in consumer applications and to bipolar digital ICs in logic functions. In 1986, linear MOS ICs accounted for only about 2 per cent of the worldwide merchant MOS IC market, but many analysts believe this will increase to 4 or 5 per cent in 1990.

Digital ICs are of basically two types: logic chips and memory chips. Bipolar digital ICs are used mainly for logic circuitry; in 1986, logic ICs accounted for 86 per cent of the worldwide merchant market for digital bipolar ICs. By contrast, the principal uses for digital MOS ICs are memory and certain complex logic chips called microprocessors and microcontrollers. Memory ICs store digital data in an array of logic gates, with each location containing a bit of binary information. Microprocessors are digital logic circuits that can execute programs in the manner of a digital computer. Microcontrollers combine this processing unit with memory and input-output circuitry on a single chip. The term "microcomputer" can refer to a microcontroller or to a set of chips, including a microprocessor and various peripheral chips such as input-output and memory ICs, that together can perform useful work without additional supporting logic ICs.

Table 1 shows the sizes of the merchant markets for MOS memory ICs and for microprocessor and microcontroller ICs in 1984 with a forecast for 1991. MOS memory ICs accounted for about 28 per cent of the world merchant market for all ICs in 1984; this share is forecast to rise slightly to 29 per cent in 1991. Microprocessors, microcontrollers, and related peripherals accounted for 15 per cent of the world merchant IC market in 1984, a share forecast to remain unchanged in 1991.

New developments in IC technology frequently emerge first in memory products. Memory devices are highly regular in structure,

Table 1 *World Merchant Market, 1984 and 1991 Forecast: MOS Memory ICs and MOS Microprocessors and Microcontrollers*

Product		1984	1991
MOS Memory ICs			
Total (Millions of Dollars)		6,175	9,000
Of Which (Percentages):			
DRAM		51%	44%
SRAM		18	21
ROM		10	7
EPROM		18	21
EEPROM		2	6
Other		1	1
MOS Microprocessors and Microcontrollers			
Total (Millions of Dollars)		3,100	6,300
Of Which (Percentages):			
Microprocessors:	8-bit	14%	3%
	16-bit	10	11
	32-bit	0	6
Microcontrollers:	4-bit	6	2
	8-bit	13	25
	16-bit	1	12
Peripherals*		56	41

Notes: * Not including standard memory ICs.

Source: Integrated Circuit Engineering Corporation (1985, 1987).

consisting of rows and columns of identical transistors; and they are also a sizable market, accounting for about a third of the total IC market.

The basic structure of a memory chip is a grid of metal conductors, with the crosstown wires insulated from the uptown-downtown wires by a spacer. At each of the nodes is one or more transistors that store one bit of information – a "zero" or a "one." In one particular NMOS technology, each node consists of only a single transistor and a tiny capacitor. The presence or absence of a charge on the capacitor determines whether the cell is storing a "one" or a "zero."

In a random-access memory (RAM), every cell can be addressed separately in order to read the current contents or to write new contents. As Table 1 suggests, dynamic RAMs (or DRAMs) account for about half the merchant-market value of MOS memory ICs. What makes a DRAM "dynamic" is that the charge representing the data storage must be periodically refreshed. By contrast, the static RAM (SRAM) does not require refreshing.

Unlike the RAM, which can be continually altered, the read-only memory (ROM) permanently stores information used repeatedly.

Some ROMs – called mask-programmable ROMs – are programmed as part of fabrication by simply connecting or disconnecting certain transistors during one of the masking steps. Other kinds of ROMs can be programmed after fabrication. In an erasable-programmable ROM (EPROM), the contents of the device can be erased, usually through exposure to ultraviolet light, and new information then entered into the device. The electrically erasable PROM (EEPROM) allows selective erasure of its contents using a specific electrical stimulus. As shown in Table 1, each of these devices has a smaller share of the MOS memory market than do DRAMs, but the forecast calls for growth in the shares of SRAMs, EPROMs, and EEPROMs.

There are three primary qualities that engineers seek in a memory chip: density (the number of bits per chip), address-access time and power dissipation. To increase density, one has to simplify the electronic circuit at the nodes and to reduce the size of the devices there. Over time, the number of transistors in the cell has been reduced from six to one. It is here that DRAMs have the advantage. Using the one-transistor-one-capacitor cell described above lowers the number of devices per cell to a minimum, but, unlike the multi-transistor "latched-logic" circuits used in SRAMS, the capacitor circuits tend to lose their charge and require constant refreshing. To improve access times, the devices must be fewer and faster – which, once again, means smaller devices. Reducing size also reduces power dissipation because smaller devices call for lower voltages and currents. CMOS, with its low power consumption, is superior in this regard to NMOS as circuit density increases into the highest ranges. In 1984, only 14 per cent of MOS memory devices were CMOS, but CMOS will likely come to dominate by 1991.[8] The fastest memory devices use speedy but power-hungry bipolar transistors.

The density or complexity of RAMs is usually characterized by the number of bits that they can store. The largest DRAM currently offered in the merchant market is the one-megabit (1M) DRAM, which can hold over a million bits of information. The 1M DRAM accounted for about 8 per cent of the worldwide merchant DRAM market in 1984, but should become the largest part of this market by 1988. The 256K DRAM accounted for about 82 per cent of the market in 1986, and the 64K DRAM for most of the remaining 10 per cent. The four-megabit (4M) DRAM is now beginning to appear. In early 1987, IBM announced production of a 4M DRAM for in-house use. Some Japanese firms, notably Toshiba, are also beginning to

[8] The Integrated Circuit Engineering Corporation (1987) forecasts that by 1991 80 per cent of MOS memory devices will be CMOS.

sell prototype 4M chips.[9] A 16-megabit chip is currently in the wings.

The size and composition of the MOS microprocessor and microcontroller merchant market in 1984 and the forecast for 1991 are also shown in Table 1. In 1984 CMOS ICs accounted for 13 per cent of this market, a share forecast to rise to 66 per cent in 1991. Bipolar microprocessors accounted for only a small part of the market, about $200 million worth in 1984.

Microprocessors and microcontrollers can process several bits of information at a time. Each chunk of bits processed is called a "word," and its length (measured in bits) determines in part the complexity of operations the device can handle. In 8-bit microprocessors, the Intel 8088 – used by IBM among others – is the largest selling design, with designs by Zilog and Motorola also of some importance. In 16-bit microprocessors, the Intel 8086 design has 75 to 80 per cent of the market, with Motorola as the only other important design. One might also note that peripheral chips (not including standard memory ICs) account for slightly more than half of the total market.

Microcontrollers are used most often in applications to consumer products. The 4-bit microcontrollers are expected to decline in sales, as most new applications utilize 8-bit microcontrollers. NEC designs are important in both of these product areas.

The 16-bit microcontroller and the 32-bit microprocessor are relatively new products that will gain in share of the market over the next years. As the 32-bit microprocessor matches the data-processing capabilities of a mainframe computer, this may be the final stage of microprocessor evolution.

Trends in Materials

The overwhelming dominance of silicon as the base material for semiconductors is the result of two factors. Silicon has a number of very desirable properties that make it a natural choice for semiconductor devices. More importantly, perhaps, the early emergence of silicon as the material of choice has endowed the industry with an enormous store of experience with that material.

Silicon possesses a higher band-gap and higher thermal conductivity than its early competitor, germanium. This means that silicon can produce higher-power junction devices. Moreover, silicon is one of the most plentiful elements on earth. It forms its own oxide readily, a property that makes semiconductor processing significantly easier.

[9] David E. Sanger, "4-Megabit Chip Set by IBM," *The New York Times*, 26 February, 1987, p. D1.

In addition, silicon is now by far the best understood semiconductor material – understood in its intrinsic properties, in its use in a variety of electronic devices, in its interaction with other materials. This base of experience makes it extremely difficulty for other materials to make inroads – even when those would-be interlopers have properties superior to those of silicon along some dimensions.

The principal challenger to silicon today is gallium arsenide (GaAs). GaAs has a slightly larger band-gap than silicon, which tends to make it good for high-temperature operation. But the main benefit of GaAs is its higher speed. The principal disadvantage of GaAs is that it does not have its own native oxide and is therefore somewhat less tractable a material than silicon.

Because of the industry's superior command of silicon technology, manufacturers have usually been able so far to reduce the size of their silicon devices to remain competitive with the speed of available GaAs devices. This is unlikely to continue. In fact, some very fast GaAs chips have already shown performance superior to that of silicon. And GaAs processing will eventually improve as experience with that material accumulates – especially to the extent that GaAs processing can benefit from knowledge gained with silicon processing.

One area in which GaAs is already clearly superior is in its use as an optoelectronic material. GaAs has a so-called direct band-gap, which means that it can be used as the basis of a laser. (Silicon, by contrast, has an indirect band-gap, and therefore cannot be used as a laser.) A considerable number of GaAs lasers are in operation in applications such as fiber-optic communications. One intriguing possibility opened up by the optical properties of GaAs is the optoelectronic circuit, in which, for example, electronic driver circuits and laser diode light-sources might be combined on the same chip.

Silicon is likely to remain the dominant material for most of the electronic chip world for some time to come. For the time being, GaAs will occupy a small segment of the market, mainly in high-speed logic and memory and in optoelectronic interfaces. Because of the knowledge base in silicon, that material still has the edge in large complex circuits; outside the laboratory, GaAs is still limited to the level of small-scale integration.

Standardization and Customization

An increasingly important aspect of IC production is the extent to which an IC is specially designed for a single application, that is, whether the IC is "customized." There are a number of levels of customization, reflecting different techniques of IC design and fabrication. Which technique is best for a particular application will depend primarily on the level of performance required and the size of the production runs anticipated.

The production of a chip typically requires from ten to twenty-five layers of masks. Each region or element of the chip requires its own mask. Many intermediate masks might be needed to provide insulation, to expose the photoresists, and so on. As the chip reaches the final stages of processing, masks are also used to define the metallic interconnections that form the circuit. The degree of customization depends on the number of mask layers that are designed specifically for the application in question.

In a full-custom chip, the masks at all layers are designed specifically for that chip. As one might expect, this is a costly procedure. Turn-around time is long. Furthermore, one can get the best performance out of a custom chip only when the designers understand the peculiarities of silicon production technology – a facility comparatively rare in design engineers, who are trained to think in terms of design schematics not process technology. As a consequence, full customization is cost-effective when performance specifications demand the ultimate or when production volume will be large. In the latter case, the up-front costs of design can be recovered in reduced materials cost over the production run.

Clearly, then, a chip is most likely to be produced using techniques of full customization when that chip can serve many uses. Examples would include RAMs and general application microprocessors such as the Intel 8086. In a sense, such chips have become standard products – they are no longer "custom" ICs in the sense of having been designed for a specific application. In general, the term "custom IC" is reserved for an application-specific product, even when the techniques of its fabrication are the same as those for a standard product.[10]

For applications with less exacting standards or with smaller anticipated production volumes, there are techniques of IC production that sacrifice performance in the name of lower design costs. One approach that falls short of full customization is the standard-cell approach. Here, standard portions or subsections of a circuit – a memory, a collection of logic gates, or even a microprocessor – are predesigned and stored in the software of the designer's computer-aided design (CAD) equipment. The designer can then call upon these predesigned building blocks to put together a circuit in less time than would be required to design the

[10] It is interesting to note that the industry classifies ROMs as standard products, even though one could legitimately view them as semicustom.

chip from scratch. As with any kind of modular construction, of course, the finished piece is not as elegant or as efficient as it would have been if custom designed.

Although not full-custom chips, standard-cell chips are considered "custom" chips to the extent that all mask layers are designed specifically for the particular application. Another approach to design is semi-customization, in which some layers are specially designed and some are not. An important type of semi-custom chip is the gate array. Here, a standard set of masks is used to define all layers except the very top ones. These masks lay out a set of standardized logic circuits called gates. A customized top layer of interconnections links the gates to form the circuit. As a result, the designer can use methods similar to those used for circuits with old-fashioned discrete devices on printed-circuit boards; he or she needs to know very little about the properties of silicon or the process of chip production. Other advantages include faster turn-around time and lower up-front processing costs because of the relatively few masks needed. The disadvantages of this approach include a limit on possible circuit complexity, low speed because of the nonoptimal layout, and high cost (relative to custom approaches) as production volume increases. An extreme variant of this approach is the fuse-programmable IC, in which *no* mask layer is customized during production: the standardized logic cells must be connected – fused together – by the user after the chip is produced.

The size and composition of the worldwide merchant market for non-standard ICs in 1984 are shown in Table 2, with a forecast for 1990. In addition to this marketed production, captive production is often focused on non-standard ICs, and merchant producers make non-standard ICs for in-house use; but no estimates are available on the value of this production.

Table 2 *World Merchant Market for Nonstandard ICs, 1984 and 1990 Forecast*

	1984	1990
Total (Millions of Dollars)	1,966	8,645
Of Which (Percentages):		
Full Custom	39%	29%
Standard Cell	6	31
Gate Array	41	26
Linear Array	3	4
Fuse-Programmable Logic	11	10

Source: Integrated Circuit Engineering Corporation (1986).

Non-standard ICs accounted for 9 per cent of the world merchant IC market in 1984, and this share is forecast to increase to 21 per cent in 1990.[11] Over this period, standard-cell ICs are expected to grow rapidly to about one-third of the non-standard IC market, while fully customized ICs and gate arrays will decline in relative importance. These trends assume continued advances in CAD technology.

[11] Integrated Circuit Engineering Corporation (1986).

3

The Economic Structure of the Industry

Semiconductor Production

The semiconductor industry is among the fastest growing of manufacturing industries, with an average annual growth rate of about 16 per cent since the late 1950s. In fact, because of price declines for semiconductor products and functions, the real growth rate of the industry is even faster. Prices generally decline as experience with production lowers unit costs. In addition, the rising complexity of integrated circuits is itself a source of decline in price per function performed. For instance, the cost of one bit of memory fell from 1 cent in 1970 to 0.01 cent in 1981 as memory devices advanced from the lK DRAM to the 16K DRAM. This cost continued to fall to 0.001 cent in 1986 for the 256K DRAM. Furthermore, the appearance of entirely new devices – such as microprocessors – opens up new functions and applications. As a result, it is not easy to calculate a price index for semiconductor devices to reflect all of these factors; but even a conservative estimate of the average rate of price decline suggests that real growth of the industry could easily be 25 per cent per year or more.

Production of semiconductors around the world (excluding Eastern Europe and the Soviet Union) totaled $34 billion in 1986. Table 3 illustrates the pattern of production for the period 1978-1986 (broken down by home-base of producing company and by product type). Production around the world approximately tripled over this period. The United States is the single largest home-base, accounting in 1986 for 50 per cent of world production of semiconductors and 55 per cent of world production of ICs. Japan is the second largest home-base, accounting for 38 per cent of all semiconductors and 36 per cent of ICs in 1986. Companies based in Western Europe accounted for 10 per cent and 7 per cent,

Table 3 *World Semiconductor Production: by Home Country of Producing Firms, 1978–84, in Millions of Dollars**

Country/Product	1979	1980	1981	1982	1983	1984	1985	1986
United States	8,625	11,135	10,900	11,210	13,620	19,115	16,260	16,915
IC	6,681	9,055	8,950	9,365	11,475	16,530	14,100	14,675
Merchant	4,671	6,360	6,050	6,205	7,850	12,250	9,300	9,800
Captive	2,010	2,695	2,900	3,160	3,625	4,280	4,800	4,875
Discrete**	1,944	2,080	1,950	1,845	2,145	2,585	2,160	2,240
Western Europe	1,650	1,620	1,540	1,725	1,975	2,720	2,635	3,240
IC	600	710	790	835	1,040	1,545	1,460	1,790
Discrete	1,050	910	750	890	935	1,175	1,175	1,450
Japan	2,930	3,840	4,170	4,585	6,210	10,440	9,430	12,755
IC	1,750	2,450	2,590	3,060	4,420	7,800	7,050	9,555
Discrete	1,180	1,390	1,580	1,525	1,790	2,640	2,380	3,200
Rest of World***	1,700	320	360	355	430	620	650	975
IC	675	130	160	165	230	370	400	650
Discrete	1,025	190	200	190	200	250	250	325
Total	14,905	16,915	16,970	17,875	22,235	32,895	28,975	33,885
IC	9,706	12,345	12,490	13,425	17,165	26,245	23,010	26,670
Discrete	5,199	4,570	4,480	4,450	5,070	6,650	5,965	7,215

Notes: * Home country as categorized by the Integrated Circuit Engineering Corporation.

** Includes both merchant and captive production.

*** Includes Eastern Europe and the Soviet Union for 1978 and 1979. Excludes Eastern Europe and the Soviet Union for 1980-1986.

Sources: Integrated Circuit Engineering Corp. (1980, 1981, 1982, 1983, 1984, 1985, 1986, and 1987).

respectively. Notice, though, that a substantial part of production by American-based companies occurs in Western Europe. Overall, about one-quarter of world merchant production of semiconductors occurs in Western Europe, with over half of this accounted for by the affiliates of American companies.[1]

For all three of the major home-bases, production of ICs has been growing more quickly than production of discrete devices. The value of production of ICs surpassed the value of production of discrete devices in 1979 for Japan and in the early 1980s for Western Europe – a milestone the United States achieved much earlier. The average annual growth rate of Japanese semiconductor production was almost 23 per cent during 1978–1986, while that of the United States was almost 14 per cent. Although production of discrete devices grew somewhat more rapidly in Japan, the major difference is in IC production, which grew at a 30 per cent annual rate for Japan and at a 16 per cent rate for the United States. It might also be

[1] Office of Technology Assessment (1983).

noted that the growth rate of American captive IC production has been slightly greater than the growth rate of American merchant IC production.

The preceding analysis is based on the categorization used by the Integrated Circuit Engineering Corporation to assign each producing firm to a "home-base." Although this categorization follows standard industry practice, several companies are arguably misclassified. Most importantly, Signetics, Fairchild, and (prior to 1985) Interdesign are all considered American companies, even though they have been acquired by European parents. Also, ITT is considered a European company. Its semiconductor operations are largely located there, but its corporate headquarters are in the United States, and it is usually considered an American-based company in its overall operations. Table 4 indicates how IC production values change for 1983 and 1986 if these four companies are categorized by the home-base of the parent firms. The adjustment reduces the US share of world IC production in 1986 to 52 per cent, and raises the European share to 10 per cent. This is a relatively large shift for Europe. The difficulty in categorizing firms by home-base is just one reflection of the rising international interdependence of the semiconductor industry.

By most accounts, the growth of the world semiconductor industry will continue to be rather strong through the early 1990s. One authoritative forecast is that of the Integrated Circuit Engineering Corporation (1987), who predict growth for all semi-

Table 4 *World Integrated Circuit Production: Alternative Definitions of Home Country of Producing Firms, 1983 and 1986, in Millions of Dollars*

	1983		1986	
Country	ICE Estimate	Adjusted	ICE Estimate	Adjusted
United States	11,475	10,752	14,675	13,805
Merchant	7,850	7,127	9,800	8,930
Captive	3,625	3,625	4,875	4,875
Western Europe	1,040	1,763	1,790	2,660
Japan	4,420	4,420	9,555	9,555
Other	230	230	650	650
Total	17,165	17,165	26,670	26,670

Note: Adjustments involve crediting the IC production of Fairchild (owned by Schlumberger), Signetics (owned by Philips), and Interdesign (owned by Ferranti) to Western Europe and crediting the IC production of ITT (headquartered in the United States) to the United States.

conductors to be about 12 per cent from 1986 to 1991, with the growth of ICs at 13 per cent and that of discrete devices at 7 per cent. They expect total production of semiconductors to be about $60 billion, including about $8 billion of captive production, in 1991. They estimate $50 billion worth of IC production in 1991.

Consumption and End-Use Demand

Table 5 displays national shares of world consumption of semiconductors for selected years during the period 1956–1986. The United States is the single largest consuming nation, but its share has fallen to about two-fifths of world consumption. Japan's share has risen to about one-third of world consumption. The share of Western Europe in world consumption rose to nearly one-quarter in the mid–1970s, but has since declined to about one-fifth. In 1986, Japan became the largest merchant market for semiconductors, though total consumption (including captives) remains larger in the United States.

Table 6 provides information on consumption of ICs in 1983. The United States consumed 61 per cent of world output of ICs in that year, including captive consumption. Japan consumed 17 per cent, and Western Europe 15 per cent. The same figure also shows the source of supply for this IC consumption. Using the categorization of the Integrated Circuit Engineering Corporation, American-based firms supplied 91 per cent of American consumption and 52 per cent of European consumption, but only 15 per cent of Japanese consumption. Japanese firms supplied 85 per cent of their own market, but only 16 per cent of European consumption and 7 per cent of American consumption. We will examine these foreign shares of national markets in more detail shortly.

Table 5 *Shares in World Consumption of Semiconductors, 1956–86*

	1956	1960	1965	1970	1972	1978	1981	1986
United States	80	76	66	53	51	46	51	39
Japan	5	7	8	14	20	23	23	34
Western Europe	8	12	18	22	22	23	18	19
Other	7	5	8	11	7	8	8	8

Sources: Finan (1975), U.S. Department of Commerce (1979), Gutmanis (1979), Integrated Circuit Engineering Corporation (1983 and 1987).

Table 6 Consumption of Integrated Circuits, 1983

Consuming Area	Value (Millions of Dollars)	Percentage Supplied by Firms with home-base* in: United States	Western Europe	Japan	Rest of World
United States	10,160	91	1	7	Z
Western Europe	2,425	52	32	16	Z
Japan	2,770	15	Z	85	Z
Rest of World**	1,230	41	4	42	13
Total	16,585	69	6	24	1

Notes: * Home country as categorized by the Integrated Circuit Engineering Corporation.

** Excludes Eastern Europe and the Soviet Union.

Z = Less than 0.5%.

Source: Integrated Circuit Engineering Corporation (1984).

Table 7 Consumption Shares by Type of Device, 1983

Type of Device	United States	Japan	Europe
Discrete and Optoelectronic Devices	16.7	33.6	33.2
ICs	83.4	66.4	66.8
Linear	12.8	26.7	28.4
Digital	87.2	73.3	71.6
Standard Logic	14.3	18.4	33.8
Microprocessors	25.9	18.2	12.9
Special-Purpose Consumer ICs	8.0	13.3	1.6
Non-standard ICs	4.8	2.1	NR
Memories	35.9	21.4	23.2
RAM	17.5	11.4	13.7
ROM	16.7	8.1	9.5
Other	1.7	2.0	NR

Notes: Apparently does not include captive consumption in the United States. Shares for categories of ICs reported as a per cent of IC consumption.

NR: Not reported separately.

Source: Electronics, January 12, 1984, as reported in OECD (1985).

Table 8 *World Demand for Integrated Circuits by End-Use Market, 1962–85, as a percentage*

<table>
<tr><th>End-use</th><th>1962</th><th>1970</th><th>1976</th><th>1980</th><th>1984</th><th>1985</th></tr>
<tr><td>Computer</td><td>0</td><td>64</td><td>45</td><td>44</td><td>39</td><td>36</td></tr>
<tr><td>Telecommunications</td><td>0</td><td>5</td><td>10</td><td>10</td><td>11</td><td>15</td></tr>
<tr><td>Industrial</td><td>0</td><td rowspan="2">26</td><td rowspan="2">30</td><td>10</td><td>13</td><td>10</td></tr>
<tr><td>Military and Aerospace</td><td>100</td><td>8</td><td>7</td><td>9</td></tr>
<tr><td>Consumer</td><td>0</td><td>5</td><td>15</td><td>28</td><td>30</td><td>36</td></tr>
</table>

Note: Excludes captive consumption.

Sources: Finan (1975), Malerba (1983), Integrated Circuit Engineering Corporation (1980, 1985, 1986).

Table 7 shows the composition of consumption by type of device in 1983 for the United States, Japan, and Western Europe. Of the three, the United States takes the highest fraction of consumption in the form of ICs. Within IC consumption, digital devices accounted for a higher share of American IC consumption, with microprocessors and memories showing particularly high shares in the United States.

The consumption of IC demand by device type is closely related to the composition of demand by end-use market, because specific devices have been developed for particular end-use markets. Table 8 shows the composition of world demand by end-use market during 1962–1985.

The military and aerospace market accounted for all demand for ICs in the first two years of production, 1961–62, and for about 90 per cent of IC sales through 1965.[2] High performance, reliability, and the ability to operate under extreme environmental conditions are crucial in this end-use application. By 1985, the share of military and aerospace demand had fallen to somewhat less than one-tenth of world demand.

The computer segment was the next application area to develop. In 1970, ICs for use in computers accounted for nearly two-thirds of world demand for ICs. The computer segment requires very reliable devices, but price is also important. Computer producers have been especially aggressive in incorporating ICs into their systems designs to increase speed, capacity, and reliability, while reducing the physical size and cost of computers. The share of computer end-use

2 Finan (1975).

in total IC demand has fallen since 1970, but it is still over one-third of the total. On average, 10 to 12 per cent of a computer system's total cost in 1984 was the cost of its ICs, somewhat higher than the average 8 per cent of cost for all electronic systems products.[3]

End-use demands by producers of telecommunications equipment and other industrial equipment accounted in total for one-fourth of total IC demand in 1985. End-use in consumer products, including radios, televisions, audio equipment, calculators, watches, and automobiles, has developed steadily since the late 1960s, and accounted for nearly one-third of demand for ICs by 1985.

Semiconductor penetration of industrial and consumer applications first occurred when transistors and other discrete devices replaced electron tubes because of their greater reliability and declining prices. The discrete devices also made possible some new products, such as the transistor radio. The IC then began to replace discrete devices, most rapidly in the industrial segment. As the complexity of ICs has increased and their prices have fallen, a variety of new product applications, such as those in automotives, have arisen. Linear ICs are particularly important in consumer applications, but the recent growth in consumer and industrial applications is focused on the increasing use of microprocessors and microcontrollers. Such expansion depends upon assistance to the end-user in programming, so that the role of marketing and customer service contacts have become more important in the semiconductor industry.

Table 9 displays demand for ICs by end-use market for the United States, Japan, and Western Europe in 1982 and 1985. American end-use demand is relatively large in the areas of computers and military and aerospace. Indeed, demand derived from US government military and space contracts was arguably of major importance to the development of the semiconductor industry, and especially to its predominance in ICs.[4] Production contracts for ICs in the early 1960s permitted firms to acquire experience, leading to cost reductions from learning economies. As unit costs fell, ICs began to penetrate other applications.

The share of military and aerospace in American IC demand fell dramatically into the late 1970s, but has since been rising somewhat as military procurement has increased recently.

In Japan, about half of ICs are used in consumer products, but this share has been falling gradually since the early 1970s. The share of end-use demand in computer products rose dramatically in the

[3] Integrated Circuit Engineering Corporation (1985).

[4] Levin (1982a).

Table 9 *Demand for Integrated Circuits by End-Use Market: United States, Japan, and Western Europe, 1982 and 1985, as a percentage*

End-use	United States		Japan		Western Europe	
	1982	1985	1982	1985	1982	1985
Computer	40	45	22	36	25	20
Telecommunications	21	10	10	13	20	29
Industrial	11	10	17	6	25	19
Military and Aerospace	17	18	0	0	5	7
Consumer	11	16	51	45	25	25

Note: Includes captive consumption.

Source: OECD (1985).

first half of the 1980s. There is essentially no military and aerospace demand in Japan.

European end-use demand is relatively strong in telecommunications and other industrial-products applications. Since the mid–1970s, the share of computer and consumer end-use demand has fallen somewhat in Europe, while that of telecommunications has risen.

National Shares by Geographic Market and by Product

One major dimension of growing interdependence is the interpenetration of national markets by firms based in other countries. The most notable shift in recent years in the semiconductor industry has been the rising penetration by Japanese firms of foreign markets.

Table 10 shows the shares of each other's markets held by American- and Japanese-based firms. American firms have held about 10–14 per cent of the Japanese semiconductor market since the late 1960s. The American share of the Japanese IC market has also been rather steady, averaging about 16 per cent since the early 1970s. In contrast, the Japanese share of American IC consumption was only 1 per cent in 1976, but had risen to 9 per cent by 1986.

American and Japanese shares of the European market are shown in Table 11. American-based firms have provided half or more of the total consumption of semiconductors and ICs in Europe. The Japanese started with a share of the European markets comparable to their low share in the American market in

Table 10 *American and Japanese Shares of Each Other's Markets, 1976–83, as a percentage*

	U.S. Share of Japanese Market		Japanese Share of U.S. IC Market
Year	All Semiconductors	ICs	
1976	11	16	1
1978	10	16	2
1980	12	16	5
1983	NA	15	7

Notes: U.S. market includes captive production.

NA: Not available.

Sources: Semiconductor Industry Association (1983), Integrated Circuit Engineering Corporation (1984).

Table 11 *American and Japanese Shares of the European Market, 1977–83, as a percentage*

	U.S. Share		Japanese Share	
Year	All Semiconductors	ICs	All Semiconductors	ICs
1977	50	64	1	3
1980	56	64	4	6
1983	50	52	10	16

Sources: OECD (1985), Integrated Circuit Engineering Corporation (1984).

the mid-1970s. Since then, the Japanese firms have steadily gained share, so that by 1983 Japanese firms provided 10 per cent of European semiconductor consumption and 16 per cent of its IC consumption. In the late 1970s, both American-based and Japanese firms were increasing share at the expense of European firms; but, in the early 1980s, the Japanese gains in market share came at the expense of American-based firms.

Another dimension of competitiveness can be seen in the national shares achieved in the worldwide markets for various IC products. Table 12 shows American, Japanese, and other (essentially Western European) shares for various IC product-areas in

Table 12 *National Shares of the World IC Market, by Product Type, 1982, as a percentage*

Product	United States	Japan	Other*
IC Total	62	31	7
MOS IC	60	35	5
Microprocessors	64	33	3
Memory	65	33	2
Logic	49	40	11
Bipolar	62	27	11
Linear	51	35	14
Digital	74	19	7

Notes: Excludes captive production.

* Mostly Western Europe.

Source: Takai (1983).

1982. In comparison with their overall share of the IC market, Japanese firms have a somewhat larger share of MOS ICs, where they have been focusing much of their research and production efforts. In contrast, the Western European firms exhibit particular weakness in the areas of MOS microprocessors and memory. In the bipolar area, American-based firms have particular strength in bipolar digital ICs, whose end-use is largely in computers. Japanese and European firms have relative strengths in bipolar linear ICs, whose use is found more in consumer products.

Japanese firms show special strength in particular MOS products. Although Japanese firms had no share in the lK DRAM market in the early 1970s and achieved only a 12 per cent share of the 4K DRAM merchant market in the mid–1970s, they captured about 40 per cent of the world merchant market for 16K DRAMs in the late 1970s, and about 60 per cent of the world merchant market for 64K DRAMs in the first half of the 1980s. Japanese firms account for about 80 to 90 per cent of the world merchant market for 256K DRAMs, and are expected to achieve a similar share in the world merchant market for 1M DRAMs.[5] In 1984, Japanese firms held about 80 per cent of the world merchant market for 4-bit microcontrollers, used largely in consumer products. Total production of this product, however, is expected to decline. Japanese firms accounted for about 35 per cent of merchant production of 8-bit microcontrollers, which are displacing the 4-bit microcontrollers in many consumer applica-

[5] Integrated Circuit Engineering Corporation (1987).

tions.[6] American-based firms maintain their dominance in the markets for 8-bit and 16-bit microprocessors, with Japanese production of these largely based on second-source manufacture of American designs.

Industrial Structure

Several hundred companies around the world manufacture semiconductors. Of the top 10 firms in 1983, 5 were American firms, 4 Japanese, and 1 – Philips (including Signetics) – European. Of the largest 30, 17 were American-based firms (including ITT, often considered European because the headquarters for its semiconductor operations is in Europe), 9 Japanese, and 4 European (including Fairchild, often considered an American firm, although, owned by Schlumberger). Of the largest 30, 4 were captives, including IBM, the world's largest producer of semiconductors and ICs. By 1984, 5 of the 10 largest producers were Japanese, 4 were American, and 1 was European.

This section presents brief descriptions of some of the leading semiconductor producers. The discussion is divided into the four types of producers noted above: American merchant firms, American captive producers, Japanese firms, and European firms. In addition, this section also briefly discusses current efforts by Korean firms to become important players in the semiconductor market. The final parts of the chapter turn to the issues of capital requirements and R&D spending in the semiconductor industry.

American Merchant Firms

There were some forty-nine major American merchant producers of ICs in 1986, of which two were actually owned by European firms. In addition, there are a number of smaller merchant producers of ICs and merchant producers of discrete devices.

Because of the great diversity in such areas as product offerings, vertical integration, diversification and other elements of strategy, American merchant firms are not easy to characterize. For instance, semiconductor sales account for about one-third of total sales by Texas Instruments and Motorola, but for three-quarters or more of total sales of such other large merchant firms as Intel, National Semiconductor, AMD and AMI. Semiconductor operations form a relatively autonomous division at such diversified producers as GE, Harris, and Rockwell, and account for rather small shares of those companies' total sales.

[6] Integrated Circuit Engineering Corporation (1985).

Another characteristic of the American merchant semiconductor industry is the substantial amount of entry and exit in comparison with the European or Japanese semiconductor industries. One important feature of the American economy that has facilitated entry of new merchant firms is the availability of venture capital provided through well-developed channels in the American financial markets. Venture capital is not nearly so readily available to independent start-up firms in Europe or Japan.

During 1966–1972, at least thirty new companies entered the American merchant semiconductor industry by focusing on IC technology – especially MOS technology – which the established American firms at first failed to develop aggressively. The rate of entry of new merchant firms declined precipitously after 1972, partly because of rising capital requirements but largely because of changes in American tax laws that eventually led to a contraction of the venture-capital market. With further changes in American tax laws in 1978 – changes affecting the tax treatment of capital gains – venture capital became more plentiful and start-ups of new semiconductor firms increased. Recently, start-ups have emphasized CMOS production technology and standard-cell, gate-array, and other non-standard product technologies. However, these firms now face relatively high and rising capital requirements for production facilities. Venture capital financing for these facilities is not easy to obtain, and the long-term viability of many of the recent start-ups is questionable.

Exit of merchant firms from the American semiconductor industry has also been significant. The business cycle often has a magnified effect on industry output, capacity utilization and profits, encouraging exit during cyclical downturns. Other firms exit as they find it difficult to keep up with the rapidly changing technology. Some of these firms later re-enter the industry. Before 1975, little exit was the result of mergers and acquisitions, but these increased noticeably in the late 1970s.

Forward vertical integration into various systems products became a part of the corporate strategies of a number of the larger American merchant producers of semiconductors in the 1970s. The firms identified several reasons to favor integration into such products as watches, calculators, and computers. First, IC design was becoming more complex, with the character of the systems product more closely determined by this design. Thus, a single firm could be more effective by internalizing and co-ordinating product development and IC design development, thereby avoiding duplicate R&D. Second, the firms saw larger markups on the systems products, and believed that their sales would be less cyclical than semiconductor sales. Third, backward vertical integration by systems producers was also increasing, threatening to shrink the merchant market for semiconductors, so forward integration was partially defensive.

Several difficulties arose to reduce the likelihood of successful forward integration. First, semiconductor firms lacked the marketing expertise needed to sell consumer and industrial goods. Second, developing systems products and marketing abilities sometimes diverted managerial and R&D efforts from semiconductors, so the firm then might lag in this fast-moving technology. Third, the margins tended to shrink as entry increased competition in the systems-product markets.

These difficulties were sufficiently important in that many of the firms who attempted forward integration had abandoned the systems products by 1977.[7] For example, Intel and Mostek both withdrew from sales of watches, and Rockwell abandoned pocket calculators. Even firms that initially showed some success in the product areas they had entered through forward integration eventually experienced difficulties and have been forced to withdraw. A major example is Texas Instruments, which achieved some success – in terms of market share, if not profitability – in products such as computers, watches and calculators. Texas Instruments has since dropped many of these products, including a costly withdrawal from the home-computer market in 1983.

American Captive Producers

Traditionally, captive producers have been defined as those that produce semiconductors solely for in-house use. However, the Integrated Circuit Engineering Corporation concluded in the early 1980s that this definition should be altered, so that in their view captive producers are now those that sell less than about one-quarter of their production into the open market, have relatively few device-development programs oriented primarily toward open-market sales and maintain the service of in-house needs as the primary goal of their semiconductor operations.

A systems firm – a computer manufacturer, for example – can obtain a number of advantages by producing its own semiconductors "in-house." Most important, the firm can develop and protect proprietary IC designs that differentiate their systems products from those of their competitors. In addition, the firm gains administrative control over quality, reliability and continuity of supply. The firm may also gain bargaining power with respect to its merchant suppliers.

[7] Borrus, Millstein, and Zysman (1983).

But captive production also has its disadvantages. The costs of capital investment and R&D have been rising dramatically (see below). The captive producer may not maintain sufficient volume to utilize capacity or to spread relatively fixed costs such as R&D. The lack of direct market feedback may lower the pressure constantly to reduce costs. In addition, the smaller captive producers may have difficulty attracting key personnel to its relatively unglamorous semiconductor operations.

The relative strengths of the advantages and disadvantages have been changing over time. The importance of proprietary IC designs to systems differentiation has clearly been rising. However, custom and semi-custom ICs are increasingly available in the open market at reasonable cost. Technology development contracts offer another way for systems firms to forge close links with their semiconductor suppliers. Thus, the rising costs of facilities and R&D appear to be restraining the growth of captive production. After increasing in the 1970s, the share of captive IC production in total IC production by American-based firms has been rather stable. Since 1980 no major IC user has begun full-scale captive IC production, although several large companies apparently have the resources to do so. By contrast, a number of captive producers are moving toward or into open-market sales. NCR has completed a shift to the status of a merchant firm with the open-market sales of several memory products and its 32-bit microprocessor.

Integrated Circuit Engineering Corporation (1987) lists seventeen American firms with the capability for full IC production in-house. They also list one Canadian captive producer, Northern Telecommunication, which has one IC production facility in Canada and one in the United States. In addition, several firms, including AT&T (Western Electric), Delco, and Hewlett-Packard, have captive production of discrete devices.

The estimated value of IC production by the six major captive producers in 1983 and 1985 is shown in Table 13. These firms are also major purchasers of ICs on the open market, as also shown in this table. Indeed, of the six companies, only IBM and AT&T produced more than they purchased in 1984.

IBM is the largest IC producer in the world and a major innovator in IC production processes and products applicable to computers. It carries out substantial basic research in semiconductor-related areas. It is the only American captive with semiconductor production facilities outside of the United States; it produces ICs in West Germany and France and has pilot production in Japan. IBM also acquired 20 per cent of Intel, an investment presumably to assure access to an ongoing supply of Intel ICs, especially micro-

Table 13 *Captive* IC *Production and Open-Market Purchases: Major American Captive Producers, 1983 and 1985, in Millions of Dollars*

Company	IC Captive Production 1983	IC Captive Production 1985	IC Open Market Purchases 1983	IC Open Market Purchases 1985
IBM	2400	3000	550	630
AT&T*	390	640	375	450
Delco (GM)	210	310	375	325
Hewlett-Packard	180	195	400	335
Honeywell	85	115	235	200
DEC	65	80	400	390

Notes: * Includes Western Electric.

NA: Not available.

Sources: Integrated Circuit Engineering Corporation (1984, 1986, 1987).

processors and related peripheral ICs, used in IBM products. IBM has obtained the rights to manufacture the Intel 8088 family of ICs and the 32-bit 80386 microprocessor. IBM also has long-standing links to Texas Instruments for IC development and supply.

As part of the recent restructuring of AT&T, AT&T Technologies has absorbed Western Electric and Bell Laboratories. AT&T was the major force in early semiconductor innovation and production. According to the 1956 consent decree resolving a US government antitrust suit against AT&T, Western Electric was prohibited from marketing products commercially within the United States. Given this foreclosure from the largest merchant market, Western Electric chose not to sell semiconductors commercially anywhere. As part of the resolution of the recent antitrust case, the restrictions of the 1956 decree have been removed. AT&T has announced plans for a drive into the merchant semiconductor markets, but its progress has been slowed by strong in-house demand for its production and by the initial weakness of its marketing capabilities. Its production of 256K DRAMs is largely consumed internally, and its sales efforts for its 32-bit microprocessor are developing slowly. In April 1985, AT&T bought Synertek, a merchant firm, from Honeywell. Through Bell Labs, AT&T has conducted substantial basic research in semiconductor technologies, but the future of this research is unclear in view of the firm's reorientation toward profitability in open, competitive markets.

Delco supplies nearly half of the semiconductor devices consumed by General Motors, and it supplies them on a cost-competitive basis against open-market suppliers. Honeywell is beginning to offer semicustom ICs on the open market. DEC recently announced that it will become the second American captive producer with a production facility abroad: it plans to build an IC manufacturing plant in Scotland.

Japanese Firms

Nine firms dominate semiconductor production in Japan, although there are also many smaller producers. To some extent this somewhat concentrated structure has been encouraged by Japanese government policies, especially with respect to R&D funding and telecommunications procurement by NTT, the state-owned telecommunications monopoly. NTT itself conducts research on semiconductor technologies but does not produce semiconductors (or other equipment).

Selected information on these nine Japanese firms for 1984 is shown in Table 14. Semiconductors account for a relatively small share – less than one-quarter – of total company sales in Japanese firms; this is in sharp contrast to many American merchant firms, for which semiconductors contribute a large fraction of total sales. All Japanese semiconductor producers are substantial exporters, although Fujitsu and Matsushita export only about 15 per cent of their semiconductor production, a figure that is somewhat misleading in that about half of the production of these two companies is consumed internally. Thus, the share of exports in merchant sales is about 30 per cent. With the exception of these two firms and Sharp, at least three-quarters of their semiconductor production is sold into the open market rather than consumed internally. It should also be noted that there is substantial trade in semiconductors among these firms, as they are also large consumers of semiconductors. Borrus, Millstein, and Zysman (1983) estimate that these nine firms and Sony, the top ten semiconductor producers in Japan, account for over 90 per cent of Japanese semiconductor production and also consume about 60 per cent of this production.

Each of the six leading producers is a huge multinational company with billions of dollars of sales. Each is a member of a *keiretsu*, a grouping of industrial firms around a large bank or one or more large firms. The firms in the group are loosely linked by equity cross-ownership, interlocking management, and buying-selling relationships. A large trading company is usually affiliated with each *keiretsu*. Flaherty and Itami (1984) conclude, however, that the only aspect of these *keiretsu* linkages that is of any significance to the semiconductor operations of the companies is the

Table 14 *Selected Sales Ratios for the Leading Japanese Semiconductor Producers: Fiscal Year 1984*

Company	Semiconductor Sales as a Percent of Total Company Sales	Exports as a Percent of Production	Merchant Sales as a Percent of Production
NEC	20%	24%	78%
Hitachi	11	40	80
Toshiba	10	23	85
Fujitsu	12	15	48
Matsushita	3*	15	50
Mitsubishi	8	25	90
Tokyo Sanyo	20	26	75
Sharp	7	20	65
Oki	19	37	86

Note: * As a percent of consolidated Matsushita Electric sales for 1981, as reported in Office of Technology Assessment (1983). Semiconductors accounted for 49 per cent of the sales of Matsushita Electronics, which is a joint venture between Matsushita Electric and Philips.

Source: Yano Research Institute (1984).

financial link. Even the importance of access to finance afforded by the *keiretsu* links appears to have declined recently.

NEC is a leading producer of communications equipment, computers, and consumer appliances. It is a member of the Sumitomo Bank *keiretsu*.

Hitachi is the largest diversified electronics systems producer in Japan, with sales of computers, communications and consumer products, and heavy industrial and electrical machinery. It is the core of its own *keiretsu*.

Toshiba is a major producer of heavy electrical equipment, instrumentation, appliances, and other electronics systems. It is a leading firm in the Toshiba-IHI *keiretsu*.

Fujitsu is Japan's largest computer manufacturer. It is a member of the *keiretsu* surrounding the Dai-Ichi Kangyo Bank.

Matsushita Electric is Japan's largest producer of consumer electronics and home appliances. Matsushita Electric owns 65 per cent of, and controls, Matsushita Electronics, which produces semiconductors. Matsushita Electric is the core of its own *keiretsu*.

Mitsubishi Electric is a major producer of business computers, appliances, industrial and heavy electrical machinery and other electronic systems products. It is a member of the Mitsubishi *keiretsu*.

European Firms

European-based producers of semiconductors are mainly large, vertically integrated producers of electronics systems products. In general, the growth rates of their semiconductor production have been below those shown by American-based and Japanese firms.

Philips is the largest European producer if the production of Signetics, owned by Philips through the US Philips Trust, is included in the Philips total. Philips is perhaps the most truly "European" of the European firms. Based in the Netherlands, it also has production facilities in West Germany (its Valvo affiliate), the United Kingdom (Mullard) and France (Radiotechnique). Semiconductors accounted for about 3.0 per cent of total Philips' sales in 1980.[8]

Until recently, Fairchild was the second-largest European-owned producer of semiconductors, although it often was and continues to be considered an American firm. Schlumberger, a French firm formally incorporated in the Netherlands Antilles, acquired Fairchild in 1979. After persistent problems and significant losses, Schlumberger agreed in October 1986 to sell 80 per cent of the company to Fujitsu of Japan. The possibility of a Japanese takeover of this sort sparked a loud controversy, with many in industry and government – including Commerce Secretary Malcolm Baldrige – voicing strong dispproval. In March 1987 Fujitsu dropped its offer for Fairchild. The company's future is unclear at the time of writing, but a management buy-out – making Fairchild once again clearly "American" – is under discussion.[9]

Were Fairchild removed from the ranks of European-owned firms, Siemens would become the second-largest European producer of semiconductors. It was the first European firm to begin production of the 64K DRAM. Semiconductors accounted for about 2.3 per cent of Siemens' sales in 1980.[10]

The two other major Continental semiconductor manufacturers are SGS of Italy and Thomson-CSF of France.

SGS is wholly owned by STET, the state-controlled telecommunications-equipment firm. In 1982, only about 17 per cent of the company's sales of semiconductors took place in Italy. Roughly one-third of its sales were in other EEC countries and one-third in the United States.[11] A high proportion of the total sales of SGS (not STET overall) is in semiconductors.

Thomson-CSF is the largest French semiconductor producer. It is nationalized and highly diversified, with semiconductors accounting for 4.8 per cent of its total sales in 1980.[12] Its IC

[8] Office of Technology Assessment (1983).

[9] Brenton R. Schlender, "Fujitsu Drops Plan to Acquire U.S. Chip Maker," *The Wall Street Journal,* 13 March, 1987, p. 3.

[10] Office of Technology Assessment (1983).

[11] OECD (1985).

[12] Office of Technology Assessment (1983).

production includes MOS memory ICs, microprocessors, logic ICs, gate arrays, standard cells, full-custom ICs, and bipolar linear and logic ICs. In November 1985, Thomson acquired the troubled American merchant firm Mostek from United Technologies.

Recently, SGS and Thomson agreed to merge their semiconductor operations. The new firm, which will be incorporated in the Netherlands, will become the second-largest chip producer in Europe, with about $800 million in annual sales and a research budget of some $200 million.[13]

The three largest semiconductor firms based in the United Kingdom are Inmos, Ferranti, and Plessey. The British General Electric Company also produces semiconductors, focusing on custom ICs.

Inmos was founded in 1978 by the UK National Enterprise Board. The British government initially invested 25 million pounds to establish an equity share of 76 per cent, with most of the rest of the equity held by two founding executives. By 1983 the government had raised its stake to 65 million pounds in cash and 35 million pounds in loan guarantees, as Inmos had accumulated losses of $100 million. Inmos established its initial research and production facilities in the United States, and then established an R&D center in the United Kingdom. With some pressure from the British government, it opened a second factory in South Wales, but ran into serious problems transferring production from the United States. Inmos achieved significant production in 1982, and sales, 85 per cent of which are made in the United States, grew rapidly. It produces high-performance 64K DRAMs, 16K SRAMs, and other memory ICs. It has developed a type of 32-bit microprocessor called a "transputer."

In July 1984 the British government agreed to sell its equity in Inmos to Thorn EMI for $124.4 million, and Thorn is expected to buy the other 24 per cent for a comparable amount. Thorn expects Inmos to help in its efforts to shift toward production of high-technology electronics products, with Thorn eventually sourcing Inmos chips in-house. The government had earlier turned down an offer from AT&T for Inmos, partly because the money offered was considered low, but perhaps largely because of the desire to keep this rather peculiar company British.

Ferranti's production focuses on bipolar gate arrays. In 1980, semiconductors accounted for 9.6 per cent of total sales. Ferranti owns Interdesign in the United States.

Plessey specializes in semiconductor devices for telecommuni-

[13] E. S. Browning, "SGS of Italy, Thomson Unit Agree to Merge," *The Wall Street Journal,* 30 April, 1987, p. 27.

cations equipment. In 1980 semiconductors accounted for about 3.0 per cent of its sales.

South Korean Firms

Four large South Korean electronics firms have invested over $1 billion to develop advanced IC-design and production capabilities.[14] Their general strategy involves creating R&D and pilot production facilities in the United States, hiring scientists and engineers, especially expatriate Koreans, in the United States, and then establishing mass production of ICs in Korea. It is interesting that Korean firms are looking primarily to American rather than to Japanese technology. The reasons for this are complex, but they probably include elements of competitive strategy as well as a distrust of the Japanese rooted in an unhappy history of relations between the two countries.

Three of the four major Korean firms – Samsung, Gold Star and Daewoo – are large producers of electrical and electronics systems products already, while one – Hyundai – has no previous experience in this area. Their move into IC production is also linked to an eventual push into computers. The Korean government is actively supporting these development efforts. A major channel of support is through government funding of R&D, including the Korean Institute of Electronics Technology. The Institute also performs some wafer fabrication.

Samsung is the largest producer of semiconductors in Korea. It has made semiconductors since the mid-1970s, with capabilities in discrete devices, bipolar linear ICs, and some other ICs. It began producing 64K DRAMs at its American affiliate in 1984 and completed construction of a VLSI production facility in Korea in 1984. In 1985 Samsung began producing 256K DRAMs in Korea.

Gold Star produces discrete devices, bipolar linear ICs, and MOS memory ICs in Korea. It acts as a foundry for several American firms, including LSI Logic and AT&T. It is using technology from AT&T to improve its IC production capabilities.

Daewoo produces discrete devices and bipolar linear ICs in Korea. It entered the IC industry by buying the electronics divisions of Taihan. Its semiconductor production remains small, however.

Hyundai focused its initial efforts on producing MOS memory products in its American affiliate, but losses forced its closure in late 1985 and subsequent sale in 1986. Hyundai's future in the semiconductor business is not clear.

[14] Integrated Circuit Engineering Corporation (1985).

Investment Behavior

Capital Requirements

The capital-intensity of, and minimum capital requirements for, entering into semiconductor operations have increased dramatically since the 1960s, as the increasing complexity of ICs has required the introduction of more precise, more automatic, often computer-controlled production and testing equipment. The incremental capital-sales ratio is now generally regarded as about one, whereas in the 1960s it was less than one-half.

The increasing cost of production equipment, clean rooms and testing equipment has led to a large increase in the capital required to set up a production facility of minimum efficient scale. A compilation of minimum investment requirements for semiconductor production by the OECD (1985) concludes that these requirements were about $100 thousand in 1954, $300 thousand in 1958, $500 thousand in 1967, $2 million in 1972, $5 million in 1976, $10 million in 1978 and $60 million in 1982. The Semiconductor Industry Association (1983) estimates the cost of entry into 64K DRAM production at $30-100 million and perhaps $160 million for entry into 256K DRAM production.

Thus, the cost of entry into the semiconductor industry has increased dramatically over the last several decades even when the above estimates are adjusted for general inflation. New entrants into the industry are increasingly focusing on narrow niches of the market, where high-cost production at less-than-efficient scale is viable, or on design activities, with actual production undertaken by other firms, often by silicon foundries.

Capital Spending

A major dimension of behavior in the semiconductor industry is capital spending on plant and equipment. The need for capital spending to expand capacity is crucial to competitiveness in an industry with such a rapid rate of growth in sales, and this need has also been increasing as the incremental capital-intensity has been rising.

Most attention has focused on a comparison of capital spending by American merchant firms and Japanese firms. Table 15 shows the capital spending on semiconductor operations by these two sets of firms for 1973–86. For Japan, the figure gives data on spending by the nine largest firms and, when available, for all Japanese firms. The nine largest firms dominate the Japanese semiconductor market and accounted for slightly more than 90 per cent of the total investment during 1978–86. Thus, spending by the largest nine is

Table 15 *Capital Spending on Semiconductor Operations: American Merchant Firms and Japanese Firms, 1973–86, in Millions of Dollars*

	U.S. Merchant Firms	Japanese Firms	
		Largest Nine	All
1973	341	112	NA
1974	410	107	NA
1975	194	73	NA
1976	358	230	NA
1977	438	175	NA
1978	665	263	290
1979	1,112	412	454
1980	1,463	636	701
1981	1,520	877	974
1982	1,357	1,014	1,124
1983	1,630	1,522	1,642
1984	2,874	3,170	3,345
1985	2,125	2,695	2,960
1986	1,685	2,230	2,585

Note: NA = Not available.

Sources: Integrated Circuit Engineering Corporation (1986, 1987), Flaherty and Itami (1984).

taken as representative of spending by all Japanese firms prior to 1978.

Both America and Japan have increased capital spending dramatically over this period. Whereas American firms were spending at least three times as much as Japanese firms in the early 1970s, spending by Japanese firms has exceeded spending by American firms since 1984. Thus, in the early 1980s, American-based firms were spending about 15–17 per cent of semiconductor revenues on capital equipment, whereas Japanese firms were spending 20–24 per cent. Based on such willingness to invest, Japanese firms should continue to gain market share from American (and European) firms.

According to the Integrated Circuit Engineering Corporation (1986), worldwide spending on semiconductor products from the merchant industry totaled about $5.6 billion in 1985. Confirming observations above, the American share of merchant semiconductor sales was 47 per cent, but its share of capital spending was only 36 per cent. For Japan the respective shares are 40 per cent and 46 per cent. For European-based firms the shares are 11 per cent and 9 per cent, suggesting that European firms are not likely to do much better than maintain their current share of the world market in the next few years. The shares for firms in the rest of the world were 2 per cent and 9 per cent respectively. New sources of semiconductor supply are emerging, especially as several South Korean firms enter the merchant VLSI market.

The highly cyclical nature of the industry is also evident in the data on capital spending shown in Table 15 above. Capital spending declined in both countries during the recession of 1974–5. The drop in the United States was particularly large, and the American industry did not recover as much in 1976. This decline and somewhat slower recovery is often cited as a reason why serious capacity shortages emerged in the American industry in the late 1970s, giving Japanese firms an opportunity to begin their penetration of the American market. The effects of the 1981–82 recession are also evident, as capital spending fell slightly in the United States. The boom conditions of 1984 drew out substantial increases in investment in both countries, but the bust of 1985 has once again led to reductions in capital spending.

Rather little is known about capital spending by types of products or processes or by types of expansion. The Integrated Circuit Engineering Corporation (1985) estimates that in 1984 about 65 per cent of worldwide capital spending went to MOS facilities, 20 per cent to bipolar (rather evenly split between digital and linear), and 15 per cent on facilities for discrete devices. For Japan the share devoted to MOS facilities was about 70 per cent.

Analyses of the role of capital in the rising competitiveness of Japanese companies have often focused on differences in the cost of capital between the United States and Japan. Such differences are difficult to estimate accurately, although the Japanese firms do appear to derive an advantage in the after-tax cost of capital because (with the exception of Matsushita) they operate at higher levels of leverage (that is, they have a higher ratio of bond and loan financing to equity financing).[15] Nonetheless, the cost of capital in and of itself is likely to play a rather minor role in the semiconductor industry, as capital costs are a small, although growing, component of total cost. Of far more importance is capital availability, given the need for large amounts of new capital spending. Here the Japanese firms do seem to have an advantage, given the high saving rate in Japan. Banks in Japan now have difficulty finding sufficient demand for their loans, and are very willing to lend to the large, diversified companies that are the major semiconductor producers in Japan. At the same time, these companies view semiconductors as one of the few areas of major growth opportunity open to them. Thus, with an increasing ability to generate funds internally and ready access to bank loans and other

[15] Flaherty and Itami (1984).

sources of external funds, the Japanese semiconductor firms are able and willing to finance substantial new investments in semiconductor facilities. Capital availability, and not simply the cost of capital, is a key to their competitive capability.

R&D spending

Spending on R&D is the other major type of investment crucial to competitiveness in the semiconductor industry. Successful R&D can lead to a significant advantage for the innovating firm, although this advantage is often eroded quickly by rivals' imitation and further technical advances. R&D is in many cases a team effort in which several professional specialties must be combined. Physicists may supply design concepts, while specialists in chemistry, optics, metallurgy, and various branches of engineering are necessary to develop successful production of a device.

A rule of thumb in the industry is that circuit design costs about \$100 per gate for the hardware. A single IC can easily cost over \$1 million for the hardware circuit design. Software costs can easily be much more than this, and the costs have been rising rapidly as IC complexity increases. Intel's initial 4-bit microprocessor cost less than \$10 million to develop; the Intel 8086 16-bit microprocessor cost \$20 million to develop; while the Intel 32-bit 80386 microprocessor cost more than \$100 million to develop.[16] Thus, the semiconductor industry is among the most highly intensive in R&D spending of all manufacturing industries.

The significant early R&D occurred mainly in the United States. In 1959, R&D spending by American firms was equal to 19 per cent of their semiconductor sales revenues.[17] As sales expanded rapidly, the rate fell to 10 per cent of sales in 1972 and 8 per cent in the late 1970s.[18] Even as the rate fell, total real R&D spending continued to rise substantially.

Estimates of spending by American merchant firms on IC R&D as a percentage of IC sales vary somewhat. The Semiconductor Industry Association (1983) reports that the IC R&D-to-sales ratio ranged from 8 to 10 per cent between 1976 and 1981. There are other estimates of 13 to 16 per cent.[19]

Semiconductor R&D spending by Japanese firms was apparently rather low in the 1960s, perhaps about 2 per cent of sales.[20] This

[16] Office of Technology Assessment (1983) and Integrated Circuit Engineering Corporation (1986).

[17] Finan (1975).

[18] Arthur D. Little (1980).

[19] Borrus, Millstein, and Zysman (1983).

[20] Tilton (1971).

Table 16 *Japanese IC Capital Investment and R&D in Relation to Sales, 1973–84*

Year	Capital Investment as a Percentage of Sales	R&D as a Percentage of Sales
1973	21.9	19.7
1974	21.2	22.2
1975	10.5	19.9
1976	21.3	14.7
1977	14.1	15.7
1978	18.2	15.1
1979	22.4	14.6
1980	24.9	12.6
1981	25.1	14.9
1982	26.6	22.7
1983	30.0	14.8
1984	30.1	14.9

Source: Japan Ministry of International Trade and Industry.

ratio increased dramatically in the 1970s. Estimates of IC-related Japanese capital spending and R&D spending, each as a percentage of IC sales, are shown in Table 16. The R&D-to-sales ratio was about 20 per cent during 1973–5, but this fell to an average of about 15 per cent during 1976–84, except for the rather high ratio in 1982 when IC sales were depressed. Since 1981 Japanese firms have been ploughing back 40 per cent or more of their IC sales revenues into IC-related capital and R&D investments.

Although comparisons should be treated cautiously because of differences in accounting methods and definitions, the intensity of R&D spending on ICs by Japanese firms is, and has been for some years, at least as great as, if not greater than, that by American merchant firms. Furthermore, according to the estimates by the Semiconductor Industry Association (1983), American merchant firms in 1976 were spending twice as much in dollar terms on IC R&D as were Japanese firms, but this had fallen to only 1.5 times as much in 1981. The differential has most probably continued to fall since then.

4

International Trade in Semiconductor Products

The usual first step in analyzing international competition and the interdependence of national industries is to examine patterns of international trade. If a country has positive net exports, economists say it has a "revealed comparative advantage" in the product under analysis. One can scrutinize the patterns of trade to help understand the reasons behind a country's competitiveness or to explore changes in competitiveness over time.

Unfortunately, this kind of analysis is much less useful in the semiconductor industry than it is in many other industries. This is so for several reasons. First, the semiconductor industry exhibits a substantial degree of what is ponderously referred to as "intrafirm international vertical integration." As we described earlier, the production of semiconductors can be divided into at least four distinct stages: design, wafer fabrication, assembly, and final testing. These stages can – and frequently do – take place in different countries. The result – international vertical integration – has an important effect on American trade flows. Many American firms engage in "offshore assembly," which immediately complicates the pattern of trade flows in their products. Specifically, trade in semiconductors comprises both trade in finished semiconductors and trade in parts – mainly wafers and packaging materials – for offshore assembly.

Second, many semiconductor firms are extensively multinational in their operations, with facilities in foreign countries involved in design and sales efforts, in assembly and in wafer fabrication. The multinationality creates a serious question about how to evaluate "national" competitiveness. Most observers of the industry conduct such an evaluation not on the basis of production that occurs within a country's borders but rather on the basis of production worldwide by firms with a home-base in the country.

This was the premise of the analysis of global production patterns discussed in Chapter 3. Unfortunately, if one bases the analysis on such a premise, then the pattern of trade in goods is of much less interest. For example, Texas Instruments fabricates a large quantity of DRAMs in Japan, a large portion of which are shipped to the United States after assembly. In the traditional analysis such imports into the United States would suggest a lesser American competitiveness, but these imports can also be viewed as reflecting a competitive strength for the United States. Texas Instruments, as an American-based firm, has the capabilities to undertake and succeed in such a complex operation.

A third factor that complicates an analysis of international trade patterns is that semiconductors are also traded indirectly, that is, after incorporation into systems products. However, any attempt to evaluate this "indirect" trade forces an examination of the competitiveness of systems producers, thus moving well beyond the issue of the competitiveness of the semiconductor industry.

This chapter first discusses the phenomenon of offshore assembly. It then provides an analysis of American trade in semiconductors and brief observations on Japanese and European trade.

Offshore Assembly

Semiconductor companies operate extensive networks of foreign subsidiaries; they also have networks of international licensing agreements, along with some international joint ventures and minority equity-ownership positions. Their multinational operations include foreign subsidiaries engaged in wafer fabrication or complete manufacturing as well as subsidiaries engaged mainly in assembly. Some assembly subsidiaries sell mainly to the local or regional market and some mainly re-export the assembled semiconductors to the home country or to third countries. The former type of assembly affiliate is especially prevalent in Europe because of the protection erected by the European Economic Community (EEC). The latter type is called "offshore assembly," which sometimes also includes final testing of the assembled semiconductors. These offshore assembly facilities are usually located in developing countries in order to take advantage of low-cost labor in labor-intensive manual assembly operations. In addition to offering low-cost, trainable productive labor, such countries may also act to some degree as tax havens; historically they have provided duty-free access to some developed country markets.

Offshore Assembly by American Firms

The major strategic factor influencing the establishment of offshore assembly by American firms in the developing countries was the goal of cost-reduction. Wages in the important host countries (except for Mexico) have been one-fifth (or less) as high as wages in the United States, although in several of these countries real wages have been rising at a relatively rapid rate. Training of workers in these countries is not costly. Assemblers can be taught the basic techniques in one day and become proficient in less than two weeks.[1] Companies report that these foreign workers are generally more willing than American workers to perform tedious assembly work. They display good dexterity and eyesight, exhibit low turnover rates, and, because they display positive attitudes toward the importance of high-quality work, they are less prone to errors than are American workers.[2] Thus, labor productivity is good and labor relations pose few problems.

Offshore assembly can provide substantial savings in relation to total manufacturing cost. Grunwald and Flamm (1985) estimate that, on average, offshore assembly reduced total manufacturing cost by about one-quarter in comparison with manual assembly in the United States. This cost saving varies with the share of assembly cost in the total cost of the device. The Office of Technology Assessment (1983) estimates that, in the late 1970s, offshore assembly would have lowered the total cost of producing discrete devices or simpler ICs by over 50 per cent – but by only 15 per cent for complex ICs. Both estimates are based on the rather conservative assumption that wages for American assembly workers are five times as high as wages for the foreign assembly workers.

The ability to transfer assembly offshore is enhanced by several aspects of the manual assembly process. First, scale economies are minor, capital requirements are modest and few learning economies attach to assembly beyond the worker-training period. Second, although package designs are continually changing, the manual assembly process itself is a relatively stable technology. Third, in view of the high growth rate of the industry, decisions about the establishment of offshore assembly were generally confronted as capacity-expansion decisions. Without sunk costs, the lower average total cost of offshore assembly was often the deciding factor.

Certain additional costs attach to the use of offshore assembly. There are certainly transport costs; but these are low because of the very high value per pound for semiconductors. Round-trip air

[1] Finan (1975).
[2] Moxon (1974).

transport from the United States represents about 5 per cent of total manufacturing costs for mature devices and much less for devices in an earlier stage of the product cycle.[3] Of course, shipping costs to and from Mexico are lower. Inventory and storage costs are also low.

Until recently, if the assembled devices were reimported into the United States, as many are, they were subject to tariff duties – but, if item 806.30 or 807.00 of the tariff code applied, to duties only on the foreign value-added, not the total value, of the devices. Item 806.30 applied to articles of metal manufactured in the United States that were exported for further processing and then returned to the United States for additional processing. Item 807.00 applied to articles assembled abroad with fabricated components manufactured in the United States, as long as the components had not been altered except by assembly and incidental processing. These items were added to the tariff code in 1963 as codifications of practices that had developed in the 1950s, and the semiconductor industry became a major user of them. The duties on foreign value-added have been minor, adding only 1 or 2 per cent to the total cost of reimported devices in the late 1970s.[4] In April 1985, the American tariff rate on semiconductors was reduced to zero, eliminating even this small cost.

A major risk involved in using offshore assembly is the risk of supply disruptions – disruptions from such events as transport or communications breakdowns, political instability, or labor difficulties. The larger American firms have responded to this risk by diversifying through the establishment of multiple offshore assembly facilities. The lower level of scale and learning economies in manual assembly permits this strategy of diversification. American firms also maintained American assembly, in part to diversify and in part to meet the requirements of the US Department of Defense for domestic production of classified products.

American firms have also used offshore assembly subsidiaries to reduce their global tax burdens. Beginning in 1967, countries including Taiwan, Singapore, Malaysia, South Korea and Mexico have offered various inducements to encourage the formation of "export platform" subsidiaries. The specific package of inducements varies from country to country, but generally includes a holiday from corporate income taxes, reduced property taxes, and duty-free imports and exports. The multinationals enhance the attractiveness of these inducements by using transfer pricing to reduce further their global tax liabilities, although their ability to do

[3] Finan (1975).

[4] US Department of Commerce (1979).

this is constrained by the tax and customs authorities in the developed countries.

American firms face two relevant alternatives to manual assembly in offshore subsidiaries: automated assembly, presumably in the United States or another developed country, and subcontracting of assembly work to independent companies in the developing countries. The chief drawback to automated assembly is not operating cost but rather the problems of adapting the machines to changes in semiconductor package designs. The machines must be flexible and reprogramming is costly. Automated assembly offers the advantage of achieving more uniform and higher levels of quality. Moreover, the desire of many firms to work closely with customers militates in favor of automated onshore assembly; the smaller distances facilitate more flexible timing of deliveries and better coordination with customers.[5] Automated assembly is being used to an increasing extent in the United States, especially by the larger merchant firms who are more able to commit capital to the automated assembly facility, and especially for the higher-volume standardized products such as MOS memory ICs. Automated assembly also appears to be used extensively by the larger captive producers such as IBM and AT&T. IBM indicates that better process control and higher quality are the major advantages.

Fairchild was the first American firm to establish offshore assembly – in Hong Kong in 1963 and in South Korea in 1964. Competitive pressure from Fairchild encouraged other American semiconductor firms to establish offshore assembly. According to a survey of thirty-two American semiconductor producers by Finan (1975), three firms followed Fairchild in 1965–67, eleven in 1968–9, and eleven more in 1970–4. By 1974, at least 26 of the 32 firms in Finan's sample had established offshore assembly operations, with many assembling in several locations. A total of 56 assembly subsidiaries were established and operating in developing countries in 1974, including 12 in Mexico, 11 in Malaysia, 8 in Singapore, 5 in Hong Kong, 5 in South Korea, and 3 in Taiwan. Since then, the Philippines, Thailand, and Indonesia have become important sites for new offshore assembly facilities, both because they began adopting policies favorable to export platform investments and because wages began to rise in a number of the locations previously favored by American firms. According to the Integrated Circuit Engineering Corporation (1984), seven of the ten largest American merchant producers of ICs had assembly affiliates in the

[5] Steven P. Galante, "U.S. Semiconductor Makers Automate, Cut Chip Production in Southeast Asia," *The Wall Street Journal*, 21 August, 1985, p. 28.

Philippines in 1984, while two had assembly affiliates in Thailand and two in Indonesia.

Grunwald and Flamm (1985) estimate that about 40 per cent of American production was assembled abroad in 1969, 46 per cent in 1971, 79 per cent in 1974, 78 to 92 per cent in 1978, and 70 to 80 per cent in 1981. Most observers believe that American firms will continue to use offshore assembly but are not likely to expand its use. As the complexity of ICs continues to rise, so does the precision needed for very minute assembly operations; this calls for increasing levels of automation to lower the labor time required for assembly and to assure quality. Furthermore, advances in automation technology are adding flexibility and precision to the automated assembly process. Thus, expansions of assembly capacity are likely to be substantially, if not fully, automated. Nonetheless, products such as non-standard ICs, with short product cycles and small production runs, will continue to benefit from manual assembly in offshore sites.

Japanese and European Offshore Assembly

Japanese and European firms must confront the same strategic issues and cost factors as their American counterparts when it comes to deciding on locations and methods of assembly. Yet those firms do not make use of offshore assembly to nearly the same extent as do American firms.

Japan has a provision in the tariff code similar to the American 806/807 items. Japanese components of certain designated manufactured imports, including various types of semiconductors, can be granted relief from duty upon reimport with the prior authorization of customs officials. But in the late 1970s reimports of foreign-assembled ICs totaled less than 5 per cent of Japanese IC production, according to Grunwald and Flamm (1985). Foreign assembly of discrete devices may be higher. For instance, Tokyo Sanyo indicated in a recent interview that it assembles 85 per cent of its transistor output in South Korea and Taiwan, and only 15 per cent in Japan. In contrast, it assembles 85 per cent of its IC output in Japan and only 15 per cent in South Korea. It is likely that a large part of the devices assembled offshore are sold in foreign markets rather than re-imported into Japan. Information on the offshore assembly subsidiaries of Japanese semiconductor producers is shown in Table 17. The lack of use of offshore assembly, in general, and especially with respect to devices reimported back to Japan, may reflect protectionist government policies, which, until the mid-1970s, also protected the Japanese market by quotas. In addition, re-export back to Japan may have been discouraged by

Table 17 *Japanese Offshore Assembly Affiliates: Offshore Affiliates of the Nine Largest Japanese Semiconductor Producers, 1984*

Company	Location	Information
NEC	Malaysia	Assembly and test of discrete devices and ICs. 1,200 employees.
	Singapore	Assembly and testing of ICs. Production of discrete devices. 300 employees.
Hitachi	Malaysia	Assembly and testing of ICs.
	Singapore	NA
Toshiba	Mexico	Production of discrete devices.
	Malaysia	Assembly and testing of ICs. Production of discrete devices.
	Korea	Assembly and test of ICs. Production of discrete devices.
Matsushita	Singapore	Assembly of ICs, and production of discrete devices, for use by local Matsushita Electric systems manufacturing operation.
Tokyo Sanyo	Taiwan	Assembly and test of ICs. Production of discrete devices.
	Korea	Assembly and test of ICs. Production of discrete devices.

Notes: Fujitsu, Mitsubishi, Oki and Sharp apparently own no assembly affiliates in developing countries. Smaller Japanese semiconductor producers with offshore assembly affiliates include Mitsumi (South Korea), Rohm (South Korea), Sanken Electric (South Korea), Toko (South Korea), and Tottori Sanyo (Hong Kong).

NA: Not available.

Source: Yano Research Institute (1984), Kimura (1986).

the discretionary authority of government officials over duty-free re-import. A factor that is probably at least as important, however, is that Japanese firms have consciously chosen a strategy that emphasizes automated assembly. This is consistent with their emphasis on higher-volume standardized products offered into the merchant markets. Even though the Japanese tariff rate was also lowered to zero in April 1985, few analysts expect any shift toward offshore assembly by Japanese firms.

European firms also make rather little use of offshore assembly, with less than 20 per cent of EEC production of ICs sent for foreign assembly and then re-imported into Europe.[6] To a large extent, this

[6] Grunwald and Flamm (1985).

reflects EEC tariff provisions that favor assembly within the EEC. The European tariff on uncut silicon wafers is 9 per cent, while the tariff on semiconductor devices is 17 per cent. This provides substantial effective protection to EEC assembly, and has led many American firms and several Japanese firms to establish assembly (or full manufacturing) operations in the EEC. Furthermore, the EEC outward processing regulations grant duty relief equal only to the tariff that would apply on the original component export in its untransformed state. Thus, the re-import into the EEC would be assessed at 17 per cent duty on its full value, with a reduction made at the 9 per cent rate for the original wafer that represents European and not foreign value-added. All transactions under these outward processing regulations must have the prior approval of the national customs authorities. Given the likely continuance of this protectionism and general industry trends favoring increasing automation of assembly, it is unlikely that European firms will expand their use of offshore assembly.

US International Trade

International trade is of major importance to the American semiconductor industry, but much of the trade is intrafirm and involves offshore assembly. Before 1968, the United States levied a tariff of 12.5 per cent on semiconductor imports. This fell to 6 per cent in 1972 as a result of the Kennedy Round of trade negotiations and to 4.2 per cent as a result of the Tokyo Round. As part of an agreement with Japan, the United States eliminated its tariff completely in 1985. No nontariff barriers affect semiconductors, although discrete devices became eligible for the generalized system of preferences (GSP) toward developing country exports only in 1981, and ICs have never become eligible. (GSP is now irrelevant, of course, since the abolition of the tariff on semiconductors in April, 1985.)

Information on American trade in semiconductors is shown in Table 18. Exports exceeded imports until 1978, but the trade deficit has widened in every year since then. In 1981, nearly three-fourths of American exports consisted of semifinished products sent abroad for assembly.[7] Historically, slightly more than half of these exports of semiconductor parts to developing countries have been re-imported into the United States, while the rest have been sold into foreign markets after assembly.

Table 18 has substantial detail on American imports of semi-

[7] Office of Technology Assessment (1983).

Table 18 *US Trade in Semiconductors, 1966–83, in Millions of Dollars*

Year	Exports	Imports			
		Total	807	806+807	806+807 Dutiable Value
1966	130	50	31	NA	NA
1967	152	50	36	NA	NA
1968	204	86	67	NA	NA
1969	336	134	106	127	58
1970	395	168	127	160	69
1971	360	187	130	178	84
1972	466	329	162	254	125
1973	888	611	223	413	226
1974	1310	953	346	684	373
1975	1071	802	312	617	326
1976	1461	1098	556	879	477
1977	1389	1358	864	1120	503
1978	1628	1775	1329	1478	592
1979	2155	2427	1852	1916	734
1980	2796	3326	2451	2506	926
1981	2791	3553	2798	2825	1023
1982	2950	4128	3106	3131	1156
1983	NA	4881	3368	3383	NA

Note: NA = Not available.

Sources: Grunwald and Flamm (1985), Finan (1975).

conductors, especially information on imports entering under items 806.30 and 807.00. These 806/807 imports are generally taken to be the re-import of devices assembled abroad by American companies. Grunwald and Flamm (1985) note several caveats to this supposition, including the facts that foreign producers, perhaps with little American content, might still use 806/807; that some American producers may forego the use of 806/807 on eligible imports, perhaps to avoid paperwork; and that some American content may become ineligible for duty-free treatment because of the way in which it is processed abroad. They believe such biases are probably small for semiconductors. They also note that customs valuations on these transactions are rather arbitrary because most of this trade is intrafirm.

As the figure suggests, imports under 806/807 have been a substantial share of total imports throughout the 1966 to 1983 period. Indeed, during 1969 through 1971, this share was 95 per cent, indicating almost no imports from sources other than the assembly affiliates of American firms. Since 1971 the share of 806/807 has fallen below 70 per cent in only 1973 and 1983, and then only to 68 and 69 per cent, respectively. Thus, the offshore assembly by American firms continues to dominate American imports of semiconductors.

The dutiable value of 806/807 imports is an estimate of the foreign value-added. As a share of the total value of 806/807 imports, the foreign value-added peaked at about 54 per cent during the 1973 through 1976 period. The share then fell to about 37 per cent during the period 1979 through 1982, the last year for which complete data are available. The reason for this is presumably that the costs of assembly are becoming a smaller fraction of the total costs of chip manufacture; as the complexity of IC devices increases, more cost is incurred in the design and wafer-fabrication stages of production.

One can also estimate the relationships of American exports to American production and of American imports to American consumption. Unfortunately, such estimates may be somewhat imprecise. Part of the problem is the complexity of the American trade pattern. But another problem is that one has to compare exports and imports with some measure of overall production. The typical measure – shipments – is not a particularly accurate measure; there appears to be some double-counting of devices as they are shipped and reshipped.[8]

With these caveats in mind, however, the following picture emerges from an analysis of the data. In 1960, American exports of semiconductors were about 2 per cent of domestic shipments. This share rose rapidly to about 10 per cent by 1965, 24 per cent in 1970, and over 30 per cent during the late 1970s. Since 1965, a growing portion of these exports has consisted of parts that are assembled offshore and re-imported into the United States. Exports adjusted for the American content of re-imported semiconductors were about 20 per cent of shipments throughout much of the 1970s.[9]

Imports as a share of domestic consumption rose from ll per cent in 1970 to nearly 30 per cent in the late 1970s. Again, however, a substantial portion of these imports represents re-imported American components. Imports adjusted for American content totaled 5 per cent of consumption in 1970, rising to somewhat less than 20 per cent in the mid- and late-1970s.[10] Furthermore, most of the 806/807 imports are controlled by American firms. The share of the American market captured by semiconductors with little or no American content is made up of imports other than 806/807 imports. These were only 1 per cent of consumption in 1970, rising to just 5 to 8 per cent later in the decade. This still overstates the penetration of foreign-based firms, because some of these imports are from the manufacturing subsidiaries of American-based firms.

[8] Grunwald and Flamm (1985).
[9] US Department of Commerce (1979).
[10] US Department of Commerce (1979).

Trade between the United States and Japan in integrated circuits is a topic that has been much in the spotlight recently. Unfortunately, the standard American sources of data on American trade are not helpful in examining this issue of bilateral trade. A substantial part of the American exports of ICs to Japan are sent first to an offshore assembly facility and then to Japan after assembly and testing; thus, American exports to Japan are seriously understated in the American data. Japanese data on US–Japan trade in ICs appear to reflect the trade situation more accurately, because the source of imports into Japan are generally traced back past the offshore assembly, and because Japanese firms make rather little use of offshore assembly. Data from Japan's Ministry of Finance show the United States with a trade surplus with Japan in ICs through 1979. Trade was roughly in balance in 1980 and 1981, but the balance shifted in Japan's favor in 1982 and beyond. The US deficit in IC trade with Japan was $133 million in 1982, $307 million in 1983, and $834 million in 1984. With the industry recession, the deficit then fell to $376 million in 1985 and about $350 million in 1986. One might recall that, even with this trade deficit, American-based companies still provide a larger share of Japanese IC consumption than Japanese companies do of American consumption.

In the late 1970s and early 1980s, perhaps about three-fourths of Japanese exports to the United States were DRAMs, but the mix has started to diversify. In the 1985, about one-third of Japanese exports to the United States were DRAMs, with other MOS memory products constituting a little more than another quarter.[11]

Japanese and European Trade

The policies toward trade of the Japanese and European governments have been rather different from those of the United States. Japan offered substantial protection to its semiconductor industry, especially in ICs, using quotas and tariffs to limit import competition and restricting foreign direct investment into Japan. These quotas and investment restrictions were liberalized and removed during the period 1974 through 1976. The Japanese tariff on imports of most discrete devices at that time was 6 per cent, with a 12 per cent tariff on imports of ICs and other discrete devices. These tariffs were reduced to 4.2 per cent in 1982 as part of the Tokyo Round trade agreements; they were eliminated completely in 1985.

[11] Integrated Circuit Engineering Corporation (1986).

Table 19 *Japanese Exports and Imports: Relation of International Trade in ICs to Japanese Production and Consumption, 1973–83*

Year	Exports as a percent of production	Imports as a percent of apparent domestic consumption
1973	2.3%	23.2%
1974	5.3	30.1
1975	11.5	27.8
1976	11.5	26.4
1977	15.2	24.0
1978	18.6	21.1
1979	28.3	26.4
1980	32.1	22.0
1981	29.0	18.9
1982	34.1	18.8
1983	37.2	17.6
1984	39.4	15.7
1985	31.6	11.6
1986	29.4	10.4

Source: OECD (1985), MacKnight (1987).

The relationship of international trade to the Japanese IC industry has shifted dramatically over the last decade, as shown in Table 19. The share of IC production exported has risen from only 2.3 per cent to about one-third between 1973 and the mid–1980s. During the same time, the share of imports in domestic consumption of ICs has fallen gradually from 30 per cent in 1974 to under 12 per cent. The jump in import penetration in 1979 apparently was the result of Japanese purchases of 16K DRAMs at the same time that Japan was also exporting substantial amounts of these. Faced with a capacity shortage, Japanese producers chose to maintain or increase exports in order to solidify their relationships with foreign customers. Japanese consumers, many of whom also produce these ICs, turned to imports temporarily to satisfy domestic demand.

Recently, about 40 per cent of Japanese IC exports have been shipped to the United States, and nearly 70 per cent of Japanese imports are from the United States (with some via offshore assembly facilities). Nearly 15 per cent of Japanese IC exports have gone to the EEC, and about 10 per cent of IC imports come from the EEC. Apparently IBM Japan accounts for a substantial portion of these imports from the EEC.[12]

Trade policy in the EEC has also been protectionist. The EEC tariff on semiconductors is 17 per cent, and this was not lowered as a result of the Tokyo Round trade agreements. This duty can be waived for devices not produced in the EEC, but one can never be sure such waivers will be granted. France and the United Kingdom

[12] Yano Research Institute (1984).

are also reported to use informal administrative quotas.[13] Furthermore, EEC Rules of Origin limit duty-free trade within the EEC to electronic products containing less than 5 per cent imported ICs. Semiconductors are eligible for duty-free entry under the EEC's Generalized System of Preferences (GSP), but the quantities permitted are extremely limited – for instance, only $9 million in total in 1978.

In contrast to Japan, European countries have generally not limited inward foreign direct investment. In fact, the relatively high tariffs, along with government procurement practices in some European countries that favor firms with local operations, have drawn in a substantial amount of investment by American firms and, recently, Japanese firms.

As an example of the danger of using trade statistics, the recent book by the OECD (1985) is instructive, especially its Table 8 showing the IC trade balances of the United States, Japan and the EEC for 1982 and 1983. In both years the combined trade deficits of the United States and the EEC far exceed the trade surplus of Japan, by about $3 billion in each year. Yet in no way does this represent some fourth player with substantial competitiveness in ICs. Rather, it shows the peculiar nature of trade in the semiconductor industry, especially the role played by offshore assembly.

13 Grunwald and Flamm (1985).

5

Technical Alliances in the Semiconductor Industry

The traditional way to understand the international aspects of economic activity – namely, through the standard categories of import and export by national firms – is increasingly limiting and misleading in the case of the modern semiconductor industry. This is so partly, as Chapter 4 explained, because of the peculiarly complex structure of international vertical integration in semiconductor manufacture. But it is also so because the conventional categories of international trade miss an important aspect of internationalization: the technical and economic linkages across international boundaries that consist in flows of know-how and capital rather than of goods.

This chapter examines the nature and extent of these connections within the semiconductor industry. In particular, we look at three categories of linkage:

1 Acquisitions of or equity investments in companies abroad;
2 International investment in semiconductor design, production, testing and assembly facilities;
3 International interfirm agreements, that is,
   - Joint ventures;
   - Technology exchanges;
   - Licensing/cross licensing;
   - Second sourcing; and
   - International private-sector research corporations.

In addition to providing a relatively clear and complete picture of the web of these activities as it is now developing, we also try in this chapter to provide some insight into the strategic and economic reasons behind such linkages.

The focus in this chapter is on private sector arrangements. We include in this the increasingly important phenomenon of university-industry co-operation, which we treat briefly in the final section of the chapter. Chapter 6 will take on the task of analyzing further the problems of competitive strategy in this interdependent world, while Chapter 7 looks at the public sector component of international co-operation, including programs to encourage co-operation as well as the broader sweep of government programs toward the semiconductor industry.

Much of the data on which this chapter draws – especially data on the various kinds of co-operative agreements – were collected specifically for this study. For a full description, see Haklisch (1986).[1]

Foreign Direct Investment and Acquisitions

Foreign direct investment (PDI) is a major dimension of competitive strategy in the semiconductor industry. The increasing cross-penetration of national industries through the establishment of production facilities by firms based in the United States, Japan and Europe is a tangible manifestation of the rising global interdependence of the industry. Acquisitions are also an important phenomenon, especially during the late 1970s. Indeed, foreign firms often have used acquisitions of local firms to establish foreign direct investment.

Acquisitions and Equity Investments

Few acquisitions of American semiconductor firms occurred before 1975, and those that did occur were of small ailing firms, often by large American conglomerates. Since 1975, the number of acqui-

[1] The database was compiled from published sources through a literature survey and a computer search of technical journals and the popular press through Predicast Prompt and Predicast F&D Indexes for the period 1978–1985. In addition, interviews were conducted with selected companies to confirm and augment the information gathered and to discuss its significance. A list of the companies interviewed and a sample interview questionnaire are contained in Appendix B of Haklisch (1986). The focus of the data collection was on semiconductors, including integrated circuits (MOS and bipolar), microprocessors, and discrete devices. Activities further downstream, in applications for information technology or consumer electronics, were therefore excluded unless they involved a semiconductor dimension. We do not represent this database as complete with respect to all firms and all activities. Nevertheless, we obtained information from a broad array of authoritative sources to be as representative as possible. Interviews and careful reviews of references suggest that this inventory is a fair reflection of the overall level of activity and involvement of participating firms.

sitions has increased significantly, including the acquisitions of several major American semiconductor firms. The acquirers, both domestic and foreign firms, are often systems producers seeking to develop or reinforce captive backward integration and, in some cases, positions in the merchant market. Thus, the buying firm views acquisitions or equity investment as a route to establish access to additional technology, especially advanced IC production capabilities, an assured source of supply, or access to the merchant market, especially the American market, through the acquired firm's marketing operation. In addition, the relatively depressed American stock market and the weak dollar may have made American semiconductor firms especially attractive to foreign buyers in the late 1970s.

The firm being acquired may also view the transaction favorably for a number of reasons. Such a firm might see an acquiring firm as a source of financial capital during a period in which capital requirements are rising but the issue of new equity is difficult. The firm may also see a potential buyer as a source of strategic guidance, of access to new end-use product markets (including the benefit of the acquirer's R&D efforts), or of access to foreign merchant markets.

Table 20 shows recent acquisitions of American semiconductor firms by other American firms. Among the important systems producers represented are Honeywell and GTE, the latter re-entering semiconductor production after a ten-year absence. Most of these investments were small in value. The largest include the acquisitions of Mostek by United Technologies, of American Microsystems (AMI) by Gould, of Intersil by General Electric, and of Synertek by Honeywell. United Technologies has since sold Mostek to Thomson-CSF of France and Honeywell has sold Synertek to AT&T. Also, GE has since acquired RCA, which has extensive semiconductor operations, but is talking about selling all its semiconductor operations.

IBM's investment in Intel is related to agreements for Intel to develop IC product technologies for IBM and to the reliance of IBM on Intel products such as microprocessors. It is reported that one reason for IBM's investment is to prevent a takeover of Intel by another firm, especially one that would not be friendly to IBM's interests. One recent fruit of this alliance is a technology-exchange agreement in which IBM will give Intel process technology and access to a library of chip designs in exchange for the right to customize Intel designs – especially microprocessors for personal computers – into IBM chips. Intel sees the agreement as inaugurating a shift away from mass production of standard devices and into

Table 20 *American Firms Buying other American Firms: Acquisitions of and Equity Investments in American Semiconductor Firms by Other American Firms, 1974–84*

Acquiring Firm	Firm Acquired	Date	Equity
Exxon	Zilog	1974	80%
Signal Cos.	Semtech	1976	12
Commodore International	MOS Technology	1976	100
Electronic Engineering of California	Siliconix	1977	NA
Standard Oil of Indiana	Analog Devices	1977	13
Borg-Warner	American Microsystems	1977	12.5
Commodore International	Frontier	1977	100
Bourns	Precision Monolithics	1978	96
Emerson Electric	Western Digital	1978	100
Honeywell	Spectronix	1978	100
Honeywell	Synertek	1978	100
General Telephone and Electric	SEMI	NA	NA
Signal Cos.	Unitrode	NA	NA
United Technologies	Mostek	1979	100
General Electric	Intersil	1980	100
Gould	American Microsystems	1981	100
Westinghouse	Siliconix	1981	38
IBM	Intel	1982	12
		1984	20

Sources: OECD (1985), Borrus, Millstein, and Zysman (1983).

customized-chip production.[2]

The most recent acquisition of one American firm by another is the purchase of Monolithic Memories by Advanced Micro Devices. Advanced Micro produces a relatively broad line of semiconductors, whereas Monolithic is more narrowly focused, specializing in programmable logic chips. The merged company is expected to have annual sales in the range of $800,000 to $1 million. The merger is widely touted as foreshadowing greater consolidation in the American industry.[3]

Foreign Direct Investment by American-Based Firms

The major American-based firms, and even some of the smaller firms, have engaged in substantial foreign direct investment. The foreign affiliates of American-based firms that are engaged in production activities can be divided into two types, those engaged in full manufacturing, including wafer fabrication, and those engaged in assembly, often with final testing as well. The assembly affiliates can be further distinguished as to whether their sales

[2] Brenton R. Schlender, "Intel Pact with IBM Is Seen Propelling Firm into Custom Computer Chip Line," *The Wall Street Journal,* 7 October, 1986, p. 4.

[3] Andrew Pollack, "Two Makers of Chips to Merge," *The New York Times,* 1 May, 1987, p. D1.

activity is mainly into the local or regional market or mainly for re-export back to the United States or to third countries. Finan (1975) calls the former type "point-of-sales" assembly affiliates, while the latter are usually called offshore assembly affiliates. The offshore assembly affiliates are located predominantly in developing countries. (We discussed offshore assembly in some detail in Chapter 4.) In addition to foreign affiliates with production capabilities, there are also affiliates that engage only in marketing and sales activities. An important type of sales affiliate is the design center, an affiliate working with customers to develop microprocessor software and/or non-standard ICs that fit the users' needs.

EUROPE

The first instance of FDI by a American semiconductor firm was the establishment of a British affiliate by Texas Instruments in 1957. (The affiliate began producing semiconductors by 1959.) A major motivation for establishing this affiliate was to qualify as a local producer in order to receive production contracts from the British government. Texas Instruments established its French subsidiary in 1960, largely to provide devices to IBM's computer-production affiliate in France.

Aside from offshore assembly, Europe has been the major focus of FDI by American-based firms. The size of the European market makes sales there desirable and profitable. Export of wafers fabricated in the United States generally would have been the preferred mode of supplying the European market in a world without frictions, because it permits the achievement of learning economies. Three factors, however, favor FDI. First, European production avoids the EEC tariff of 17 per cent as well as various nontariff barriers to semiconductor imports. Second, a local marketing effort, if not complete manufacturing, permits the firm to co-ordinate better with European buyers, a factor the importance of which has grown as IC designs become more complex. Third, the operation of local production improves the firm's chances of acquiring government contracts in countries where discriminatory government procurement policies pose a nontariff barrier to imports.

FDI into Europe by American-based firms grew throughout the 1960s and in the 1970s. A survey of 32 American semiconductor producers[4] indicated that by 1974 these 32 had established in Europe 19 wholly owned subsidiaries and 3 joint ventures engaged

[4] US Department of Commerce (1979).

in full manufacturing, as well as 24 subsidiaries engaged in assembly. The affiliates engaged in full manufacturing represented 71 per cent of the thirty-one affiliates worldwide identified by the survey as being engaged in full manufacturing.

The analysis by Finan (1975) of the FDI into Europe found several interesting patterns. First, in many cases there was a progression of activities by the affiliate. The affiliate was often initially engaged in design and sales activities. A facility for assembly and final testing was then constructed and put into operation, using imported wafers fabricated in the United States. Sometime thereafter the operations would be extended to wafer fabrication, resulting in a subsidiary engaged in full manufacturing.

Second, the large American semiconductor producers were responsible for all of the subsidiaries with full manufacturing capabilities. Indeed, only large firms with multiple American production plants had transferred wafer fabrication abroad. These firms had experience in transferring learning economies, the most difficult part of the technology to transfer. In most cases only well-established production processes were transferred, but slight differences in the composition of raw materials still created problems in achieving acceptable yields.

Smaller firms seemed to avoid FDI other than assembly because they could satisfy foreign demand, especially for their more innovative products, through export; because they were unwilling to commit and risk the necessary financial capital; and because they tended to concentrate on the American market as a sufficiently large challenge. Incidentally, this relationship of firm size to the extent of multinational investment is consistent with the results of more general research on the pattern of American FDI.

FDI by American-based firms into Europe has continued to grow in recent years, and joint ventures between American and European firms have also become prominent. Two locations, Scotland and Ireland, are of increasing importance for wholly owned facilities.

Scotland has become known as "Silicon Glen." Among the attractions for foreign semiconductor firms are the availability of technical personnel, related to the presence of several good local universities; the availability of production workers; and government efforts to promote investment. (These attractions are in addition to the general reasons for investing within the EEC noted above.)

Four American firms have established semiconductor production in Scotland. General Instrument, established in 1968, focuses on non-standard ICs. National Semiconductor engages in full manufacture of memory, linear, and logic ICs, as well as microprocessors. In 1986, Motorola shifted from assembly and test to full manufacture, including automated assembly, of a range of NMOS and CMOS ICs. Hughes designs and fabricates non-standard ICs, with an emphasis on CMOS and hybrid ICs sold into the European military end-use market.

A major attraction of Ireland is the favorable tax treatment of profits and other government programs promoting FDI into Ireland. Analog Devices established its Irish subsidiary in 1975 and engages in full manufacturing of linear ICs. Sales by its Irish affiliate accounted for about one-sixth of total company sales in 1983. Mostek established a production facility in 1979, with an emphasis on memory ICs. AMD has announced construction of a facility to engage in full manufacturing, with a focus on CMOS ICs. In addition, several American-based firms produce discrete devices in Ireland.

A number of joint ventures between American-based and European firms have been established recently for production in Europe. Harris and Matra (France) established a joint venture to produce non-standard and specialized ICs in 1979. Harris supplies the design and process technology, while Matra, with French government assistance, provides the finance. American Microsystems established a joint venture with Voest-Alpine (Austria) for the development, production, and marketing of ICs in 1981. American Microsystems holds a 51 per cent interest. The facility was opened in 1983. Mostek established a joint venture in 1982 with AEG-Telefunken, which was in serious financial difficulties, to take over the semiconductor production facilities of Telefunken and inject Mostek technology in the areas of NMOS, CMOS and non-standard ICs.[5]

In this same period, one major joint venture was formed and sold. In 1978, National Semiconductor formed a joint venture with St. Gobain (France) called Eurotechnique. In 1983 Thomson-CSF acquired National Semiconductor's 49 per cent share and then St. Gobain's 51 per cent share.

JAPAN

Foreign direct investment into Japan is at much lower level than into Europe. Until the mid–1970s, Japanese government policy

[5] Mostek, which was owned by United Technologies Corporation, fell into serious financial difficulties during the slump of 1985. UTC shut down production and then sold Mostek to Thomson-CSF of France in November 1985 at a considerable loss.

Table 21 *Foreign Direct Investment in Japan by American-based Merchant Firms**

American Company	Year Established	Information
Texas Instruments	1968	Three factories fabricate MOS and bipolar ICs. 3,000 employees in 1981.
Motorola	1980	Acquired 50% of Aizu Toko to establish joint venture to manufacture MOS ICs. Raised share to 100% in 1982.
Fairchild**	1972	Assembly and test of bipolar ICs opened in 1984. Expansion to full fabrication in 1987.
Analog Devices	1980	Assembly and test of bipolar ICs.
Raytheon	pre-1969	Joint venture (33%) with Japan Radio (67%) in New Japan Radio, which produces bipolar linear ICs, diodes, transistors, and other discrete devices.
International Rectifier	pre-1969	Joint venture (33%) with Kyosan Electric (67%) in International Rectifier Corporation of Japan. Produces rectifiers, diodes, and other discrete devices.
American Microsystems	1983	Joint venture (51%) with Asahi Chemical (49%) in Asahi Microsystems. Design and eventual manufacture of custom MOS ICs. AMI provides technology, Asahi provides finance and marketing.

Notes: * Affiliates with production facilities only.
** Owned by Schlumberger, a French firm.

Sources: Yano Research Institute (1984), OECD (1985), Tilton (1972).

required approval of all foreign direct investment into Japan in the semiconductor industry. Such investment was very difficult and generally permitted only if the foreign firm transferred significant technology into Japan and if the foreign firm accepted a minority interest in a joint venture with a Japanese company.

Texas Instruments was the only American company to mount a clear challenge to this policy. TI held a number of important IC patents, and in the early 1960s requested the right to establish a wholly owned subsidiary for IC production in Japan. The Japanese government rejected this request. Texas Instruments then refused to license its IC patents, preventing the Japanese IC producers from exporting without threat of suit. Sales of TI ICs by Japanese producers were legal within Japan because the Japanese government was very slow in approving Texas Instruments' applications for Japanese patents. In 1968 a compromise was reached in which Texas Instruments was permitted a half share in a joint venture with Sony on condition that it would license its patents and agree not to capture more than 10 per cent of the Japanese IC market. In 1972, Texas Instruments was permitted to obtain full ownership, with the market share restriction remaining.

Table 21 shows the current status of American-based firms with production facilities there. Texas Instruments remains the most important American producer in Japan. It operates three factories, one at Miho producing MOS memories, especially DRAMs; one at Hatogaya producing MOS microprocessors, digital ICs, and memory ICs; and one at Hinode producing bipolar digital and linear ICs. The Miho factory is being expanded to double its size. The value of shipments by Texas Instruments Japan is estimated at $59 million in 1979 and $130 million in 1983.[6] In early 1984, 80 per cent of Texas Instruments' worldwide production of 64K DRAMs came from the Miho plant.[7] Texas Instruments reportedly achieved noticeably higher yields on this product in Japan. The higher yields are apparently due not to differences in process or product technology but rather to the quality of effort of the Japanese production workers, especially their attention to details such as the maintenance of high standards in clean-room operations.

Motorola recently established fabrication of MOS ICs in a joint venture that was later taken over fully by Motorola. Fairchild expanded its assembly facility to full fabrication, but is seeking to sell this facility, perhaps to another American firm. Analog Devices has an assembly facility in Japan. Two joint ventures, one involving Raytheon and the other International Rectifier, were established before the liberalization of the 1970s and focus on the production of discrete devices. American Microsystems established a joint venture with Asahi Chemical in 1983 for non-standard MOS ICs.

In addition to these production facilities, a number of American semiconductor firms, including American Microsystems, Advanced Micro Devices, Signetics, Intel, Zilog, Mostek, National Semiconductor, LSI Logic, Harris, and Micron Technology, have sales offices in Japan, and some of these include design centers.

Foreign Direct Investment by Japanese Firms

Japanese firms have generally followed a cautious approach to FDI. This reflects in part their rather recent emergence as important factors in the IC markets outside of Japan and in part earlier

[6] Yano Research Institute (1984) and Yano Economic Research Institute (1982).
[7] Integrated Circuit Engineering Corporation (1985).

Table 22 *Acquisitions of American Semiconductor Firms by Japanese Firms*

Acquiring Firm	Firm Acquired	Date	Equity	Value*
Hatori (Seiko)	Micropower Systems	1971	77%	3
Toyo**	Exar	1971	53	1
Mansei Kogyo	Maruman IC	1976	60	3
NEC	Electronic Arrays, Inc.	1978	100	9
Toshiba	Maruman IC	1980	100	NA

Notes: * Millions of U.S. dollars
** Now Rohm.
NA Not Available.

Sources: Moxon (1980), Borrus, Millstein, and Zysman (1983).

government controls on FDI out of Japan. But perhaps the most important reason for the reticence of the Japanese in FDI is their fear of production outside of Japan – a fear grounded in a perception that foreign workers pay less attention to quality than do their Japanese counterparts, along with a general concern about the difficulties of managing foreign operations. In the late 1970s, less than 5 per cent of the value of semiconductor production by Japanese firms took place outside of Japan.[8]

UNITED STATES

As Table 22 suggests, until recently only four American firms had been acquired by Japanese firms, and these have all been rather small in value. Table 23 provides information on all FDI by Japanese firms in American production facilities. By the end of 1984, only two Japanese semiconductor producers had American affiliates engaged in full production, and both of these were based on acquired operations.

Fujitsu's recent aborted attempt to acquire an American semiconductor firm has received wide publicity. But that firm has been actively investing in the United States for some time. Fujitsu established an assembly facility at San Diego in 1980, focusing on memory ICs. Fujitsu Microelectronics also has six gate-array design centers, in Santa Clara, Boston, Dallas, Chicago, Minneapolis and Atlanta. In addition, Fujitsu owns 49.5 per cent of Amdahl, a

[8] Office of Technology Assessment (1983).

Table 23 *FDI in the USA by Japanese Semiconductor Firms**

Company	Year Established	Information
NEC	1978	Production of memory ICs, using facilities acquired from Electronic Arrays. Now reduced to assembly of ICs.
	1984	Large, highly automated plant at Roseville for full production of memory ICs, gate arrays, and microprocessors.
Hitachi	1978	Assembly of memory ICs. Expanding to full manufacture.
Toshiba	1980	Production of LSI devices and assembly of memory ICs and microprocessors, based on facilities acquired from Maruman.
Fujitsu	1980	Assembly of memory ICs.
Mitsubishi	1985	Assembly of memory ICs, especially DRAMs.
Oki	1985	Assembly of gate arrays and DRAMs.

Note: * Affiliates with production facilities only.

Sources: Integrated Circuit Engineering Corporation (1987), Yano Research Institute (1984).

computer maker that is also a captive producer of gate arrays for in-house use.

In September 1984 Fujitsu announced plans to build two plants in Oregon, including a semiconductor fabrication plant that would cost $130 million, employ about 500 people and begin production in 1987. This announcement occurred one month after Oregon repealed its worldwide unitary tax on corporations operating in Oregon. Fujitsu cited this development, as well as a generally favorable tax climate, the availability of skilled labor, an excellent system of higher education, and pleasant living conditions, in discussing its choice of Oregon as the location for these new facilities. However, with the advent of the industry recession, construction of the semiconductor plant has been postponed indefinitely.

In October 1986, Fujitsu agreed to buy 80 per cent of the American Merchant firm Fairchild from Schlumberger. The move was widely perceived as a forerunner of increased Japanese acquisitions of American firms. The decreasing value of the dollar made American merchant firms – many of which were suffering depressed stock prices – good buys for the Japanese. Moreover, the Strategic Trade Agreement, the price-fixing arrangement signed by the American and Japanese governments in July 1986, created an incentive for Japanese firms to produce in the United States where prices would not be controlled. The Strategic Trade Agreement never lived up to the hopes of its American proponents, however, and the proposed Fujitsu deal sufaced at a time when many in American industry and government were accusing the Japanese of failing to honor the pact. Commerce Secretary Malcolm Baldrige quickly pronounced himself opposed to the deal, and, although the government now possesses no direct power to block such acquisitions,[9] it announced it was prepared to throw any number of roadblocks in the way.[10] In March 1987, Fujitsu unexpectedly rescinded its offer, leaving the ownership of Fairchild in doubt.[11] The would-be acquisition has since been transmogrified into a long-term contractual relationship between Fujitsu and Fairchild.[12]

Among the Japanese producers, NEC has perhaps the most clearly defined and most ambitious strategy for penetrating the American semiconductor market. It began its push in 1976–77, when it added sales centers and multiplied revenues, especially through sales of 16K DRAMs. In 1978 it acquired Electronic Arrays, a move that NEC believes helped it to penetrate the American market more effectively. A new facility at Roseville, California began production in 1984, producing mainly memory ICs at first, with eventual production of gate arrays, microprocessors, and custom ICs expected. This facility incorporates state-of-the-art automation and is probably the most automated of any American IC fabrication plant. NEC also has a design center in Sunnyvale, California, focusing on gate arrays, and a design center in Boston, focusing on microprocessor applications. NEC currently transmits the designs back to Japan for fabrication.

In 1978, Hitachi established a facility in Irving, Texas, for the assembly of DRAMs and SRAMs fabricated in Japan. Hitachi Semiconductor announced in June 1984 that it would invest $45 million to establish a fabrication facility at Irving.

Toshiba acquired bankrupt Maruman IC in 1980 from another Japanese firm, Mansei Kogyo, that had previously invested in Maruman. Toshiba wanted production facilities for fast penetra-

[9] Some of the recent trade proposals emanating from Congress have included provisions that would explicitly allow the President to block foreign acquisitions. Leonard Silk, "Some Perils in Trade Bill," *The New York Times,* 27 March, 1987, p. D2.

[10] Peter T. Kilborn, "U.S. Asked to Block Japan Deal," *The New York Times,* 12 March, 1987, p. D1.

[11] Brenton R. Schlender, "Fujitsu Drops Plan to Acquire U.S. Chip Maker," *The Wall Street Journal,* March 17, 1987, p. 3.

[12] Brenton R. Schlender, "Fujitsu, Fairchild Semiconductor Plan Ventures Even Though Merger Is Ended," *The Wall Street Journal,* 18 March, 1987, p. 3.

tion of the American market. Toshiba replaced the top executives and top marketing staff, hoping to keep most of the rest of the company's personnel. But the disruptions and effects of the imposition of a different "corporate culture" resulted in the loss of 90 per cent of management within one year. These losses prevented the rapid expansion of production that Toshiba desired and prolonged the financial losses.

Toshiba Semiconductor now operates fabrication and assembly facilities in Sunnyvale, focusing on DRAMs, SRAMs, and other memory ICs. It is opening two design centers, one in Sunnyvale and the other near Boston, to establish itself in the American market for gate arrays. Terminals at these design centers will be linked via satellites to computers at the design center in Tokyo, with production of the gate arrays in Japan. Toshiba is reportedly planning the establishment of a large new fabrication facility in the United States.

Mitsubishi is constructing a facility for the assembly of DRAMs at Durham, North Carolina, that is expected to begin production in 1985. Oki is spending about $10 million to establish an assembly facility and is also reportedly searching for a location for a large fabrication facility.

In addition to these facilities in operation or under construction, Sharp announced an agreement with RCA in April 1985 to establish a joint venture in the United States to develop and produce CMOS VLSI devices. The company, named RCA Sharp Microelectronics, was to have been owned 51 per cent by RCA and 49 per cent by Sharp. The initial facility created was to have been a design center, and there were plans for a highly automated $200 million production facility in Washington State. This agreement was called off, however, soon after RCA was acquired by GE in 1986.[13]

Overall, the cautious approach of the Japanese firms toward FDI in the United States is seen in both the methods of entry and expansion and the types of products produced. Of the entries by major Japanese semiconductor producers, only two involved acquisitions, and these were relatively small. Although NEC views its acquisition positively, the problems encountered by Toshiba appear to be influencing the decisions of other firms, such as Oki, to enter *de novo*.

Interestingly, the products emphasized in the American production of Japanese firms – mainly DRAMs and other memory ICs – are precisely those the Japanese firms also export very successfully.

[13] Janet Guyon, "GE Abandons Joint Venture by RCA Unit," *The Wall Street Journal,* 11 July, 1986, p. 4.

These are high-volume standardized devices with little need for technical interactions with customers. Japanese FDI production thus is not yet oriented toward improving on weaknesses in software development, circuit designs, and customer interactions outside of Japan. One possible reason for this product emphasis is that the Japanese firms are responding to the threat of American protection against imports of Japanese memory ICs. Perhaps at least as important, the Japanese may be using production of memory ICs to accumulate experience in American production while minimizing risks.

Japanese firms have cited a number of advantages of American production, including access to American production equipment at somewhat lower cost; access to American software engineers; the ability to lay off workers during cyclical downturns in business; American wage rates that are similar to Japanese rates; and the low level of unionization in the American industry, which allows flexibility in the management of resources.[14] At the same time, Japanese firms view American production as more risky than Japanese production. One worry is the yield problems that often accompany inter-plant transfers of production. More importantly, perhaps, the Japanese also see risks in their ability to organize and manage in the United States. For instance, American workers are not considered to be as fastidious in attending to the details of production, which could result in lower yields. Thus, the transfer of production of memory ICs appears to be an attempt to gain experience in production with a product whose production is more straightforward and more easily managed.

Manufacture in the United States of products such as gate arrays and advanced microprocessors, which might help Japanese firms in improving their American technical service and marketing efforts, is still at a low level. In part this may reflect satisfaction with the operation of the design centers that co-ordinate customer interactions and then transmit designs back to Japan for production. But this also appears to be a stage in the evolution of the international strategies of the Japanese semiconductor producers. NEC in particular recognizes that there would be advantages to producing products requiring close customer interactions in the United States, especially advantages from avoiding language problems. And NEC does in fact expect its new Roseville plant to move into the fabrication of logic devices.

[14] *Business Week*, "Can Semiconductors Survive Big Business?," 3 December, 1979.

Table 24 *FDI in Europe by Japanese Semiconductor Firms*

Company	Location	Information
NEC	Ireland	Assembly and test of ICs, with major exports to NEC's West German sales affiliate. Opened 1974.
	Scotland	Assembly and test of ICs, especially memory and microprocessors. Opened 1983. Now expanding to full fabrication.
Hitachi	West Germany	Assembly and test of ICs, especially memory. Operations began 1982.
Toshiba	West Germany	Assembly and test of ICs, especially SRAMs and DRAMs. Opened 1984. Expect to add wafer fabrication.
Fujitsu	Ireland	Assembly and test of ICs, especially DRAMs. Operations began 1981.

Sources: Integrated Circuit Engineering Corporation (1985), Yano Research Institute (1984).

EUROPE

Table 24 provides information on FDI in Europe by Japanese firms. The strategies pursued here seem similar to those used by Japanese firms in their investments in the United States. Only the four largest Japanese semiconductor producers have production facilities in Europe. All of these currently are assembly affiliates, with expansion to full production underway or planned in some cases. NEC also has a design center for gate arrays in West Germany.

Foreign Direct Investment by European and Other Firms

European and other firms have also been rather less involved with FDI than have American firms, with the exception of Philips. In addition to a certain amount of FDI within Europe, most FDI by European and other firms has been in the United States. Very little FDI by European and other semiconductor firms has been in Japan, although one exception is the joint venture between Siemens and Fuji for the assembly of ICs in Japan.

In contrast with Japanese FDI into the American semiconductor industry, European FDI is more diverse in its motivations, methods and outcomes. Most notably, European FDI is more often effected through acquisitions, including two acquisitions of major American semiconductor firms. Table 25 lists acquisitions of American semi-

Table 25 *Acquisitions of US Semiconductor Firms by European and other Firms*

Acquiring Firm (Home)	U.S. Firm Acquired	Date	Equity	Value*
Northern Telecommunications (Canada)	Monolithic Memories	1969	12%	0.3
Siemens (W. Germany)	Dickson	1973	100	NA
Philips (Netherlands)	Signetics	1975	100	49
Northern Telecommunications (Canada)	Intersil**	1977	24	11
Siemens (W. Germany)	Advanced Micro Devices	1977	20	27
Siemens (W. Germany	Litronix	1977	100	16
VDO (W. Germany)	Solid State Scientific	1977	25	5
Ferranti (U.K.)	Interdesign	1977	100	4
Bosch (W. Germany)	American Microsystems***	1978	25	14
Lucas (U.K.)	Siliconix	1978	24	6
Siemens (W. Germany)	Microwave Semiconductor	1979	100	25
Schlumberger (France)	Unitrode	1979	14	10
Schlumberger (France)	Fairchild	1979	100	397
Thomson-CSF (France)	Solid State Scientific (Power Transistor Div.)	1979	100	NA
Siemens (W. Germany)	Databit	1979	100	NA
CIT-Alcatel (France)	Semiprocess	1980	25	NA
Siemens (W. Germany)	Threshold Technology	1980	100	NA

Notes: * In millions of U.S. dollars.
** GE subsequently acquired Intersil.
*** Bosch subsequently sold half of its share to Borg-Warner, and then Gould acquired American Microsystems in 1981.
NA: Not available.

Sources: Moxon (1980), Arthur D. Little (1980), Gresser (1980), OECD (1985).

conductor producers by European and other non-Japanese firms through the early 1980s. The bulk of these acquisitions occurred during 1977–9. This clustering of foreign acquisitions has also been noted in the aggregate, and it is often attributed to the relatively weak international value of the dollar and relatively depressed American stock prices during this period.

ACQUISITIONS BY EUROPEAN FIRMS

In 1975, Philips acquired Signetics, a major American producer, through the US Philips Trust. Philips has allowed Signetics to function with substantial autonomy, and Signetics is sometimes still categorized as an "American" firm. Communications and technology exchanges between parent and affiliate are generally considered to be good, but slow decision-making may be adversely affecting Signetics, which is considered to lag in the introduction of new product technologies. Signetics' production in 1983 was $435 million, nearly as large as all other Philips semiconductor production. Signetics produces mostly bipolar ICs but is attempting to build its MOS capabilities by transferring MOS technology from Philips.

With its acquisition of Fairchild in 1979, Schlumberger, which has no other semiconductor production, became the second-largest semiconductor producer among the European firms. Schlumberger's major business had been the provision of oil-field services, but it was attempting to diversify into new business and strengthen its existing electronics product-areas.

Fairchild had been plagued with strategic and operating problems before the acquisition. After the acquisition Schlumberger tried to address Fairchild's problems, but in many ways may have made them worse.[15] Schlumberger provided substantial capital to Fairchild, investing about $250 million in R&D and $500 million in new plant and equipment. At the same time, however, Schlumberger installed a new president at Fairchild who had had no semiconductor experience. There were three major reorganizations of management in the first four years after the acquisition; morale suffered as a result, and Fairchild lost key engineering and management personnel. The company decentralized much of its decision-making, but decisions about new products seemed to remain slow and more centralized. The firm also implemented more financial controls, held down salaries, and reduced or eliminated many of the fringe benefits and incentive-payment schemes typical in the industry. Nonetheless, Fairchild has suffered losses every year since its acquisition. As noted earlier, Schlumberger agreed in October 1986 to sell 80 per cent of Fairchild to Fujitsu for an estimated $250 million – a deal that the Japanese partner scuttled amid controversy. The future ownership of Fairchild is unclear, but a management buyout is said to be under consideration. Despite its foreign ownership, Fairchild, like Signetics, is often still categorized as an "American" producer, a status that will be made official if a management buyout does occur.

Siemens has not made a major acquisition but rather a series of

[15] *Business Week*, "Is the Worst Over for Fairchild Camera?" 14 November, 1983, and *Wall Street Journal*, "Schlumberger's Slip: Oil-Fields Highflier Finds Turbulent Skies in the Chip Business," 26 August, 1983.

small acquisitions and investments. Siemens' acquisition of Litronix has experienced serious problems. Litronix had been operating at a loss before the acquisition, and Siemens found the problems larger than expected. In addition, the American market for light-emitting diodes began to decline in 1977, and Litronix sales fell by one-half over the next several years. The company finally regained its 1979 sales level in 1984, and this is the first year since the acquisition that Litronix showed a small profit. Siemens' investment in AMD is of a much different character. The investment was part of a number of agreements reached between the two, including licensing and cross-licensing of technologies and a joint venture that has since been taken over by AMD. Siemens' major goal was to gain access to AMD technology in order to improve Siemens' IC capabilities. AMD acquired capital and access to Siemens' marketing and in-house demand for ICs. In June 1986, Siemens purchased Hyundai's wafer-fabrication facility in California.

A number of the smaller acquisitions shown in Table 25 have a similarity to Siemens' investment in AMD.[16] VDO acquired 25 per cent of Solid State Scientific in 1977 in order to assure access to technology and production capacity to meet the semiconductor needs of its automotive-systems production. Lucas, which had recently started captive production in Europe, acquired 24 per cent of Siliconix to meet the semiconductor needs of its automotive and aerospace products. In both of these cases the small American semiconductor firms acquired capital and a more assured demand for their products. The investment in AMI by Bosch, which had already started its own captive production in Europe, was part of a five-year joint IC-development effort. Gould, an American firm, acquired AMI in 1981.

Through its acquisition of Interdesign in 1977, Ferranti intended to launch a line of Ferranti's semi-custom designs in the United States. But Interdesign's own business grew so rapidly that the designs could not be introduced until 1982.

DE NOVO FOREIGN DIRECT INVESTMENT BY EUROPEAN FIRMS

The most unusual European FDI into American semiconductor production is Inmos, founded in 1978 by the UK National Enterprise Board. The initial operations of Inmos were set up in Colorado Springs in order to tap the American pool of scientific and engineering talent. The development center and factory in Colorado Springs employed about 800 people in 1984, before the industry recession hit.

[16] Borrus, Millstein, and Zysman (1983).

SGS, the Italian firm, recently announced that it is building a $90 million facility in Phoenix that will account for about a third of its total semiconductor output. This seems to represent a clear break from the approach of other major European firms to effecting entry into American production. SGS considered entry by acquisition, but instead chose *de novo* entry in order to have state-of-the-art facilities that met its needs closely.

FOREIGN DIRECT INVESTMENT BY SOUTH KOREAN FIRMS

Four South Korean firms have recently established subsidiaries in the United States.[17] Through these American facilities, the Korean firms hope to tap the American labor pool, circumventing the shortage of top-quality engineers in South Korea, and to learn American IC technology more quickly. The Korean firms are also actively recruiting scientific and engineering talent, especially Koreans now working for American companies, for positions back in South Korea. They are also sending Koreans to their American affiliates for training.

Samsung, through Tristar, its American semiconductor affiliate, invested about $30 million to establish facilities for research and prototype production in California, employing about fifty American and Korean-American engineers. Tristar began production of 64K DRAMs in 1984, based on a design purchased from Micron Technology, and began production of 256K DRAMs in 1985.

Hyundai, through Modern Electrosystems, invested about $40 million to establish research and prototype production facilities in Santa Clara, California. Production of ICs began in October, 1984, with an emphasis on SRAMs. In 1986, Hyundai sold this facility to Siemens.

Daewoo initially established IDFocus in Santa Clara to develop non-standard ICs for in-house use, but the company has since shifted emphasis to developing the technology for producing 64K and 256K DRAMs. In early 1986, Daewoo bought a controlling interest in Zymos. Gold Star is investing about $60 million in a design center in Sunnyvale, which is also being used to co-ordinate efforts with its American partners, especially its joint venture with AT&T.

[17] *The Wall Street Journal*, "South Korean Firms Honing Their Skills in U.S.'s Microchip Mecca, Silicon Valley," October 3, 1984, and *Business Week*, "Lucky-Goldstar: Using Joint Ventures to Sprint Ahead in the High-Tech Race," 9 July, 1984.

Table 26 *Profile of Companies and Agreements in Sample Pool*

Area	Number of firms	Number of agreements	Average number of agreements per firm
U.S.	12	100	8.3
Japan	10	64	6.4
Korea	4	19	4.8
Europe*	15	53	3.5

Note: * Signetics and Fairchild are included as European here.

Source: Haklisch (1986).

Interfirm Technical Agreements

In order to trace the trends in patterns of technical exchanges among semiconductor firms, we constructed from published sources an inventory of 121 agreements involving 41 firms in the United States, Europe, Japan and Korea.[18] Table 26 provides a profile of the firms and agreements by country.

Patterns and Trends

An examination of this inventory reveals a number of interesting patterns. First of all, the number of agreements appears to be increasing. Our data show a rise since 1981, with a sharp increase in 1984.[19] (See Table 27.) Second, the principal emphasis in these agreements is technology co-operation, especially co-operation tied to current and near-term interests. By contrast, research co-operation seems to be pursued primarily through other mechanisms with the focus on longer-term technical development.

The geographic distribution of the agreements is shown in Figure 4. Alliances between American and Japanese companies predominate with fifty-two agreements signed. There are thirty-five links between American and European firms, reflecting a preference for European companies to seek partners across the Atlantic rather

[18] For a fuller description of this data base, see Haklisch (1986), Table 1 (Appendix A).

[19] To date the agreements, we used the year associated with the agreement in published sources. Of the total 121 agreements, 106 had dates associated with them for the period 1978–1984. Obviously, since our sampling technique may have some biases inherent in it, the exact figures should be taken with some caution. But we believe the trend is real and not an artifact of the data sample.

Table 27 *Sample Pool Agreements by Year*

Year	Number of Agreements
1978	2
1979	1
1980	4
1981	22
1982	19
1983	16
1984	42
TOTAL:	106

Note: 15 of the 121 agreements could not be associated with a specific year.

Source: Haklisch (1986).

Figure 4 *Geographical Distribution of Agreements*

	U. S.	Japan	Europe	Korea
U. S.	--	52	35	13
Japan	52	--	9	3
Europe	35	9	4	3
Korea	13	3	3	--

Note: Firms located in the United States but wholly owned by European companies (e.g., Signetics and Fairchild) are here considered European firms.

Source: Haklisch (1986).

than across more proximate borders at home – we discovered only four pacts within Europe.

In the United States, the leaders in international agreements – Intel with 14, Motorola and Zilog with 8 each – are all important producers of microprocessors. Most of the international agreements in which these firms are engaged involve the transfer of microprocessor-design technology from the American firm to the partner. The majority of the agreements are for second-sourcing,[20] with the bulk of the remainder involving joint development of microprocessor designs.

In Japan, NEC (12 agreements), Hitachi (9), and Toshiba (9) are the most active in international agreements. Here the nature of the agreements is a bit more balanced, but transfer of microcontroller designs – in both directions – remains important. As one might expect, many of the agreements signed by the Japanese firms are for licensing of American microprocessor designs, while others involve the transfer to the United States and Europe of Japanese production technology. What is more surprising is the extent to which the Japanese firms are beginning to license their own indigenous microprocessor and microcontroller designs.[21]

Among the Europeans, the firms most active in international agreements are Philips with eight, Siemens with seven and Matra with six. There does not seem to be as clearcut a pattern in the nature of the technology flow in these agreements. Overall, the Europeans seem to be most interested in joint research and development projects of various kinds.

The growing participation of Korean firms in the international arena is also interesting. We uncovered 19 international ties in 1984, of which 13 were agreements between American and Korean firms. As we saw in Chapter 3, Korea probably has the strongest technological potential of any developing Asian nation, and is widely expected to become a major hotbed of IC production. The Korean firms seem clearly motivated in these agreements by a desire for a rapid infusion of technology. The technology-transfer process occurs several ways in these agreements: a Korean company can manufacture a product for an American company or can purchase the technology directly. This strategy is widely perceived as an attempt by the Koreans to copy the approach Japanese companies used a decade or more earlier.[22] The strategy seems so far to have been an effective – perhaps even a startlingly effective – one, helping firms such as Hyundai to develop from scratch in a matter of two or three years a capability in memory chips approaching that of the Americans. But licensing American technology and subcontracting production for American firms is only part of the strategy. As we saw earlier, the Koreans are also

[20] For example, in 1981 there were 9 second sources (3 unlicensed) for the Intel 8086 chip, 7 second sources for the Motorola 68000, and 5 second sources for the Zilog Z8000. See Haklisch (1986, Figure 2.6, p. 59).

[21] For example, Zilog is second source for NEC's proprietary V-series microprocessors and peripheral controllers, while Motorola is second source for two of Hitachi's eight-bit CMOS microcontrollers.

[22] On which see Finan (1982).

investing in American facilities – especially design facilities – in an effort to tap into American (especially Korean-American) personnel and know-how. For their part, American firms are motivated to form alliances with Korean firms by a desire to take advantage of low-cost production and to gain a foothold in the expanding Korean market.[23]

Technical Areas and Partnerships

The technical subjects of agreements span a broad spectrum, but there does seem to be some clustering in a few areas: microprocessors, memories and gate arrays, with CMOS technology a pervasive ingredient. Most agreements reflect a bilateral blending of technical strengths.

MICROPROCESSORS

Overall, microprocessors, microcontrollers and peripherals are the major technical foci in the accords we surveyed; they are part of at least 45 of the 121 agreements.[24]

American companies have asserted a dominant position in microprocessors. Indeed, by one estimate, 99 per cent of all microprocessors sold in 1984 were designed in the United States.[25] The Japanese, for their part, have mastered CMOS technology. As we saw earlier, CMOS holds a number of advantages for semiconductors in general and for high-density microcontrollers and microprocessors in particular.[26] The respective strengths of American companies in design and of Japanese firms in CMOS lie behind a significant number of US–Japan agreements in microprocessor and microcontroller technology. Here are some examples.

- **Intel–Oki** Under agreements in 1981 and 1984, Oki is to produce CMOS versions of Intel's microprocessors and microcontrollers.
- **Intel–Fujitsu** Since 1981, these two partners have co-operated on a number of Intel's microprocessor lines, including the

23 This is, of course, quite apart from more general motives for technical liaisons. For example, Zytrex licensed its semiconductor technology to Samsung under the pressure of bankruptcy.

24 Note (1) that fifteen agreements did not specify a technical area and (2) that agreements may include more than one technical subject as the focus of interest.

25 Bro Uttal, "Now the Japanese Challenge in Microprocessors," *Fortune*, 8 July, 1985, p. 10. In the same year, American companies accounted for 63 per cent of microprocessor sales, while Japanese firms accounted for 30 per cent and European firms for 7 per cent.

26 See section 2.3.1.

iAPX 86, the iAPX 88, the 8086, the 8088 and the 8089. They are now collaborating on the development of Intel's 80286 and 80386 microprocessors. Fujitsu is also second-sourcing Intel's 16-bit microprocessors.

- **Motorola–Hitachi** Under a 1981 agreement, Hitachi described its high-performance CMOS process in exchange for Motorola's 68000 mask sets. In a 1984 agreement, Motorola will second-source two of Hitachi's CMOS eight-bit single-chip microcontrollers.
- **Zilog–NEC** Under a five-year agreement (1984–9), Zilog will second-source NEC's V-series microprocessors and peripheral controllers. Zilog is thus the first American alternative supplier of a Japanese microprocessor. NEC will second-source the Z8000.
- **Zilog–Toshiba** Through a 1982 agreement, these partners established a ten-year cross-licensing arrangement for Zilog's Z80/Z800/Z8000 families. In exchange for its designs, Zilog obtained advanced CMOS versions of its Z-series microprocessors as well as process technology for CMOS fabrication.

A central feature in these and other accords involving microprocessors is second-sourcing, a mechanism for providing a customer with the security of an alternative supplier. Among the forty-five microprocessor-related agreements in the sample pool, about half involve second-sourcing. Second-sourcing can be a key mechanism for technology transfer, since design specifications as well as mask sets for lithography may be provided, enabling a company to acquire a new technology without developing it in-house. When combined with marketing strength and the availability of peripherals, second-sourcing can also be a strategic mechanism for establishing one's design as an industry standard.

One of the most interesting agreements in the area of microprocessors is that between Intel and NEC. Intel is the world leader in microprocessors and microcontrollers, with their designs accounting for about 60 per cent of industry sales.[27] NEC is the largest Japanese supplier in this field and is striving for a larger share of the global microprocessor business through its V-series. While Intel and NEC have collaborated on a cross-licensing, second-sourcing, and technology-exchange agreement for microprocessors, they are also crossing swords in court over whether NEC has violated Intel's copyright on the instructions for activating the basic functions of the 8086 and 8088.[28]

27 Uttal (1985), *loc. cit.*

28 *Electronics News,* 30 September, 1985, pp. 41, 48.

Another dimension to note in agreements about microprocessors and microcontrollers is the role and significance of peripherals. In the 1984 market for MOS microprocessors, microcontrollers, and peripherals, peripherals accounted for 56 per cent of sales as against 24 per cent for microprocessors and 20 per cent for microcontrollers. Peripherals can determine the saleability of a microprocessor or microcontroller since they are the control and interface for memory, logic, and general system functions. In order for a microprocessor or microcontroller to be accepted in the market, it must be accompanied by adequate peripherals, since these are the key to providing software and support, both of which are expensive in dollar cost, manpower and expertise. The importance of peripherals is reflected in a pact between Motorola and the Signetics division of Philips in which Philips agreed to produce adapted versions and peripherals for Motorola's 68000. Another illustration is NEC's network of agreements – NEC–Corvus Systems, NEC–Digital Research, and NEC–Tektronix – with each accord established to develop support families for NEC's V series.

MEMORIES

Memory chips – SRAMs, DRAMs, ROMs, PROMs, etc. – are also an important subject of technical agreements, but to a lesser extent than are microprocessors and microcontrollers. About fifteen accords in the sample pool were focused on memories, with CMOS memories a key ingredient. Examples include the technology exchange agreements Ricoh has with two American firms; the agreement by Japanese startup firm NMB Semiconductor to license 256K CMOS DRAM technology from Inmos of Great Britain; and the agreement by the Italian firm SGS to license CMOS technology from Toshiba.

As a group, Korean firms show the most interest in memories as a topic for international ties. These links are forged primarily with American firms. There appear to be only a few examples of links between Korean and Japanese firms despite the pronounced Japanese strength in this area. Overall, there seems to be a pattern of co-operative US–Japan ties and US–Korea ties in memories. Korean–Japanese accords are much more limited, perhaps reflecting, among other things, the potential competitiveness between the two in manufacturing capabilities.

An important characteristic of memories is that they are normally the locus of state-of-the-art advances in process technology, and their production can serve as a learning guide for the manufacturing of other types of ICs. The underlying reason is that memories do not require simultaneous mastery of manufacturing and design complexity, since the designs are repetitive and relatively less complicated than the process technology. Thus, capital and technical resources can be concentrated on manufacturing complexity, with the lessons learned transferred to other, more design-intensive, IC products.[29] Here lies the apparent rationale for the agreement signed between Philips and Siemens, a five-year (1984–9), $900-million joint R&D venture. It is the largest industrial R&D agreement on record in terms of funds committed and resources allocated. The agreement's focus is the development of one-megabit and four-megabit memories, and the endeavor has thus been dubbed the Mega Project. Funding will come from Siemens (30 per cent) and Philips (30 per cent), with the balance (40 per cent) from the German and Dutch governments. The major technical purpose of this accord is to accelerate the drive of Philips and Siemens to the forefront of submicron CMOS technology. Philips will develop a one-megabit SRAM and Siemens will develop a four-megabit DRAM. There will also be some exchange of laboratory personnel.

NON-STANDARD ICs (CUSTOMIZED PRODUCTS)

Non-standard ICs – which include gate arrays, linear arrays, standard cells and full-custom chips – were the subjects of about twenty agreements in the sample pool. The market for non-standard ICs is an area of increasing attention, particularly among captive American producers and vertically integrated Japanese firms who supply their own products. It is also of interest to merchant producers capable of close customer interaction.

Among the agreements in the sample pool, gate arrays were of most interest in the category of non-standard ICs. Fujitsu's activity in this area is especially pronounced in view of its equity interest in Amdahl and its six gate-array design centers in the United States. An agreement between Fujitsu and Texas Instruments involves mutual second-sourcing of CMOS and bipolar gate arrays. Texas Instruments provides bipolar gate arrays and Fujitsu provides them in CMOS. Monolithic Memories also has a second source agreement with Fujitsu and will supply 2.3- and 2.8-micron double-layer-metal CMOS silicon gate arrays.

Perhaps the agreement deserving the most attention in this area is the joint venture between Fujitsu and the British computer maker ICL,[30] which provides an example of a customer–supplier

[29] We will have more to say about the significance of this in the next chapter.

[30] This discussion of the ICL–Fujitsu agreement is drawn from John Lamb, "Teamwork with Tokyo," *Datamation*, 1 January, 1985, pp. 64–14 to 64–16, and from an interview with ICL.

Table 28 *Other Gate-Array Agreements*

Agreements	Comments
Hitachi(J)-Microcircuit Engineering(US)	Joint venture in gate arrays
Oki(J)-Thomson CSF(E)	Mutual second-sourcing of CMOS gate arrays
Ricoh(J)-Custom MOS Arrays(US)	Ricoh provides CMOS wafers in exchange for gate-array-design technology
LSI(US)-SGS(E)	SGS licensed gate-array technology from LSI Logic. They fit well since both use Toshiba CMOS technology.
LSI(US)-Toshiba(J)	Joint venture in CMOS gate arrays

Note: US = United States; J = Japan; E = Europe.

Source: Haklisch (1986).

relationship in gate arrays that has turned into a partnership. Originally established for the period 1981–8, the arrangement has been extended to 1991. ICL is reported to have paid $25 million to Fujitsu to supply gate arrays as well as CMOS and other technologies for their product lines. Under this agreement, Fujitsu produces an 8,000-gate CMOS chip for ICL. Fujitsu's largest CMOS gate array prior to this was a 2,000-gate chip. ICL also used Fujitsu's basic logic chip to design the microprocessor for its Estriel computer. The pact specifies an exclusive contract relationship for chips between ICL and Fujitsu. However, Fujitsu may supply other buyers. Another dimension of this relationship is that Fujitsu bought ICL's West Gorton, Manchester semiconductor facilities, which it now uses to supply gate-array logic chips to other customers in Europe. The partnership involves a number of technology-transfer mechanisms. There are close contacts between technical personnel in the two companies, maintained through six-month visits, frequent meetings, and high-speed facsimile between Tokyo and Manchester. This year, the agreement was extended to 1991 to cover collaboration on GaAs chips, fifth generation architectures and super computers.

Table 28 provides a sampling of other agreements involving gate arrays.

STANDARD CELLS

Standard cells are currently not a topic of great interest in technical agreements. However, given the potential of this market, it may become a subject of greater co-operation in the future. The accord between Philips/Signetics and Texas Instruments is the major example of collaboration in the area of standard cells. Under the terms of this arrangement, no money or technology is to be transferred. The partners will develop an Electronic Design Interchange Format (EDIF), a common customer-interface language that will facilitate semiconductor design. This pact establishes the most complete standard-cell library announced to date.

Patterns and Motivations

A closer look at the details of all these agreements reveals some interesting points. About forty accords in the sample pool are limited to the transaction of one company licensing technology from another. However, the dominant pattern is the exchange of technology for technology, a bilateral flow rather than a unilateral one. Moreover, the flow typically involves technology of comparable sophistication moving between technical peers. This is evident in four types of relationships.[31]

- Technology-sharing agreements.
- Accords for joint and/or complementary development.
- Customer–supplier partnerships.
- Joint-research pacts.

Technology-sharing agreements in the sample pool most often involve an exchange of comparable technical expertise, a two-way flow. A major example is the US–Japan agreements in which American design capabilities have been traded for Japanese competence in CMOS-fabrication technology. The following agreements illustrate this type of relationship (although they may not be limited solely to technology sharing).

AMI – NEC
Fujitsu – Texas Instruments
Hitachi – Motorola
Oki – Intel
Oki – Standard Microsystems
Oki – Thomson-CSF
Ricoh – Custom MOS Arrays
Ricoh – Rockwell
Toshiba – Zilog

[31] This section draws in part on OECD (1985).

One exceptional arrangement provides an example of a technology-sharing agreement in which technology is not actually exchanged: the agreement between Philips/Signetics and Texas Instruments to establish a joint standard-cell library. However, while no technology *per se* is being exchanged in the agreement, this collaborative approach is innovative, with the result, potentially, of a significant asset in an area with a projected high growth market.

A second type of relationship is focused on development and may involve a joint effort directed to a single technology, such as collaboration on a group of logic devices or a particular microprocessor, or, alternatively, co-operation involving complementary tasks in which one partner may work on a specific microprocessor and the other on its related family of peripherals. Some agreements that contain this ingredient are the following.

SGS – Toshiba
Siemens – AMI
Siemens – Intel
Matra – Harris
Philips – Motorola
Philips – RCA
Intel – Fujitsu
NEC – Tektronix
National Semiconductor – Oki

Another category of relationships is customer-supplier partnerships. What distinguishes these arrangements from the typically close customer-supplier relationships in the semiconductor industry is the formalization of a link that reflects a significant reliance of the partners on one another. It may or may not involve an equity interest and may or may not involve an exclusive relationship. Its primary feature is that it responds to the intensifying systems dimension of components and provides a mechanism for leveraging critical technical and financial resources for the partners. The principal illustration described here is the ICL–Fujitsu venture in which ICL has an exclusive contract with Fujitsu to "intercept" certain technologies for its product lines. ICL depends on Fujitsu for its silicon foundry, while Fujitsu obtained ICL as a key first customer for its CMOS components. Other examples of customer–supplier partnerships include:

Nixdorf – Ferranti
Goldstar – ATT

Amdahl – Fujitsu
Zilog – Olivetti
GS – IBM

A fourth category, research relationships, has only one major entry – the Philips–Siemens agreement – even though co-operation in research is clearly a factor in most joint-development accords and customer–supplier relationships. The scale of the research component of the Siemens–Philips agreement stands in contrast to that of the balance of co-operative ventures in the sample pool, thus pointing to a principal characteristic of these agreements: almost all of the activities center on technology co-operation rather than on research co-operation. Research co-operation, when it occurs, appears to be conducted primarily through mechanisms other than interfirm agreements, such as research corporations or university-based research centers (see below) or consortia established under national programs (see Chapter 7).

Having looked at what *is* happening in company-to-company technical agreements provokes the question: "what is *not* happening?" On a specific level, the principal subjects of technical interest in these accords are microprocessors, memories and gate arrays; and the major form of co-operation is technology co-operation. By contrast, there is scant indication of international research co-operation taking place between firms. In addition, topics not tied to current markets of some size – topics such as EEPALs,[32] standard cells and GaAs – are not subjects of much interest.

More broadly, there is considerable technical co-operation occurring in a complex network, but in parallel with independence. Companies are not unilaterally licensing technical advances central to their competitive thrust; co-operation occurs primarily on the basis of mutual and equitable exchange. Moreover, companies are pursuing a variety of linkages, with each firm establishing a portfolio of technical links to achieve its objectives. In addition, no projects are so large that, if the project fails, the company fails. Not even the Philips–Siemens venture falls into this category. Even at the peak of spending, for instance, the financial commitment of Philips would not exceed 20 per cent of their worldwide R&D expenditure in ICs.[33]

In addition, for American firms, these international agreements between firms parallel a system of relationships established on a

[32] EEPALs or EPALs are electrically erasable or erasable PALs (logic devices). This is a new, innovative device designed to offer reconfigurable logic ICs.

[33] Private communication with Nico Hazewindus of N.V. Philips, November 1985.

national level. There are within the United States significant technical partnerships that are similar to the international ones in terms of the scope, focus and length of the agreements. Our sample reveals the following characteristics of agreements among American firms.[34]

- Just as it is the most active at the international level, Intel is the firm most active in establishing national accords. AMD, National Semiconductor, and Texas Instruments are also active in signing agreements with other American companies.
- A series of agreements and/or long-term accords are as much a part of relationships among American producers as they are at the international level. Two examples are Intel-AMD and National Semiconductor-Texas Instruments.
- As in the international agreements, microprocessors and microcontrollers are the principal subject of technical interest in the national agreements; similarly, there is little attention devoted to GaAs in the accords. However, one national agreement was concluded with EPALs as the technical focus (Intel–Altera, 1984) Also, the agreements signed in 1984 show a strong interest in standard cells. Memories play a much smaller role in intra-American agreements than they do at the international level, presumably because those devices are increasingly a Japanese specialty.
- The types of relationships evident in the international sample pool are also present at a national level. Examples include: (a) technology-sharing agreements (AMD–LSI Logic); (b) accords for joint and/or complementary development (Fairchild–National Semiconductor); and (c) customer–supplier partnerships (Texas Instruments–IBM). However, there were no joint-research pacts among the national agreements; American firms appear to pursue co-operative research primarily through mechanisms other then interfirm relationships.
- Finally, international agreements do not seem to be supplanting national agreements among American producers.

Other Collaborative Arrangements for Research

Research Corporations

Research corporations are private-sector joint-R&D ventures that conduct their own research. They are thus a new mechanism for

[34] For more detail, see Haklisch (1986, Figure 2.7).

technical co-operation. Two have recently been established that merit examination, one international – the European Computer Research Center (ECRC), and one national – the Microelectronics and Computer Technology Corporation (MCC) based in the United States. Several features distinguish these corporations from other mechanisms such as industry consortia or research associations. The research corporations have set up separate laboratories and research facilities, staffed by scientists and engineers from the member firms as well as by new hires. The research focus is on generic technology that directly relates to the competitive interests of member firms. These research corporations may perform both proprietary and non-proprietary research, thus limiting the diffusion of at least a portion of the research findings. The work is ongoing and ultimately has a clearly commercial focus.

The ECRC was established in 1983 as a separate company by ICL of the United Kingdom, Bull of France, and Siemens of the Federal Republic of Germany to conduct research in artificial intelligence, computer-aided design, voice and network software. The main emphasis will be on expert systems. The Center, whose facilities are located in Munich, is funded jointly by these three computer mainframe manufacturers at a current level of about $7.5 million annually. About 80 per cent of the staff are scientists and engineers.[35]

Although not international, the MCC is similar in form to the ECRC. Established in Austin, Texas in 1983, it has a decidedly national purpose: "to help maintain US technological preeminence and international competitiveness in microelectronics and computers."[36] The MCC is owned by twenty-one American shareholder companies in both microelectronics and computers.[37] The technical program is focused on packaging, software technology, VLSI/CAD, and advanced computer architecture. This last area is the largest area of interest and will span a ten-year effort devoted to parallel processing, database-system management, human-factors technology and artificial intelligence/knowledge-based systems. The MCC is much larger than the ECRC, with a $50 million technical budget in 1985 and a staff of scientists and engineers that will exceed 300 by the end of 1986. About 45 per cent of the MCC's research program is related to semiconductors: packaging, inter-

[35] This section draws on OECD (1985).

[36] MCC press release, 1984.

[37] One of these shareholders is another research corporation, Bell Communications Research, Inc. or Bellcore, the research arm of the seven regional telephone companies recently divested from AT&T.

connect and CAD. The comparable fraction of ECRC's activities that are related to semiconductors is not available.

In view of the youth of these corporations, it is too early to assess their success or effect on the technical base of the participating companies or the industry in general. Nevertheless, the fact that a number of profit-oriented companies are willing to invest in these organizations suggests that they have at least the potential of becoming important mechanisms of, and models for, technology generation and diffusion. (We will have more to say on this in Chapter 7.)

Industry–University Research Groups: The American Example

Private-sector research corporations are a novel institution for R&D in the semiconductor industry. But there is an older and better-developed set of institutions that have been operating toward the same ends since the beginning of the industry: university research sponsored by industry. In the last few years, the network of university–industry ties has not only expanded but also changed significantly in form. In the United States, the university-based research group is becoming the dominant form of university–industry research interaction.

This section takes a look at a sampling of university-based groups that are pursuing semiconductor-related research with the support of industry. Our purpose is to examine the extent and focus of these interactions; to discover the part they play in the scheme of technical co-operation; to determine which companies interact with this resource; and to see how these activities relate to the rest of the R&D network.

Our results here are based on a survey[38] of university-based research groups receiving industry support.[39] The seventeen research groups in our survey are funded at approximately $81 million for 1984 and $93 million for 1985.[40] Thirteen of the 17 were founded since 1977; of these, 9 have annual budgets of $2 million or more. Within this group of 9, 6 indicate 16 or more corporate

[38] The survey was conducted between December 1984 and April 1985. We sent twenty-nine university groups a questionnaire asking for the following information: (1) year of establishment; (2) technical budget for 1984; (3) projected technical budget for 1985; (4) a list of corporate sponsors; and (5) areas of research interest. Seventeen groups having at least two corporate sponsors each responded within the time constraint of the study. For a detailed discussion, see Haklisch (1986). This section also draws on Fusfeld and Haklisch (1985); Peters and Fusfeld (1982); and Haklisch, Fusfeld, and Levenson (1984).

[39] Many of these groups also receive government support.

[40] There is some overlap of SRC funding in these figures since the SRC supports all of the institutions represented in this survey but not all of the research groups.

sponsors. By funding, the two largest groups are the Microelectronics Center of North Carolina and Stanford University's CIS, each with projected technical budgets for 1985 of $25 million. The National Submicron Center at Cornell and the Semiconductor Research Corporation (SRC) have the most participating companies, with thirty-seven each.

As the following examples suggest, the organizational characteristics of these groups fall into several different categories.

- The Semiconductor Research Corporation (SRC) is a non-profit industry association established "to promote basic research by universities in the scientific fields underlying semiconductor technology by pooling company membership fees and contracting with universities throughout the country for the creation of major research centers and specific research projects."[41] The SRC performs no research itself; rather, it serves as an organizational vehicle for channeling support from SRC member companies to universities for conducting research in fields of priority interest to the SRC. Funds are also used for improving educational programs and upgrading scientific equipment. Contracts have been awarded on three levels: major research "centers of excellence," major research programs, and individual university research projects.
- The Microelectronics Center of North Carolina (MCNC) is a state initiative representing the combined resources of five universities and the Research Triangle Institute, a non-profit research institute. The bulk of support is provided by the State of North Carolina, with the balance coming from industry; over the period 1981–85, the MCNC will be financed at a level of approximately $50 million, of which $43 million will come from the state and $7 million from industry affiliates.
- The Stanford University Center for Integrated Systems (CIS) and the University of Minnesota Microelectronics and Information Sciences Center (MEIS) are multidisciplinary research centers located at a single university that draw most of their support from industry and the federal government. A distinctive feature of the Stanford Center is its level of funding – about $25 million for 1984 – and the construction of a $14 million research facility to house it. Each of the twenty sponsoring firms will assign a company scientist to work at the Center. The Center anticipates training 100 Masters and 30 Ph.D. candidates per year.

[41] Erich Bloch, former chairman of the board of the SRC, written statement before the Senate Finance Committee, 24 February, 1984.

The element, however, that is common to all of these groups is a single set of objectives: "accelerating the progress of research in semiconductor technology, broadening the university base, and increasing the supply of qualified personnel for the industry."[42] John Young, President of Hewlett-Packard, articulates the industry perspective well in explaining his company's sponsorship of Stanford's CIS.[43]

> CIS is a version, in our own culture, drawing on our own institutions, of [the] co-operative-yet-competitive model. It will enable US electronics companies to discuss and coordinate our research objectives and to gain leverage on our expenditures. Even companies as large as Hewlett-Packard, with half a billion dollars to spend on R&D every year – and IBM, with much more – sense that this kind of co-operative effort is going to be necessary for us to succeed in the competitive international environment between now and the end of the century. Support for education isn't altruism on our part; we recognize that without a substantial research base, we're out of business.

Our survey inquired into areas of research under seven headings: Function, Technology, Process, Quality, Design, Integration Level and New Developments. A number of patterns emerged from the responses.[44]

- **Function** Digital ICs are a topic of major interest with 14 of the 17 groups, with logic ICs receiving special emphasis. There is a fairly high interest in memory ICs relative to microprocessors; this reverses the pattern of technical focus we saw in the international technical agreements, in which microprocessors receive the most attention.
- **Technology** Significant strength in silicon, the cornerstone of the industry, is evident in the responses (15 out of 17), with MOS of greater interest (14) than bipolar (9). This interest in silicon is a fairly recent development, however. The SRC points out that, in 1982, only $7 million of the $70 million given to universities for semiconductor research was devoted to silicon. By 1984, $23 million was being spent on silicon-related research. Gallium arsenide is also a subject of research interest in more than half of the groups, another pattern that contrasts

[42] SRC 1984 annual report.

[43] Quoted in Frederick H. Gardner, "The Center for Integrated Systems," *Hewlett-Packard Journal*, November 1983, p. 24.

[44] For a fuller description, see Haklisch (1986, Figures 3.3 and 3.4).

with the low level of interest in GaAs as a technical focus in the cross-country interfirm agreements.

- **Process** The survey groups indicate a strong focus on process technology, particularly in lithography (especially optical and electron-beam) and chip fabrication. Three groups mention research on the disposal of toxic chemicals generated in the semiconductor-fabrication process.
- **Quality** Almost all of the groups report some activity in this area, with the primary focus devoted to testing and reliability.
- **Design** Computer-aided design (CAD) is a subject of widespread interest: 16 of the 17 groups are involved in CAD research. Thirteen indicate special attention to design style, with full custom chips the subject of most attention (12) and gate arrays the subject of least emphasis (3).
- **Integration level** VLSI is clearly the area of most activity in this category. In addition, 10 groups are pursuing work in discrete devices and 7 are focusing on wafer-scale integration.
- **New Developments** Twelve of the 17 report research in this area. Five of the groups indicate work in both superlattice devices and three-dimensional ICs. These were subjects of scant interest in the international agreements.

The 17 groups in our survey had 96 major sponsors. A scan of the list of supporting firms[45] reveals widespread interest in semiconductor research. *Business Week* groupings represented by participating companies include: aerospace, automobiles, chemicals, conglomerates, electrical, electronics, fuel, information processing (computers, office equipment, and peripherals), instruments, leisure-time industries, metals and mining, semiconductors, and telecommunications.

Twenty-three firms[46] support three or more groups. These companies represent primarily those sectors most directly related to microelectronics – electrical, electronics, information processing, semiconductors and telecommunications. Of these 23, 4 are merchant semiconductor firms. The most active corporate sponsors are IBM and GE. They each support nine survey groups. The most active semiconductor merchant firm is Motorola, which supports 6 groups, followed by Texas Instruments (5), Harris (4), and Intel (4). Several foreign firms also support US university-based research: NEC supports work at Cornell's MCSR group, Philips/ Signetics supports work at Cornell's National Submicron Facility and Stanford's CIS; and Hitachi supports work at Texas A&M's

45 Haklisch (1986, Figure 3.5).

46 This includes the SRC.

TMRC. Among American firms, Motorola and National Semiconductor are the companies most active in co-operative mechanisms of all sorts: each has reported four or more technical agreements with both American and foreign partners, each is a member of the MCC and SRC, and each supports university research groups outside the SRC. These firms thus exemplify active participation in a mix of linkages for research and technology co-operation. In addition, AMD, Harris, Intel, RCA and Texas Instruments also represent active involvement.[47]

[47] See Haklisch (1986, Figure 3.6).

6

Patterns of Competitive Strategy

The preceding chapters have attempted to depict the technological and economic patterns of interdependence in the worldwide microelectronics industry. This chapter begins to tie some of these strands together. In particular, the chapter begins to ask the next questions: how have the corporate strategies of individual firms influenced these patterns? And, perhaps more interestingly, what implications do these patterns of interdependence have for the formulation and execution of strategy in the microelectronics industry?

In order to answer these questions, we have to begin by setting up a framework on which to analyze competition and competitive strategy. One of the most prominent of such frameworks is that developed by Michael Porter.[1] We begin by reviewing the Porter framework and then applying it to the microelectronics industry. The review pays special attention to the roles that technical alliances play in the strategic process. We also discuss the limitations of Porter's approach as a way of understanding – and formulating – strategy in this industry. Finally, we undertake a detailed comparison of the dominant strategic tendencies in the United States and Japan.[2] This comparison, we believe, will help to sharpen the issues in the ongoing debate over international competitiveness. For it is our (somewhat provocative) thesis that international differences in strategic approach account in large part for

[1] See especially Porter (1980) and (1985). Porter (1983) applies the approach specifically to technology strategy and innovation.

[2] The descriptions and arguments used in this comparison are based on information collected partly in an intensive review of research studies and current articles on the microelectronics industry and partly in interviews within eight American and eight Japanese microelectronics firms. (Similar interviews were conducted in European firms, but the results will here be kept in the background to focus the comparison between the United States and Japan.) A comprehensive account of this research is being published as a separate report (Egelhoff, 1986).

the emerging pattern of international competitiveness. All of this will set the stage for our discussion, in Chapter 7, of government policies toward the microelectronics industry.

Competitive Strategy: The Framework

At the broadest level, a competitive strategy is an integrated set of policies designed to create a sustainable competitive advantage for the firm adopting the policies. Students of corporate strategy normally divide the strategic process into two parts: strategy formulation (the business of choosing a strategy) and strategy implementation (the business of getting the chosen strategy to work as planned). For the moment, we will be concerned primarily with the formulation of strategy.

General Strategies

According to Porter, there are two fundamental dimensions to strategy. Along one dimension is the choice between a strategy emphasizing *low-cost* production and along another dimension a strategy emphasizing *product differentiation*. The former option emphasizes supply-side capabilities, that is, the ability to produce the product cheaply; the latter option, while not implying a complete neglect of cost considerations, nonetheless tends to emphasize attention to the demand side of the market, that is, to knowing and meeting customer needs effectively. Along the second dimension lies a choice between an *overall* approach and what is called *focus*. In the overall approach, the firm attempts to market a full-line of products and/or to sell to all types of customers. With focus, the firm targets a particular customer segment (perhaps defined by type of customer, by geography, or by product type), or emphasizes, for instance, a particular channel of distribution.

In many industries a variety of strategies are feasible and viable, but the number of distinct strategies, whether they be pure types as defined above or mixtures of these pure types, is limited. In these cases, rather clearly defined strategic groups then arise, with firms within a group following approximately the same strategy, and firms in other groups following substantially different strategies. Such strategic groups are particularly meaningful in terms of economics if there are so-called mobility barriers, that is, if firms in at least some of these groups would face substantial impediments in attempting to alter successfully their strategies in order to move into another, perhaps better-performing, group.

Applications to the Microelectronics Industry

Wilson, Ashton and Egan (1980) identified four major strategic groups in the American merchant semiconductor industry. One dimension they used distinguished between full-line firms, those adopting an overall approach to their product offerings, and specialized firms, those adopting a focused approach to their product offerings. The other dimension distinguished between those firms that often emphasized major innovations in their pursuit of new products and production processes and those firms that typically emphasized incremental and adaptive changes in their technologies. (This is essentially the distinction between technological leadership and followership that we discuss further below.)

Wilson, Ashton and Egan conclude that, through the late 1970s, Texas Instruments and Fairchild constituted a strategic group of full-line producers that often emphasized major innovation. Intel, Mostek and, possibly, RCA belonged in the group of specialized firms that often emphasize major innovations. Motorola, National Semiconductor, and Signetics formed the group of full-line producers that largely pursued incremental innovations. And a large number of firms, including AMD, AMI, Intersil, General Instrument, Rockwell and Zilog, formed the fourth group of specialized producers pursuing incremental innovations. The large size of this last group is consistent with the proposition that entry barriers are relatively the lowest into this group, so that start-up firms usually enter the industry in this group. Mobility barriers then often prevent such firms from shifting into one of the other groups, or at least make this shift difficult – both costly and risky. Indeed, this group of firms exhibited the lowest profitability, defined as the after-tax rate of return on equity, of any group averaged over 1972–8. Profitability was highest for specialized, high-innovation firms.

Since the Wilson, Ashton and Egan study appeared, there seems to have been some shifting of strategic positioning among the firms. It is now somewhat questionable to call Fairchild and Signetics full-line firms in view of their weaknesses in producing and marketing MOS ICs. Texas Instruments has de-emphasized the production of discrete devices, somewhat diminishing its status as a full-line firm. Motorola has arguably become somewhat more innovative, especially in the areas of microprocessors and advanced discrete products. Zilog has also been innovative in the area of microprocessors. AMD and AMI suggest that an additional dimension should be added to the scheme – the extent to which firms pursue significant differentiation in their product offerings. AMD has been emphasizing the development of proprietary designs tailored to the needs of specific customer groups, while AMI has emphasized production of custom ICs for individual buyers.

AMD claims that 40 per cent of its semiconductor sales are in truly proprietary products. It has used about 100 engineers to identify opportunities in market niches and to design ICs to meet these specific needs. Such ICs are generally more profitable, as there is little initial competition. AMD reports that, while the average selling price for ICs in the industry was $1.02 in 1983, its own average selling price was $3.19. However, there are also clear risks in this strategy. If sales in the market-segment become large enough, more than one firm can fit into the niche. Entry by other suppliers then becomes likely, whether based on imitation or on designs incorporating technological improvements. The "local monopoly" is lost. Another risk is that the ability to continue to define and design for new niches may decline over time.

AMI has been the world merchant leader in fully custom-designed chips, with over half of its semiconductor sales in this area. It also has strength in non-standard approaches such as gate arrays and standard cells. Thus, AMI has adopted a strong form of the product differentiation strategy.

Imai and Sakuma (1983) summarize recent research on the major Japanese semiconductor producers. They suggest defining strategic groups in light of the vertical links between a company's microelectronics efforts and its systems products. One group thus defined, comprising NEC, Fujitsu, and Oki, is focused on communications equipment and computers. A second group, comprising Hitachi, Toshiba, and Mitsubishi, produces general electric equipment. A third group, comprising Matsushita, Tokyo Sanyo, Sharp, and Sony, focuses on home electric appliances. These vertical links influence the semiconductor product-lines of the firms, both in the emphasis on discrete devices versus ICs and in the mix of IC products. The groups also tend to vary in the share of their members' semiconductor production consumed in-house and in their strategies toward plant and equipment investment. Imai and Sakuma suggest that the major mobility barriers isolate the third group from the first two.

Kimura (1986) has recently re-examined competitive strategy in the microelectronics industry. His analysis begins with the proposition that there are instead only *two* major strategic groups in the Japanese semiconductor industry. The first group includes NEC, Hitachi, and Toshiba, while the second includes Matsushita and Tokyo Sanyo. Based on an analysis of data for the years 1978–82, Kimura argues that the key variable that distinguishes these two groups is the breadth of product line, with the first group producing a broader line, and especially producing substantial quantities of MOS memory ICs. The second group is focused on ICs for applications in consumer products, and this is clearly related to the vertical linkages with the consumer electronics products produced by these firms. Further analysis suggests that, assuming that other major Japanese semiconductor producers should be categorized into one or the other of the groups, Fujitsu and Mitsubishi belong in the first group and Sharp belongs in the second group. Thus, Kimura modifies the conclusions of Imai and Sakuma by collapsing their first and second groups into a single group, and verifies this grouping using rigorous statistical testing.

Kimura also discusses and analyzes several recent efforts by Japanese firms to shift their strategic emphases. The one clear shift that he is able to document is that of Oki. In 1978, 1979, and 1980, this firm appears to be a member of the second strategic group, the one focusing on ICs for consumer products; from 1981 on, however, Oki seems more appropriately lumped with the first strategic group, the one with more emphasis on a broader line and on MOS memory ICs.[3] In the late 1970s, Oki focused on ICs for telecommunications equipment and for watches and clocks; the firm, however, recognized that the growth rate of demand for telecommunications equipment by NTT, the major purchaser of such equipment incorporating Oki's ICs, was slowing. A study concluded that ICs for computer and industrial applications fitted with the resources and assets that Oki already had, and that a number of these types of ICs could also be used in systems products produced by Oki. Thus, Oki moved late but aggressively into production of the 64K DRAM, emphasizing the very high reliability of its product. Oki also began to emphasize sales of other memory ICs, especially the 16K SRAM and recently the 64K SRAM. The firm moved to enhance its capabilities in CMOS technology and in the production of custom ICs. Oki was the first company to bring a CMOS 8-bit microcontroller into commercial production, based on the Intel design.

The apparently successful shift in strategic groups suggests that mobility barriers are not overwhelmingly high. At the same time, though, one can argue that Oki began with a favorable position for such a shift, based on its initial strength in ICs for telecommunications applications, which are usually regarded as within the general category of industrial applications.

Another effort at a strategic shift is that of Mitsubishi. Mitsubishi had often been regarded, at least up to the late 1970s, as a member of the second strategic group, the one that focuses on ICs for

[3] This is, of course, under the assumption that Oki does in fact fall into one of the two groups.

consumer products. In about 1979, the firm began a concerted effort to build up its sales of ICs for computer and industrial applications. Mitsubishi moved aggressively into the market for memory ICs, especially DRAMs, became a second-source producer of Intel's 8086 16-bit microprocessor, and invested resources to strengthen its capabilities in CMOS technology. Simultaneously, the company de-emphasized production of discrete devices, bipolar linear ICs, and MOS ICs for watches and clocks. These shifts in strategic emphasis resulted from a study Mitsubishi conducted to investigate how to position itself for higher growth. The study concluded that the firm should emphasize ICs within the sales of the whole company, and computer and industrial ICs within the semiconductor division.

Mitsubishi's shift has been largely successful. Indeed, Kimura's analysis suggests that even by 1978 Mitsubishi was best categorized as belonging to the first group. Thus, as with Oki, Mitsubishi began with certain characteristics and assets that allowed it to surmount any barriers to mobility in its efforts to alter the emphasis in its strategy.

Oki and Mitsubishi are not alone in trying to get out of the strategic group emphasizing ICs for consumer products; most of these firms seem to recognize that the potential for growth is higher in the area of ICs for computer and industrial applications. But there is evidence that several of the firms that remain in the consumer-IC group are having a more difficult time making the transition. For instance, Tokyo Sanyo has considered a shift in strategic emphasis. The company announced entry into the market for the 64K DRAM, but then decided to drop this effort. Tokyo Sanyo did develop an 8-bit microcontroller of its own design, but it was oriented to consumer applications. For computer applications, the company has become a second-source for 8-bit microcontrollers and 16-bit microprocessors designed by Intel, but production volumes for these products are expected to remain small. Thus, Tokyo Sanyo has faced difficulties in attempting a strategic shift, although it has accomplished some change in its product orientation. This experience presumably demonstrates that there are at least some mobility barriers in the Japanese microelectronics industry, barriers based on technological gaps, lack of appropriate company resources and the difficulties of changing an established corporate orientation.

Wilson, Ashton and Egan (1980) and Kimura (1986) both document the existence in the microelectronics industry of strategies that focus on particular product areas. But there is also evidence of other kinds of focus in strategy. Although the semiconductor industry would generally be regarded as a global industry, for example, certain firms do pursue a distinct geographic focus. This appears to be especially true of a number of European firms. These firms focus their efforts within the protected EEC market. Indeed, it is often suggested that their efforts are concentrated on their respective home national markets, a focus that is criticized as too narrow. Some semiconductor firms concentrate on particular customer groups. For instance, Harris derives nearly half of its semiconductor sales from applications in military equipment. Plessey focuses on devices with applications to telecommunications. Fujitsu, with its policy of limiting open-market sales of its ICs to a relatively small number of large buyers, would seem to have a focus based on distribution channels. In addition, most of the smaller firms producing ICs follow a strategy of focus in order to mobilize their limited resources effectively.

Thus, the general analysis of strategy and strategic groups advocated by Porter can be applied successfully to the semiconductor industry. But several cautions are in order. First of all, one generally cannot categorize a firm as following exclusively a strategy of low-cost production or of high product differentiation. The choice of strategy will often vary across products within the same firm. Second, Porter suggests that a firm generally cannot follow a low-cost and a high-differentiation strategy simultaneously. However, this need not be true for some products in the semiconductor industry, once dynamic effects are recognized. The innovator of a new product may gain advantages in the differentiation of its product and at the same time achieve low-cost production based on experience effects as it begins building cumulative volume earlier than its competitors. Furthermore, current efforts, often called "design-in quality" are intended simultaneously to lower cost by achieving high yields in production and to achieve product differentiation by establishing a reputation for high-quality products.[4] Signetics has recently been promoting its efforts to "design in quality," and a number of the Japanese producers also indicate that they utilize this approach. A final caveat is that the height of mobility barriers varies substantially across firms with different initial strategic positions and strengths. Thus, there are noticeable shifts over time in some firms' strategies, while others are seriously impeded in any effort to shift their strategies. One implication of this is that it appears to be difficult to divide the American semiconductor producers into a few distinct, stable strategic groups.

[4] To some extent, though, this approach does involve a tradeoff between higher design costs and lower production costs.

Technology Strategy

Technology strategy is perhaps the most important aspect of a firm's competitive strategy in the semiconductor industry. Strategy in other functional areas such as marketing can be viewed as supporting the firm's technology strategy.

TECHNOLOGY AND GENERIC STRATEGIES

Generally, both product and process technologies contribute to the successful implementation of any of the generic strategies discussed above, but the emphasis of the technology efforts is likely to vary by the generic strategy chosen.

If a firm is pursuing a low-cost strategy, process technology clearly can contribute, and firms typically will favor automation and achieving experience effects. These generally require that large volumes of production be achieved and maintained. Product technology also has a role to play. For instance, product design can be tailored to facilitate mass production and to permit mass distribution with a minimum of costly assistance to customers. Japanese semiconductor firms generally excel in the range of products, especially memory ICs such as DRAMs, where this strategy is viable. For instance, the 64K DRAM is a high-volume product. Japanese firms tailored their designs to facilitate high volume and automated mass production. Little customer assistance is necessary for this rather easy-to-use commodity product, and design and production emphasized high quality and reliability, characteristics that allow rather low-cost marketing efforts to be successful in achieving sales.

If a firm is pursuing a strategy of high product differentiation, the emphasis of its technology efforts is likely to be on product technology. The firm will attempt to enhance the features and performance of its product. It may attempt to design special product features in order to lock-in customers by raising the costs to these customers of switching to the products of its competitors. Process technology also has a role in strategy. The firm may attempt to develop process technologies that permit lower volume production at reasonable unit cost. Innovative process technologies may be needed to support flexibility in product features, in order to permit the firm to market several variants of its basic product, each targeted to particular customer needs. In the semiconductor industry, Texas Instruments has been attempting to pursue this latter strategy for 256K DRAMs. The company is developing process technology that will permit a flexible final production step; this will allow TI to offer variable characteristics in the product on order.

TECHNOLOGY LEADERSHIP AND FOLLOWERSHIP

A major issue in the area of technology strategy is the *ex ante* choice by the firm between technology leadership, where the firm strives to be the innovator or "first mover," and technology followership, where the firm deliberately chooses to imitate, adapt and incrementally improve other firms' innovations. Porter suggests that certain conditions in an industry favor the choice by one or more firms to try to be a leader, while other conditions favor a strategy of waiting and becoming a follower. He identifies three general conditions that favor a strategy of leadership.

First, an industry with *high technological opportunities* is more likely to have some firms seeking to be technology leaders. It is in this type of industry that an innovative firm can create a substantial technological gap in order to generate the returns (profits and sales growth) that justify the risky allocation of resources to innovative technology development.

Second, within such an industry, some firms will be better positioned than others to become leaders. That is, history has left firms with different *skills and capabilities* for technological development. Some firms will have capabilities more appropriate to innovation aimed at opening technological gaps. Indeed, once these capabilities are in place, they may permit the firm to continue to innovate and to reopen gaps in the face of imitation by its competitors. If such capabilities are difficult to acquire, they create mobility barriers that maintain the strategic group of innovators separate from the group of imitators.

The third general characteristic that favors a strategy of leadership is the existence of *first-mover advantages* that can also create mobility barriers. Such first-mover advantages arise from intertemporal effects that tend to perpetuate the competitive advantages of technology leadership and innovation. Sometimes product differentiation – through innovation – can affect not only demand now but demand in the future as well. For instance, innovation can establish or enhance reputation and brand image, and in many industries such intangible goodwill assets depreciate slowly. A customer who is satisfied with the performance of an innovative product may forego the costs of gathering information about imitative substitute products, and instead continue to buy the original. The innovator may deliberately enhance the likelihood of repeat purchases by designing features into an innovative product that raise the costs of switching. Intertemporal dependence of this sort can also arise on the cost side. An innovator who is able to build volume rapidly can maintain a cost advantage by staying ahead of imitative competitors on the experience curve.

Porter identifies a number of factors that favor the *ex ante*, deliberate choice to be a technology follower. First, greater *uncertainty* over the cost or success of the technological effort to develop an innovation is likely to favor a followership strategy. Greater uncertainty over market reaction to the innovation also favors followership, especially if the investment in production capacity by the innovator is irreversible or not easily converted to other uses. Second, *discontinuities* can negate the intertemporal advantages of leadership discussed above. Changes in process technology can negate the intertemporal dependence of cost, and changes in the needs of customers or their purchasing patterns can negate the intertemporal dependence of demand. If the likelihood of such discontinuities is high, firms may forego the effort to be an innovator, especially if the investment in production capacity is irreversible, so that the firm would then be stuck with outmoded capacity.

The third characteristic that favors a strategy of technology followership is the existence of *leadership externalities*. These leadership externalities or spillovers are investments by the leader that become public goods that benefit the followers as well. The followers may face some costs of adaptation, but even if they do not get a "free ride," they still derive advantages from these spillovers.

One form of leadership externality is technological – the development costs of an imitation are often much lower than those of the innovation. Such technological externalities may be achieved by reverse engineering or hiring ex-employees of the innovating firm; in other cases, the spillover occurs through the purchase of production machinery that embodies the innovation or facilitates its successful manufacture. Beyond the cost of imitation, though, the timing is also important. The leader may attempt to slow the imitation by maintaining secrecy for as long as possible or by acquiring and defending patents. On the other hand, the leader may accept imitation as inevitable, and instead attempt to derive benefits from imitation through licensing or cross-licensing of the innovative technology.

The other form of leadership externality is market-oriented. The innovator of a new product must incur the costs of informing and convincing customers of the appropriateness, effectiveness, reliability, and value of the new product. These costs may take the form of promotional and educational cost or the form of lower margins accompanying penetration pricing. Followers benefit to the extent that their products are viewed as close substitutes for the now accepted innovative product. The innovator also may face the costs of gaining government regulatory approval for new products and processes and other similar costs.

Application to the Semiconductor Industry

The application of this framework of technology leadership and followership to the semiconductor industry reveals the complexity of strategy formulation in the industry. Almost all of the factors cited above apply to the industry, and a number of them are prominent and important.

There are clearly advantages to a strategy of technology leadership. The industry is one of high technological opportunity, and certain firms have developed resources that are oriented toward technological innovation. More important, there are first-mover advantages, especially for a generation of a product. On the demand side, innovators benefit from the tendency for producers of systems products to design these products around specific semiconductor devices, especially ICs. This creates switching costs, and a new design effort may not be undertaken until the next generation of ICs appears. For instance, IBM adopted the Intel 8088 8-bit microprocessor in its personal computer products. This propelled Intel past Zilog and Motorola in this product area. IBM (and producers of IBM-compatible machines) are now essentially locked-in to the Intel design. On the cost side, experience effects generally are proprietary to the individual firm, and often specific to a particular plant. Such specificity arises from the fact that minute differences in materials, machinery, or environmental conditions can have large effects on yields and probably on the most effective path for achieving yield improvements through small engineering changes in the production process or product design.

A major issue in evaluating these first-mover advantages is the extent to which they carry over to the next generation of the product or to other products produced by the firm. The question of carry-over advantages to the next generation of the IC product is essentially one of the extent of discontinuities from one generation to the next. Discontinuities on the demand side can arise when the systems producers create new designs based on the higher performance of the next generation of ICs. Competition in the next generation then may begin with a "clean slate," and a reputation with the previous generation may be of little value. In other cases, systems producers design new products based on more advanced versions of ICs that they are familiar with and have used previously. Sales of Intel's 8086 16-bit microprocessor apparently benefited from the widespread adoption of Intel's 8-bit 8088.

On the supply side, the next generation of product begins with a new experience curve, but there is some carry-over of process technology from one generation to the next. In some cases the firms that are successful in one generation can attempt to enhance this carry-over. For instance, the product design of the next generation may be a rather straightforward evolution of that of the former generation. Not only can this reduce design costs but it also may permit similar or only somewhat more complex process technologies to be used. This is the approach taken by most of the Japanese producers when they moved from the 16K DRAM to the 64K DRAM. Thus, they were able to achieve high yields in the 64K DRAM rather quickly. As another example, technology carry-over can be enhanced by installing and using advanced production equipment to produce the current generation, equipment that later can be used to produce the next generation. NEC apparently adopted this strategy: for several years before moving to mass production of the 256K DRAM, the company produced 64K DRAMs using equipment and processes suitable for the 256K DRAM. Thus, NEC gained experience with the production equipment that enhanced its ability to achieve high yields on the more complex product. Indeed, NEC felt sufficiently sure of its capabilities that it did not include "redundancy" in its design of the 256K DRAM, an "insurance" that other merchant producers adopted.

In other shifts from one generation to the next, the carry-over of experience appears to be much less than in the examples cited above. Unfortunately, there is rather little general evidence beyond the anecdotes regarding the magnitudes of these carry-over effects.

A somewhat different issue is technology carry-over from one IC product to a different IC product. In the semiconductor industry, the paradigmatic example is that of DRAM technology. The state-of-the-art DRAM at any time generally incorporates the most dense packing of elements on the chip and thus the most exacting tolerances and line widths. The DRAM is the vehicle for new achievements in feature size and for innovations that permit processing of such complex chips. It is generally believed that the experience gained in producing these DRAMs can be carried over to other products, especially other MOS ICs, as their density and complexity rise over time. Therefore, semiconductor producers have a strong incentive to be leaders in DRAM technology, or at least to be fast followers, in order to achieve production advantages in other product areas through these carry-overs.

There are also factors in the semiconductor industry that favor a strategy of technology followership. Uncertainty is a key issue, perhaps especially the uncertainty of the yield achievable if a new production process is undertaken. For instance, for the 64K DRAM several American producers attempted to implement innovative product designs that required new and relatively complex production processes, especially in lithography. Some of these producers – most prominently National Semiconductor – ran into serious problems in achieving acceptable yields.

Leadership externalities are clearly important in the semiconductor industry. It is often difficult to maintain innovative technology as proprietary, that is, to prevent its dissemination. Equipment suppliers often quickly spread any advances in process technology. And competitors routinely engage in reverse engineering to learn innovative product designs. If a firm already possesses the process technology, it can often imitate a rival's product within six months. Thus, a design that cost tens of millions of dollars may diffuse at a cost of perhaps half a million dollars.

More generally, scientists and engineers from different companies communicate with each other, both face to face and through their writings. In the United States, a high level of mobility of technical personnel also enhances technology diffusion. Historically, patents and copyrights have not been used much in the industry. This resulted partly from AT&T's early decision (codified in the consent decree of 1956) to license its semiconductor patents to anyone interested, which fostered a rather liberal atmosphere in the industry. Another contributing factor is the speed of technological change in the industry in relation to the slow movement of the wheels of justice. A third factor is the rather close link of the industry to its scientific base, with the attendant encouragement of publishing the results of research.

Nonetheless, there has been a shift in the approach of firms in the industry toward the protection of proprietary technology, especially in the area of product design. For instance, both Intel and Zilog sued NEC for copyright infringement involving "unauthorized second-sourcing" of 8-bit and 16-bit microprocessors. The cases were settled quickly out-of-court, with NEC acquiring formal second-source agreements.

In addition, the United States enacted a law in October 1984 to provide specific legal protection of IC designs, often called layouts or masks. This law clears up what had been a gray area in the law. The IC designs can be registered with the copyright office of the Library of Congress. In contrast with the patent law, this involves no lengthy investigation to prove originality. The protection against unauthorized reproduction and sale is similar to that of a copyright, but it lasts for only ten years rather than for the typical seventy-five year duration of a copyright. Damages for infringement of the IC design can be up to $250,000, much higher than under a copyright. Thus, chip designs have achieved a special legal protection somewhat different from a copyright or a patent. In May 1985 Japan enacted a law providing protection for IC design patterned after the American law and providing essentially the same protection. A number of other countries are adopting similar laws.

These laws should provide clear legal protection for chip designs, and firms are becoming more aggressive in asserting and defending their proprietary rights. Thus, more formal second-source agreements, and less "informal" outright imitation, is likely in the future. In addition, several firms, including NEC, are likely to pursue more aggressively the development of their own designs for ICs such as microprocessors, thus injecting new competition over innovation in these product areas.

There are also leadership externalities in the marketing area. If a follower can produce a copy of an innovative product or a compatible device, the follower can often take advantage of the technical assistance already provided by the leader, thereby gaining follow-on orders without the initial costs of marketing and assistance.

Thus, there are factors that favor both leadership and followership strategies in the semiconductor industry. A good example is the strategy used by different companies in the market for 8-bit and 16-bit microprocessors. Zilog, Intel, and Motorola have the leading designs in 8-bit microprocessors. Intel and Motorola have the leading designs in the 16-bit microprocessors, while National recently introduced a design with very good hardware architecture. A large number of other producers are producing these designs as licensed second-sources, or are producing designs compatible with the leader's products. Indeed, the range of product offerings and technologies is sufficiently complex that the same firm often pursues technology leadership in some product areas and followership in others.

The strategy and timing of entry into a product area by a firm that is not an initial pioneer in the area is an issue closely related to the choice of technology leadership or followership. Essentially, the non-pioneer firm faces a choice between entry as a follower to the pioneer or entry as a leader in a subsequent generation or in a subsequent refinement of the technology in this product area. The latter option is often called technology "leap-frogging."

The choice to enter as a follower is favored by several conditions, including relatively unimportant first-mover advantages; relatively important leadership externalities; rapid, low-cost diffusion of the pioneer's technology; relatively stable or evolutionary product and process technology; and relatively stable buyer behavior. These are the factors we discussed above. The follower often will attempt to enter into this product area using a low-cost strategy. This appears to be the approach taken by the Japanese firms in the 4K DRAM and 16K DRAM markets.

Entry through a strategy of later leadership would be favored by other factors, including discontinuities in product or process technology or in buyer behavior and large first-mover advantages or low leadership externalities applying to the leader in the next generation. The discontinuities may particularly favor later leadership if the pioneer has made specific, durable, and irreversible investments in the initial technology.

Later leadership is clearly viable in the semiconductor industry – indeed, complex shifts in positions can occur over time. For instance, Fairchild was the pioneer in 8-bit microprocessors, but its position did not carry over to 16-bit microprocessors. Indeed, Fairchild could not sustain its dominance in the 8-bit product. Zilog, Intel, and Motorola subsequently introduced designs that were substantial improvements on the Fairchild design.

Competition in the developing market for 32-bit microprocessors illustrates the pursuit of strategies of later leadership, often linked to an effort to enhance product differentiation. National Semiconductor was the first merchant firm to achieve volume production of a 32-bit microprocessor design. Perhaps the major question surrounding National's effort is its ability to improve its previously weak technical support offered to potential users of its microprocessors, that is, support in both hardware and software. National has reached a technology-sharing and technology-development agreement with Texas Instruments to shore up its capabilities in support and in development of peripheral chips. Inmos has chosen a clear leadership-differentiation strategy with its development of the 32-bit "transputer," microprocessor, a device that is capable of parallel processing of instructions in a manner similar to that of large computers. Inmos is a rather clear example of technology "leap-frogging," as it has little previous experience relevant to the microprocessor market. Indeed, a major question is whether its marketing and technical people can provide adequate support for this advanced product.

Competition, Co-operation, and Strategy

The approach to strategy advocated by Porter provides a useful framework for analyzing the strategies and strategic choices of firms in the semiconductor industry. But, as we have already suggested, the microelectronics industry does not always fit snugly into this framework. This is so for several reasons.

- First, pursuit of a pure overall strategy appears to be difficult – because of the breadth of products offered, the complexity of strategic choices available, and the rapidity with which technology advances.
- Second, the strength of proprietary, product-specific experience effects suggests that a strategy of product differentiation can also become a low-cost strategy as the innovator of the differentiated product rides down the learning curve ahead of its subsequent imitators.
- Third, the analysis indicates that the complexities of the industry permit a diversity of viable strategies. The diversity is so large that it appears difficult to identify clearly a small number of strategic groups in the industry. This is particularly significant in the case of the American merchant firms in the industry. Moreover, the complexity of strategic behavior among American merchant firms is a reflection of their ability not only to pursue mixed strategies across product areas but also to shift emphasis over time (for instance, with respect to leadership versus followership in particular product areas).

This last consideration – the fact of strategic diversity – is particularly important in understanding the nature of competition and the strategic role of co-operation in the industry.

Strategic diversity and strategic-group complexity hold two divergent implications for the intensity of competition in the industry. To the extent that the strategic groups are actually isolated one from another, competition can be intense within each group but weak between groups. Such isolation may occur because the groups differ in their technological capabilities or approach (supply-side mobility barriers) or because they tend to serve distinct customer groups or needs (demand-side mobility barriers). Indeed, groups can be sufficiently isolated that they are effectively different industries. In the semiconductor industry, such isolation has been apparent in the area of logic ICs, where bipolar technology has been dominant. Japanese firms, with their emphasis on MOS digital ICs, have not posed a serious competitive threat to American firms in this area. However, in an industry as technologically dynamic as semiconductors, such insulation can deteriorate over time. For instance, CMOS logic chips will very likely begin to challenge bipolar logic chips for a variety of applications over the next few years.

The second implication of strategic-group complexity follows from this example. To the extent that firms from two or more strategic groups attempt to serve the same customer group(s), cross-group competition is likely to be especially intense. Firms in other groups are not likely to be playing by the same "rules of competition." Cost conditions may differ, and the objectives may also vary, for instance, in the trade-off between pricing for current profitability and pricing to achieve sales volume and growth in anticipation of future profitability. In such a situation there is less likelihood that an oligopolistic consensus will arise over the acceptable bounds of rivalry. (We will suggest below that competition between American and Japanese firms in many sectors of the industry can be understood precisely as inter-group competition of this sort.)

Strategic diversity and strategic-group complexity also have implications for the nature and extent of co-operation among semiconductor firms. Leadership in technology is often subject to rapid erosion.[5] The riskiness of a leadership strategy has been increasing as the costs of research into and development of, increasingly complex product designs and production processes rise, and as the costs of investment in facilities for production with these increasingly complex and demanding processes rise. In such a setting, the innovator is increasingly likely to try to mitigate risk, through such means as joint development efforts and licensing of product designs to achieve quicker, more certain returns and to spread the risk of investment in production facilities. Furthermore, as the technology advances and becomes increasingly complex, new demands are placed on the resources and capabilities of individual firms. They may then seek out the complementary resources and capabilities of other firms, and the incidence of on-going technology sharing agreements and joint ventures in development increases.

The spillover advantages (or positive externalities) of close followership, if not outright leadership, in some product areas creates a serious concern about falling too far behind in these areas. This is especially true in the area of DRAM technology. A firm in such

[5] It is said of semiconductor firms that "you can always tell the innovators – they're the ones with the arrows in their backs and their faces in the mud". Obviously this is true some, not all, of the time.

an area may be compelled to use technological co-operation to assure – or regain – its position. For instance, National Semiconductor licensed Oki technology for the design and production of the 64K DRAM after National's own original technology approach failed to develop successfully. Similarly, Siemens is pursuing a co-operative venture with Philips to develop future memory products, especially the 1-megabit and 4-megabit DRAMs, and has also contracted with Toshiba to license the latter's technology in the same product areas. The Toshiba agreement can be viewed as an "insurance policy" against falling too far behind.

Another incentive for technology co-operation arises from the mobility barriers arising from technological capabilities. Such barriers may prevent, or least make very costly, an effort by a firm to engineer a shift in strategic emphasis through purely internal development. Technological co-operation may then allow the firm to gain such technological capabilities at a reasonable cost. The firm may nonetheless still face the problem of acquiring the capabilities to keep up with continued technological changes.

Thus, certain incentives toward technological co-operation can be understood within the framework of strategy advocated by Porter. Of course, there are also disincentives to co-operation that can be understood within this framework, such as the desire to exploit fully the advantages of technology leadership or product differentiation by denying to rivals access to such proprietary advantages. The actual incidence of technology co-operation is the result of the interplay of these influences. Yet the evolution of technology and strategy in the semiconductor industry does suggest that such co-operation is likely to be of increasing importance, even while competition among these firms remains intense.

Strategy and International Competitive Advantage

One of the most highly publicized aspects of competition in the microelectronics industry is the rivalry between American and Japanese firms. The last decade has witnessed a good deal of cyclical volatility in the demand for semiconductor devices, leading to periods of significant excess capacity in the industry. During these periods, American firms have systematically abandoned to the Japanese the market for standardized, high-volume products, perhaps the most volatile segment of the semiconductor business. Increasingly, American firms on the whole have focused much of their attention – and research – on smaller but rapidly growing specialty markets in which product innovation is crucial. This trend of abandoning large segments of the markets – with its implication that few if any American firms will ever be able to compete in such markets – has even led some to question the long-run viability of the American microelectronics industry.[6]

More specifically, there seem to be three general questions in the air.

- Will specialty products and markets be large enough to support a large, broad-based American microelectronics industry (especially if Japanese firms continue rapidly to standardize those products with high-volume potential)?
- How much of an advantage is superior product innovation by itself, especially in view of the well-developed mechanisms for rapid transfer of product knowledge across national borders?
- Can a firm maintain technological leadership if it produces only specialty products? As we suggested above, there is a widespread feeling in the industry that the high-volume standardized products (especially large-scale memories) drive a firm's process technology and that the experience and knowledge gained in their production cannot be readily transferred into a firm from the outside.

In order to begin formulating answers to these questions, one has to examine the strategies of American and Japanese firms in greater detail.

A Comparison of American and Japanese Competitive Strategies

We stressed above the diversity of strategies in the industry, especially among American merchant firms. But if we focus on the comparison between the typical strategic characteristic of American as against Japanese firms, some clear dividing lines appear.

In the broadest sense, we might say that the principal difference between American and Japanese strategies is that American firms have chosen a focused, differentiated-product approach whereas Japanese firms have taken a full-line, low-cost approach. This is probably true as far as it goes. But there are a good many subtleties that this broad-brush characterization misses, subtleties that have not emerged clearly from previous comparative studies. Our analysis and interviews suggest five specific dimensions along which American and Japanese strategies typically differ.

[6] See for example Scott (1984).

UNIQUE PRODUCT OR MARKET ADVANTAGE

American microelectronics firms generally seek to differentiate their products from those of competitors through innovative product design, which normally means innovative circuit design. As a product line becomes mature and more difficult to differentiate from similar products produced by competitors, firms attempt to bring out the next generation of the product with improved performance characteristics. Another mechanism for product differentiation is to develop families of chips that work together to satisfy systems applications; then, by regularly developing peripheral chips that extend the family and its applications capability, a company can continually attempt to maintain uniqueness.

It is not surprising that American firms developed the semicustom design techniques that permit the economical design and manufacture of application-specific ICs and that these ICs figure prominently in the strategies of nearly all American firms. Of course, the degree to which American firms achieve the advantages of product differentiation varies considerably. Firms with more innovative product research realize the advantages to a greater degree than do firms with capabilities only for incremental product development. Yet nearly all firms try for some kind of uniqueness, even if only a relatively minor performance characteristic that might make the product more attractive for certain applications. Very few American firms pursue low cost as their primary competitive strategy.

By contrast, Japanese firms place considerably less emphasis on developing differentiated products. The major producers all attempt to offer broad product lines that concentrate on covering the high-volume segments of the market. Smaller producers have more of a niche strategy, usually emphasizing products that impart some special advantage to the systems products of the company. But even these companies produce large quantities of basic products (such as memory chips) in direct competition with the broad product-line firms. Their rationale is that volume production of these basic items is necessary for manufacturing economies of scale and to stay near the forefront of process technology. Thus, the strategies of Japanese firms can be characterized as either (1) a broad product-line strategy heavily oriented toward basic, undifferentiated products or (2) a niche strategy coupled with a limited line of basic, undifferentiated products.[7] Egelhoff (1986) calls the latter an enhanced niche strategy.

[7] Notice that these two strategies quite well characterize the two Japanese strategic groups identified by Kimura that we discussed earlier.

WITHDRAWAL DECISIONS

Consistent with the emphasis they put on product or market advantage, American firms tend to withdraw relatively quickly from products and market segments in which they cannot gain or maintain such an advantage. An example of this is the widespread withdrawal of American firms from the DRAM segment of the memory market. Despite the general belief among technical managers that a viable presence in this product area is critical to staying in the forefront of process technology, most American firms have strategically repositioned themselves out of this highly competitive segment in which the only available strategy is one based on high quality and low price.

Japanese companies, on the other hand, seldom withdraw from a significant product line or market segment – even if it is losing them money. If they view the product or segment as important, their strategy will tend to concentrate on restoring profitability, even if this requires a very long time-horizon. Japanese firms tend to view products and market segments as important if (1) they support the wider company strategy of vertical integration; (2) the product or segment is large or will grow rapidly; and (3) a reasonable number of internal or external customers have come to depend on the company for the product. As a result of these views, Japanese firms place substantially higher barriers in the way of withdrawal decisions than do their American counterparts; this makes strategically repositioning a firm by deliberate withdrawal from unattractive products or markets an option much more available to American managements than to Japanese managements.

THE ROLE OF PROCESS TECHNOLOGY

Since the manufacturing processes in microelectronics are complex, capital-intensive, and still evolving at a rapid pace, there is considerable room for significant differences in the capabilities of firms. And, in fact, the strategies of American firms vary considerably in the importance attached to process technology. The strategies of some American firms – usually the larger ones – call for staying at the forefront of process technology as an important part of competitive advantage. For other firms, those with strategies that rely heavily on product and market differentiation, the role of process technology is less important, and the technology in those firms can be two or three years behind the leading edge.

By contrast, both the large broad product-line and the smaller limited product-line Japanese firms pursue strategies that call for staying at or near the forefront of process technology, both in terms of technology development and capital investment. The cost of this approach would be too great for most limited-line or niche-strategy firms in the United States. In Japan, this strategy is facilitated because (1) the limited-line producers tend to be divisions of very large electronics systems companies (which can absorb the research expense and provide the capital) and (2) all of the limited-line companies have entered and maintained a significant presence in a number of high-volume basic products (which provide experience effects and economies of scale).[8]

It is interesting to observe that the internationalization of the American microelectronics market has made Japanese process technology the relevant standard of comparison for American companies. The standard had once been large low-cost merchant firms such as Texas Instruments.[9] Since forefront Japanese process technology has been improving more rapidly than its American counterpart, many American companies have been forced to alter the role of process technology in their competitive strategies. Firms that previously had forefront process technology as part of their strategy have suddenly found themselves behind the new standard of comparison, and many are having to formulate business strategies that are viable with technology that is two or three years behind the forefront. Companies that cannot do this may well be forced out of business.[10]

SOURCES OF PROCESS TECHNOLOGY

American and Japanese firms frequently have different strategies with respect to their sources for, and methods of, acquiring new process technology. Many American firms depend to a considerable extent on external sources of new process technology, concentrating their internal research and development efforts more on circuit design in order to support strategies that emphasize unique or differentiated products. Equipment manufacturers are an important source of new process technology for small and large firms alike. Many smaller firms will depend almost entirely upon

[8] Our interviews turned up a number of managerial and organizational mechanisms in Japanese companies that strongly support the dominant role that process technology plays in the strategy of nearly all the firms there. Elaborating these mechanisms is beyond the present scope, but see Egelhoff (1986).

[9] IBM is generally thought to have the best process technology in the United States, but since it is entirely a captive producer it has not been a relevant standard of comparison for other firms in the industry.

[10] Some feel that the recent shutdown of Mostek was an example of this. The company had positioned itself largely in the high-volume basic-product (DRAM) market, where forefront process technology is a must. When Mostek's process technology fell behind that of its Japanese competitors, and it could not reposition itself into other products, its strategy was no longer viable.

such suppliers for innovations in process technology. Larger firms will often collaborate closely with an equipment manufacturer during the development stage of new equipment. As we saw in the last chapter, there are two major industry groups – MCC and SIA – that sponsor research in process technology for their members. This work is typically several years from the commercialization stage. It is not yet clear how important such collaborative research will be for the development of new process technology.

A third external source of process technology available to American firms is the trading of process technology among firms. Our research indicates that this is usually done in conjunction with a transfer of product technology. Firms will license other firms to produce certain products, as Intel, for example, did with its 8088 microprocessor. Some process technology may also have to be transferred in order for the licensee to manufacture the product properly. Licensees will then sometimes convert the designs to run on newer technologies (as from a bipolar to a MOS technology) and, as part of the agreement, will transfer the modification back to the licensor. Such transfer of technology, however, tends to operate behind the forefront and is primarily a means of efficiently diffusing nonleading-edge process technology.

The relative importance of external sources for new process technology varies widely across American firms. Some large firms have extensive internal research and development operations and even equipment-building operations committed to keeping the company at the forefront. But other relatively large firms pursue strategies that emphasize innovations in product technology and a reliance upon external sources for most new process technology. Small firms tend also to pursue this latter strategy. Thus, although there is considerable variance, most American firms are quite dependent on external sources for improvements in process technology.

While Japanese firms once depended heavily on external sources for new process technology (primarily American firms and equipment manufacturers), today they rely most heavily on internal development. The abortive Sharp–RCA agreement to engage in joint technology development and manufacturing was an exception to what otherwise appears to be a do-it-yourself approach in Japan to the development of process technology.[11] Only one other smaller Japanese firm indicated a potential willingness to collaborate with other firms in developing new process technology. In

[11] It is probably significant that Sharp is in Kimura's second strategic group – the one emphasizing consumer products – rather than in the group emphasizing a broad IC line.

general, Japanese firms consider leading-edge process technology the key strength of their strategies, and, consequently, they have little incentive to collaborate with other firms pursuing similar strategies (especially other Japanese firms). Thus, inter-firm technology co-operation is likely to involve a Japanese firm with an American or European partner, and the Japanese firm is more likely to be the source rather than the receiver of innovations in process technology.[12]

The importance of government-sponsored research projects, which once played an important role in improving the process technology of Japanese firms, is rapidly declining. The magnitude of government-sponsored research has tended to remain fairly level over the years, so that the rapid build-up in company-sponsored research has greatly reduced its relative importance. While nearly all companies indicated an interest in continuing to participate in long-range government-sponsored projects as a potentially useful external source of technology stimulation, several raised questions about the value of such programs in the future. Not only has company-sponsored research eclipsed government-sponsored research in magnitude – in some cases the time-horizons of company-sponsored research have begun to exceed those of the government-sponsored projects. Thus, the strategies of Japanese microelectronics companies seem to be moving increasingly toward self-sufficiency in process technology.

THE IMPORTANCE OF VERTICAL INTEGRATION

All significant Japanese microelectronics producers are subunits of larger electronics systems-products companies. These firms originally entered microelectronics because they wanted to gain more control over the components that made up their final products. This strategy of vertical integration is still very strong in Japanese firms, even though internal sales may only account for 20 to 25 per cent of total microelectronics sales. Thus, there is a strong tendency for Japanese firms to attempt to manufacture many of the key microelectronic components that go into their final products, even when such components are readily available in the marketplace at prices that are competitive with the cost of internal manufacture.

Many American microelectronics firms are independent companies, dependent on the merchant market for all of their sales. Such firms are obviously not motivated to make products because

[12] The 1985 agreement between Toshiba and Siemens alluded to earlier would appear to be an example of this. Toshiba will largely transfer process technology to help Siemens make the one-megabit chip, and will receive money and product designs in return.

they further a strategy of vertical integration and reduced external dependency. Instead, they are driven by strategies of low cost or product differentiation. Even when American microelectronics producers belong to larger companies that use microelectronics as components in their end-products, the vertical integration strategy involved is somewhat different from that in Japanese companies. In American firms, vertical integration strategies are confined largely to supplying user divisions with components that contribute to the uniqueness of their electronics systems products. Except in the few microelectronics firms that are solely captive suppliers, it is unlikely that an American microelectronics division of a larger company will manufacture standardized basic products for the systems products division unless it is already making these products for the external market.

Strategy and the Nature of Competition

There are, then, a number of important differences between the strategies of American microelectronics firms and those of their Japanese counterparts.

American firms tend to emphasize product differentiation and seek to capture some unique advantage in a product or market. They place relatively less importance on process technology and, as a consequence, they avoid competing on the basis of low cost and high quality. This kind of business strategy has contributed to an unusually high degree of strategic diversity in the American industry, with most firms pursuing niche strategies and with even the broad product-line firms varying considerably in their strengths and their coverage of the market. American firms tend to withdraw relatively quickly from products and markets with too much competition or when they miss a technological change. As a result, price competition tends to be moderate.

By contrast, the strategies of Japanese firms emphasize forefront process technology, with only a secondary and much lower emphasis on product differentiation and unique product or market advantages. Low cost and high quality are the most important bases for competing. This kind of business strategy has led to a relatively low degree of strategic diversity among Japanese firms. Even companies with niche strategies tend to compete with the broad product-line producers on price and quality for much of their sales volume. Since there is little tendency for Japanese firms to withdraw from products or markets, and even a tendency for them to enter product areas or markets after they are quite saturated,[13]

[13] The desire to enter markets that are already mature and highly competitive may seem confusing and irrational, especially from the perspective of American

competition over price and quality in the standardized basic-product areas is intense.

These differences in strategy translate into differences in competitive behavior. American firms generally attempt to manage competition by strategic repositioning or seeking the advantages of uniqueness. There is very little standing one's ground against competitors or new entrants who seek to expand their market share aggressively. Japanese firms tend to compete against other firms with very similar strategies. They do not withdraw or try to avoid head-on competition by strategic repositioning. This low strategic diversity (or strategic similarity) means that firms cannot readily compete against one another by having a superior strategy. As a result, Japanese microelectronics firms compete not so much at the level of strategy as at the level of *strategy implementation.* This is perhaps best reflected in the fine-tuning of process development and manufacturing activities, whereby a firm seeks to gain a small, incremental cost or quality advantage over its competitors, all of whom are trying to do the same thing.

Although a detailed discussion of how Japanese firms implement strategies lies beyond the present scope, our research revealed considerable diversity in the mechanisms firms use for transferring new technology from research lab to process development, to pilot line, to production line. The diversity is interesting, considering that all of these firms are trying to race down the same learning curve to develop a sub-micron technology capable of efficiently producing the 1-megabit and eventually the 4-megabit memory chip. Our view is that it is primarily at this level – the level of strategy implementation – that differences occur, advantages are sought, and competition really takes place.

The differences in the strategies and the competitive behavior of American and Japanese firms provides a somewhat novel perspective on the growing confrontation between the two groups. With the internationalization of the American market, the two strategies have come into direct competition. As one would predict, firms pursuing the typical American strategy have withdrawn rapidly from products and market segments soon after they were assaulted by Japanese producers. The American firms have attempted to reposition themselves into more innovative product areas such as EEPROMs and application-specific ICs. The Japanese firms have rapidly gained a large share of the abandoned markets, only to find themselves facing charges of unfair competition and the threat of

---

strategic thinking. But it appears less irrational when looked at in light of the Japanese firm's strategy of vertical integration.

protectionist action by governments. The sentiment among many American microelectronics executives is that the Japanese firms have not played the game the way it should be played. Discussions with Japanese executives also uncovered a feeling that the game was not being played properly. Several were puzzled that strong American firms abandoned product areas so quickly, that they had allowed their process technology to slip so far behind, that they would clamor for government protection. This is not the way the game would have been played among Japanese companies, where no one expects the competitors to retreat or cave in when the competition becomes intense.

7

Government Policies Toward the Microelectronics Industry

However international the microelectronics industry becomes, it must still operate in a world of national governments. Many – if not all – those governments view this fast-growing industry as a key to industrial development, and most have attempted in one way or another to foster the development of their "national" industry and to assist it in gaining a competitive advantage over others. This chapter takes a look at the nature and effects of government policy in the increasingly international microelectronics industry. We attempt to place the current policy scene in context, and to examine, or at least call attention to, the salient issues that are emerging or are soon likely to emerge.

We begin by describing in some detail a number of the significant recent programs around the world aimed at fostering technical advance in microelectronics. These current programs, we argue, have recognizable connections with earlier ones. Then we briefly describe the evolution of policies regarding microelectronics in the United States, Europe, and Japan, and examine the goals and assumptions which have lain behind these policies. Later in the chapter we return to the present situation and explore what is new – and not so new – about the current context. In brief, two things are new about these present-day policies. The first is the general governmental enthusiasm for "co-operative" research and development. The second is the implicit, if on-and-off, acceptance by the United States of a position long argued in Europe and Japan – that support for research and development by the American Department of Defense can be viewed as a backdoor industrial policy. Another new development on the scene relates not to the features of the policies but to the structure of the industry. As we have tried to document throughout this report, microelectronic companies and the projects they are undertaking are becoming international as never before. We speculate on what all this entails. To anticipate a bit, one conclusion is that government policies aimed expressly to help a national or a regional industry will be increasingly frustrated by the international nature of the industry. Another is that the overlap of military and commercial technologies is going to make American policy schizophrenic and confused.

Public-Sector Programs to Support Industrial Research

As we saw in chapter 5, co-operation in technology and in semiconductor research is taking a wide variety of paths within the private sector – through company-to-company alliances and through university–industry ties. In parallel with these activities are programs recently formulated at the national level involving government support of co-operative research conducted and partially funded by industry. Over the last six years, programs such as the Fifth Generation Computer Project in Japan, the Very High Speed Integrated Circuit Project (VHSIC) in the United States, the Alvey Program in the United Kingdom, the Filière électronique in France, and the European Strategic Program for R&D in Information Technology (ESPRIT) have appeared on the scene with the express purpose of accelerating technical progress in semiconductors and the related area of information technology. What is common to all these government programs is a perceived link between national competitiveness and R&D programs funded and coordinated by government.

The programs, however, bear distinguishing characteristics that flow from each country's broad economic strategy, from its R&D culture, and from its orientation to the relationship of government and industry. Policy approaches vary – in taxation, .targeting, procurement, antitrust, and trade – as do institutional mechanisms – in banking, finance, planning councils, and government ministries. Thus the patterns of national R&D programs vary both between and even within countries.

The purpose of this chapter is to examine briefly a few examples of R&D efforts involving semiconductors that are coordinated at the national level with government support.[1] What are the objectives? What are the areas of research? Who are the performers? What are the conditions of participation? What is the level of funding? What are the mechanisms for – and the likely

[1] All the non-American programs are focused rather broadly on information technology. We are most concerned with the semiconductor portion of these efforts.

extent of – technology diffusion? Do these activities compete or conflict with other technical co-operative activities?

Both similarities and differences are evident in the key features of these collective research programs.[2] We will be particularly concerned with the implications of these programs for the industrial technical network – the partnerships formed, the priorities established, the breadth of participation. The five programs mentioned above are used as illustrations for this discussion.[3] Four are national: the Fifth Generation Computer Project (Japan), VHSIC (US), the Alvey Program (UK), and the Filière électronique (France). One is international: ESPRIT.

Japan: The Fifth Generation Computer Project

The launching of Japan's Fifth Generation Computer Project (5G) in 1981 precipitated a swell of reaction in the microelectronics and computer industries in Europe and the United States. Coming as it did on the heels of another Japanese collaborative effort, the much-discussed Very Large Scale Integrated Circuit (VLSI) program of 1976 through 1979,[4] the 5G project produced widespread worries of Japanese ascendancy in technology, along with an equally widespread assumption that research collaboration is in large part the source of – and the appropriate defense against – Japanese success in trade. Not surprisingly, the responses to the 5G project take the form of programs of research coordination and collaboration. The Alvey Program and ESPRIT are perhaps the two best examples in the public sector, and the Semiconductor Research Corporation (SRC) and the Microelectronics and Computer Corporation (MCC) in the United States are two major examples in the private sector.

The 5G project is a ten-year effort funded jointly by government and industry at a total level of about $426 million. The goal is the development of a new generation computer with so-called artificial intelligence. The project is based on the separate but parallel development of two "engines" and their related software (see Figure 5).

There are three broad functions central to this development approach: (1) a problem-solving and inference function; (2) a

[2] See Haklisch (1986, Figure 4.1).

[3] The research for this section consisted of a literature review, an examination and analysis of documents provided by the offices administering the national programs, and a series of interviews (See Appendix B of Haklisch (1986) for a list). The information was gathered over the period 1 October, 1984 to 1 June, 1985. This section also draws on Haklisch, Fusfeld, and Levenson (1984) for the discussion of ESPRIT and the Japanese Fifth Generation Computer Project.

[4] For an excellent discussion of this program, see Sigurdson (1986).

Hardware	Software
A parallel-inference machine	inference system for problem solving and processing problems
A knowledge-based machine	knowledge-based management system for accumulating and managing knowledge

Source: Haklisch (1986)

Figure 5 *The Parallel Tracks of the 5G Project*

Phase 1 (1982-84)	To develop the enabling technologies in hardware and architecture as well as related software
Phase 2 (1985-88)	To apply the results of Phase 1 to develop inference function and knowledge-base function mechanisms on a small scale (subsystems)
Phase 3 (1989-91)	To integrate the knowledge-base function and inference function in a single prototype system

Source: Haklisch (1986) and references cited there.

Figure 6 *The Plan of the 5G Project*

knowledge-based management function; and (3) an intelligent-interface function.[5] The project falls into the three phases depicted in Figure 6.

There are several interesting features of this project:[6]

- International involvement is a stated policy of the project, thus marking a change in the direction of R&D policy at MITI.[7]
- The project is oriented toward basic rather than applied research.
- There is greater coordination in the government bureaucracy for this project than for other previous efforts.
- The research results are being published in English.

The project will be carried out by a research association of eight computer and microelectronics companies and two national laboratories. As in the VLSI project, a central organization is conducting the R&D at its own facility; in this case, the organization is called the Institute for New Generation Computer Technology (ICOT),

[5] The specific areas of focus for the 5G program are shown in Haklisch (1986, Figure 4.2).

[6] Bloom (1984).

[7] The implementation of this policy, however, has been regarded with skepticism by other countries. Nevertheless, foreign researchers are working at the central research facility of ICOT. Of these, about two-thirds are software experts.

founded in 1982. While the bulk of research will be performed at ICOT, contracts will also be let to Japanese industry for making and testing hardware and software prototypes. The Institute is responsible to MITI, which sets policies for the project.[8]

The logic behind this form of organization is generally seen to be the same as that for the VLSI project. One report put it this way.[9]

> Major R&D savings were possible not only because the government subsidized much of the research, but because government coordination eliminated duplicative research by individual firms, permitting more efficient use of research personnel and more rapid and widespread diffusion of basic research findings. The VLSI Project promoted extensive cross-fertilization of ideas between and among Japanese firms and at the same time gave each participating firm access to advanced technological know-how at a very low cost. One participating company, NEC, commented that without the VLSI programme, Japanese manufacturers would have spent five times as much on R&D in the development of electron beam technology.

Unlike the objectives of the VLSI project, however, the specific aims of the 5G Project are not to advance semiconductor technology *per se* but rather to use that technology in generic research for computing and artificial intelligence. Semiconductor research is a component in the program, not the focus of it.

The main line of co-operative semiconductor research appears to be taking place in other associations, primarily the Optoelectronics Integrated Circuits (OEIC) Project and the New Function Elements Project, which is partially integrated into the 5G Project. Both of these projects are also jointly funded by government and industry and fall under the policy direction of MITI. The OEIC effort involves nine participating companies plus a central research laboratory; the nine firms plus MITI scientists are collaborating at Fujitsu's laboratories in Kawasaki. The New Function Elements Project is a ten-year program, funded at about $114 million, with eleven participating companies collaborating through the Research and Development Association for Future Electron Devices (FED). There are three areas of concentration: superlattice devices, three-dimensional ICs, and fortified ICs. An interesting feature of this project is the presentation of research findings in regularly scheduled symposia open to foreigners.

[8] A discussion on the role of MITI in Japanese national research projects is beyond the scope of this paper. For a detailed treatment, see Bloom (1984), Wheeler *et al.* (1982), and Sigurdson (1986).

[9] English and Watson Brown (1984).

Taken together, the VLSI Project, the Fifth Generation Computer Project, the Optoelectronics Integrated Circuits Project, and the New Function Elements Project represent a substantial co-operative effort. The combined multiyear funding from government and industry for all projects is modest, less than $1 billion, or the equivalent of about four months R&D spending by IBM in 1984. However, the coordination and concentration of the research, the leverage of R&D expenditures, the technology transfer, particularly among scientists and engineers in central laboratories, and the commercial orientation of the projects and partners imply a substantial impact for the participating firms. Not surprisingly, Fujitsu, Hitachi, Mitsubishi, NEC, and Toshiba, the big five in the VLSI Project, are involved in all four programs. However, what is also apparent is the widening of private-sector participation to other firms less strong in technology following the VLSI project. In the FED effort, for example, there are six other firms involved besides the 11 major companies listed.[10]

A recent report by the Congressional Office of Technology Assessment underscores three distinct features of the Japanese approach to co-operative R&D:[11]

> Compared with other countries, Japan's approach to aid for electronics is unique in at least three ways: 1) government-supported programs are multiple but carefully coordinated with one another; 2) they are oriented toward facilitating the activities of industry, rather than telling industry what to do; and 3) the time horizons are unusually long. The last point is critical: *the 8- or 10-year planning horizons for many current Japanese R&D projects – with every indication that, while projects will be adapted to evolving circumstances, continuity will be preserved – point to the depth of the government's commitment*. (Italics in original.)

An additional point to note, however, is the absence of explicit policies to forge close university–industry linkages. Contract research and consulting with university researchers are conducted on a much more limited scale than in the United States. There are also no Japanese analogues of American university-based centers, although the University of Tokyo has some computer and semiconductor facilities primarily for fabrication of discrete devices and small-scale ICs. (In addition, there are no courses at the university covering LSI design.)[12]

10 Haklisch (1986, Figure 4.4).
11 Office of Technology Assessment (1983).
12 Okimoto *et al.* (1984).

United Kingdom: The Alvey Program

The Alvey Program for Advanced Information Technology, named after John Alvey, the chairman of the commission that proposed it, is viewed as the United Kingdom's national response to Japan's Fifth Generation Computer Project – minus the establishment of a central research facility. The project is a government–industry joint venture consisting of a specified research plan in key areas of information technology (IT). The program is intended to reinforce existing technical strength rather than move into new areas. It calls for the establishment of company–company, company–university, and/or company–research establishment consortia to perform the work. These features address a primary finding of the Alvey Commission:[13]

> Compared with our competitors, our overall effort is badly fragmented. The interface between industry and the research community is nowhere near as productive as in the United States for example. And our industry does not collaborate on basic research to the same extent as Japan.

Alvey is thus "concerned with making the most of the UK's considerable expertise in IT research"[14] through research co-operation.

Launched in 1983, the Alvey Program will run for five years with approximate total funding of £350 million. About £200 million will come from government: £40 million from the Ministry of Defence (MOD), £50 million from the Science and Engineering Research Council (SERC) and £110 million from the Department of Trade and Industry (DTI) and other government sources. The program is administered through DTI in collaboration with MOD and SERC. Mechanisms for channeling funds in the contract process reflect this administrative structure: the SERC handles support in the program for academic institutions, MOD lets contracts related to VLSI, and the DTI manages the balance. The program is designed to operate as a British effort with technical information shared among participating partners. A main objective is the exploitation of results by British industry. Thus, Alvey's policy is to allow participation of non-British companies only when they have special assets to contribute and only so long as the technical information is unlikely to "leak" from the United Kingdom.[15] This approach is reflected in

[13] Quoted in Dickson (1983)

[14] Alvey Program annual report 1984, p. 4

[15] "An Alvey Survey: Advanced Information Technology in the U.K.," *Fifth Generation Computer System Journal*, vol. 1, 1984, pp. 69–78.

Table 29 *Breakdown of Projects in the Alvey Program*

Areas of Research Concentration	Number of Projects	Approximate Allocation of Funding
Information Knowledge-Based Systems (IKBS)	36	10%
Very Large Scale Integration (VLSI)	36	27%
VLSI Architecture	7	3%
CAD for VLSI	8	9%
Software Engineering	28	18%
Man-Machine Interface (MMI)	8	15%
Large Scale Demonstrators	4	9%
Infrastructure and Communications	2	6%
		97%
Contemplated: Declarative Architectures and Systems		6%
TOTAL:	129 *	103% **

Notes: * This is the total number listed in the Alvey Program Annual Report 1984. However, DTI notes an additional four in an update, making the total 133.

** Rounding error.

Source: Haklisch (1986).

the limited participation of non-British companies. For example, IBM and Philips, through their British subsidiaries, participate in only one project each.

Currently there are eight technical areas of concentration in the program, with a ninth area being formulated. Table 29 lists the categories of technical interest and the approximate allocation of funding.

The formation of consortia composed of companies, university teams, and research establishments is a requirement for participation. The average consortium consists of four or more partners, two or three companies, and one or two universities. The university link is pervasive: a university is involved in almost every project in the program. In those cases in which the academic research is long term and speculative, a company participates as an "uncle" to articulate evolving areas of interest to industry as well as opportunities for commercial application.

As of December 1984, 133 projects had been approved out of

Table 30 *Participation in Alvey Projects, December 1984*

Participants	Number
Companies	53
Universities	40
Polytechnics	6
Research Establishments	5
TOTAL	106

Source: Alvey Directorate, DTI.

about 360 proposals. Seventy-seven of the total were all-industrial projects and 56 were primarily academic. Table 30 shows the overall distribution of participation in these projects.

A review of individual projects and partners shows that of the 53 firms participating, 16 are involved in more than one project; GEC is represented more than any other company, with participation in 28. Within the academic sector, 31 of the 40 universities are participating in more than one project, with Cambridge participating in 16.

While the concentration of the Alvey Program is on information technology, the linkages among research performers and the coordination of research tasks suggest important implications for semiconductor technology. Twenty-seven per cent of Alvey Program funds is allocated to 36 projects in the area of VLSI. The technical focus of individual projects in this category is concentrated primarily in different areas of process technology in silicon, both MOS and bipolar. There does not seem to be any work in gallium arsenide. These efforts are augmented by seven projects in the category of VLSI architectures and eight projects in CAD for VLSI. The technical objective of this VLSI effort is to accelerate to 1990 the production and testing of silicon chips that are approximately one centimeter square and contain about one million logic gates capable of one nanosecond switching delays.

While partnerships in the program change in composition and number throughout the eight areas, a review of firms participating in the VLSI category shows that GEC is the most active company in this category with participation in nineteen projects. Conspicuous in their absence from participation in the VLSI area are ICL and Inmos. As we mentioned in Chapter 5, however, ICL sold its West Gorton silicon foundry to Fujitsu, and no longer maintains a silicon VLSI production activity. Nevertheless, ICL's interest in CAD for VLSI is reflected in the firm's participation in six out of eight projects in that category. Inmos, recently acquired by Thorn EMI, pursues its VLSI research outside the United Kingdom. But Inmos is involved in two CAD-for-VLSI projects and is thus a participant in the Alvey Program.

One additional feature of the VLSI research area is that most of the funding for these and VLSI/CAD projects comes from the Ministry of Defence. This connection is reflected in a mechanism in which the ministry monitors the projects, specifies areas of particular interest and provides advice when needed. While the thrust of Alvey is civilian commercial advances, the role of the MOD in this area is apparently related to both internal ministry needs and to those of the defense-export industry as well.[16]

The design of the Alvey Program addresses a major concern of the Alvey Commission: the fragmentation along the R&D spectrum among those who generate technical advances and those who convert them to use. The large number of approved projects and formation of research consortia suggest that the program has catalyzed on a national level at least some interaction among the country's research performers. Perhaps the most important function of this teaming up is the burgeoning number of university–industry ties, a feature that distinguishes Alvey from Japan's approach.

Another difference between the two is the Japanese establishment of a single central research facility, which may tend to limit the dissemination of technical information to those ten organizations immediately involved. The Alvey Program is developing an elaborate communication infrastructure with electronic messaging to facilitate exchanges among the 106 companies, universities, and research establishments participating, although the intent is to restrict the flow outside the United Kingdom. Nevertheless, the underlying motivations of leveraging funds and manpower and of facilitating technology transfer within the circle of participating partners is an obvious similarity. One interesting possibility is some collaboration and technical exchanges between the 5G Project and Alvey. Discussions are underway to explore potential co-operation on parallel computer languages and on machine translation capabilities.[17]

The European Communities: ESPRIT

Another significant program of collaboration in semiconductor technology is a major co-operative venture in information technology (IT) research launched in 1983 by the European Economic Community (EEC) and private industry. The European Strategic

[16] Interview and subsequent correspondence with Dr. W. Fawcett, Director VLSI and MOD liaison, Alvey Program, January and March 1985.

[17] Private communication with W. Fawcett of the Alvey Program, 7 March 1985.

Program for Research and Development in Information Technology (ESPRIT) focuses on long-lead-time R&D in basic underlying technologies, or "precompetitive" technical areas, related to advanced microelectronics, data and knowledge processing, and office and factory automation. The stated objective is "to provide the European IT industry with the technology base it needs to become and stay competitive worldwide in the next ten years."[18] Envisioned, therefore, as a ten-year effort, the program's first five-year phase is being funded at approximately 1.5 billion ECU[19] or about $1.25 billion, of which half is coming from the EEC and half from industrial, academic and/or institute research performers.

The stated impetus for ESPRIT is the combination of several interrelated trends. In view of a growth rate of 8 to 10 per cent per year projected through 1990, information technology is becoming one of the world's largest manufacturing sectors. However, market-share indicators have been pointing to rather bleak prospects for a strong European position in this development. In 1975, the Community had a trade surplus in IT products. By 1980, the surplus had become a $5 billion deficit, which doubled by 1982. As a whole, European industry supplies less than 40 per cent of its own market and about 10 per cent of the world market. The implications are that the European share of the $500 billion world market for IT is only about 15 per cent. In addition, the framers of ESPRIT perceived a number of other problems affecting the competitiveness of the European electronics industry: (1) generating sufficient R&D funds for long-term projects in the face of declining sales and a recession; (2) coping with a home market less innovation-minded and fragmented into national units often protected by national governments; and (3) overcoming traditional political and economic rivalries to achieve collaboration.[20] These issues, coupled with sharpening competition from the United States and Japan, led to the formation of a roundtable of twelve leading European IT companies a few years ago. With the EEC, they developed and defined "the entire ESPRIT project with respect to concept, size, scope of research, management, and legal

[18] "Bulletin of the European Communities Supplement, 5/83: Prospects for the Development of New Policies: Research and Development, Energy, and New Technologies," Luxembourg: Office of Official Publications of the EEC, 1983, p. 29.

[19] The ECU is the monetary unit of the European Communities. Its value is calculated from a weighted average of the values of certain EEC currencies.

[20] Dickson (1984, p. 28) and interview with Nico Hazewindus of N.V. Philips, 25 April 1984.

questions."[21] These twelve companies, which represent 70 to 80 per cent of European industrial research facilities in this field, thus constituted the principal engine for ESPRIT.[22]

The view that coordinated research is a key aspect of competitiveness is evident in the stated rationale for the program.[23]

> The main drive for such a large scale programme has come from industry. Facing the formidable competition of Japan and the USA, Community industry has acknowledged that, in order to reverse the trend of increasing reliance on importing technology, only joint strategic long-term research planning and the concentration of resources through the definition and funding of technology goals of common interest on a Community scale, can have a good chance of redressing the situation gradually but in a lasting manner by: (i) ensuring that research teams achieve the critical mass to obtain results; (ii) enabling optimization of resources that will result in reducing duplication and widening the spectrum of research tackled; (iii) reducing the timelag effect caused by reliance on imported technology; (iv) paving the way to the definition and adoption of standards of European origin.

The program is divided into five technical areas (see Table 31). Two areas are oriented towards applications where the greatest economic impact for the IT market is anticipated – the office and the factory. The support base for these applications consists of three areas concentrated on "enabling" technologies. Thus the structure of the program consists of five areas, with funding to be allocated on a fairly even basis among them.

Two features of the program are particularly important. First, total funding will be distributed between two categories of projects: "A" projects, which are large-scale, systems-oriented, and ongoing and thus require substantial manpower and financial resources, and "B" projects, which require a smaller-scale concentration of resources and address short-term needs that can be either near the frontier or closer to development. For each of the five technical areas, approximately 75 per cent of the budget is available for "A" projects and 25 per cent is available for "B" projects. Second, a major criterion for participation in ESPRIT is a partnership between at least two research performers, one of which may be

[21] Horst Nasko, "European Common Market," *IEEE Spectrum*, November 1983, p. 72.

[22] For a list of the companies, see Haklisch (1986, Figure 4.8).

[23] "Bulletin of the European Communities," *op. cit.*, p. 83.

Table 31 *ESPRIT Technical Areas and Applications*

Technical Areas	Focus
Advanced microelectronics	Development of submicron MOS and bipolar IC technology and the related CAD tools
Software technology	Development of a new generation of modular and reusable software-production tools that can also be used in other sectors of the program
Advanced Information Processing (AIP)	Development of new human-to-machine communications linkages, knowledge-processing techniques, and novel computer structures
Office Automation	Research into work-stations and related communication and data links for office systems
Computer-Integrated Flexible Manufacturing	Development of systems for factory automation involving the architecture of integrated systems, robotics, sensors, and transducers

Source: Haklisch (1986)

"commercially oriented" and "preferably an EEC industrial company."[24]

Several characteristics of ESPRIT are distinctive.[25] First, it is an international program whose clear underlying objective is to establish links among the research resources of member countries. It provides a strong impetus to broaden the network for collaboration. Second, ESPRIT was developed specifically with European industry in mind. It therefore has at least the potential for serving the needs of that industry. Third, the emphasis on knowledge-based systems resembling human association and inference, supported by advances in microelectronics design and information science, is a counterpart to efforts in the United States and Japan focused on artificial intelligence systems. Fourth, the 75 per cent/25 per cent distribution of A/B projects reflects a *de facto* division of the pie for both large companies and small to medium-sized enterprises. This is in part a political concession to members of the EEC (for example, Greece or Ireland) who lack a Philips or a Siemens, but it also directs specific attention to incorporating the

[24] Giles Merritt, "'Telematics' to Get R&D Boost in Europe," *Europe*, January/February 1984, p. 19.

[25] This section draws upon insights gained from a series of interviews at the European Community and with several companies associated with ESPRIT, 5–8 March, 1984. It also reflects a critique provided by the Center's Advisory Board.

contributions of smaller firms, which are commonly viewed as being more flexible and innovative.

ESPRIT's five-year expenditure plan is roughly equal to one year of R&D spending at Philips. Compared with the R&D budgets of the other twelve major ESPRIT companies, it also represents a fairly modest level of effort. ESPRIT has thus been characterized as accounting for only 6 per cent of EEC spending in IT. Nevertheless, it will probably account for about 30 per cent of all EEC spending on *precompetitive* research in that area. Moreover, it focuses on R&D in information technology, which is currently a relatively minor portion of the R&D programs in several companies. Another point to note is that the availability of funding for the extensive software requirements in the program will complement the traditional "hardware" concentration of several of the major partners.

What, therefore, are the major effects of ESPRIT likely to be? Clearly the development of a more co-ordinated network of linkages is a prime objective. The ostensible goal is to bring together major electronics companies, universities, research institutes, and small high-technology firms. One interviewee noted that, in practice, the primary thrust of the program is on industry–industry connections. Thus while universities and research institutes participate, university–industry co-operation is not likely to be the linkage strengthened the most under this program.

With these observations in mind, it is interesting to view the profile of ESPRIT's first call for proposals announced in January 1985. A total of 104 projects were approved, representing an EEC

Table 32 *Profile of Projects and Participation in ESPRIT*

Total Number of Approved Projects	104
Distribution by Technical Area	
--Advanced Microelectronics	28
--Software Technology	14
--Advanced Information Processing	20
--Office Systems	23
--Computer Integrated Manufacturing	19
Average Number of Partners Per Project	5
Total Number of Participants (Industry, Academia, Research Institutes)	270
Distribution of Participation in Projects	
--Universities and Institutes	75%
--Small Companies	50%
--Large Companies (500+ employees)	70%

Source: Compiled from EEC Press Report, 24 January 1985, and Review of First Call for Proposals

Table 33 *ESPRIT Project Participation, Advanced Microelectronics*

Firm	Number of Projects in Area I, Advanced Microelectronics, First Call
AEG	8
Bull	4
GEC	10
Philips	5
Plessey	4
Siemens	6
STET	2
Thomson	9

Source: Haklisch (1986)

financial commitment of about $150 million and thus a total effort of about $300 million. Table 32 summarizes information reported by the EEC on the projects and participants in this phase.

As in the Alvey Program, concentration in advanced microelectronics is a major focus in ESPRIT, accounting for more projects (twenty-eight) than any other area in the first call for proposals.[26] The projects reflect a strong interest in silicon, CMOS, and bipolar, with one project in GaAs. Most of the effort is devoted to process technology.

Among the twelve firms of the ESPRIT roundtable, four companies are not participating in projects in the advanced microelectronics area; they are CGE, ICL, Nixdorf, and Olivetti. The remaining eight are involved in this area as shown in Table 33.

As ESPRIT unfolds, there seem to be "clusters" of firms developing, which may lead to an interesting pattern of synergism. Two pairs of companies provide illustrations of partnerships formed under the auspices of ESPRIT that may be models for continuing co-operation: GEC and AEG Telefunken, and Philips and Siemens. GEC is the most active firm in this area with ten projects, a mirror of its pronounced involvement in Alvey. AEG is collaborating in eight projects. The two are partners in five of the total they each pursue. In combination with the other four areas in the first call of approved projects, GEC participates in a total of 19 projects and AEG in 17. Of these, they are collaborators in ten.

[26] This section is based on the list of first-call approved projects released by the EEC in January 1985.

The linkage of Philips and Siemens under ESPRIT is also a partnership to examine. Philips is involved in five projects in Advanced Microelectronics and Siemens in six. Of these, they are partners in four. Their co-operation extends through the remaining four areas; in all, Philips has 16 projects in the first call and Siemens 15. Of these, they participate jointly in seven, or about half, of the projects.

ESPRIT is clearly intended to benefit European industry. The participation by non-European companies has not been prohibited, but it has been specifically limited to those non-European firms with large R&D capabilities in Europe who can find European partners and who are willing to participate but not transfer technology out of the EEC back to their home country. The list of first-call proposals shows only two non-European participants, both in the Computer Integrated Manufacturing Area: the AT&T–Philips joint venture (one project) and IBM Germany (two projects).

For the British companies, particularly GEC, ICL, and Plessey, there is the possibility of participating in a national program, Alvey, as well as an international program, ESPRIT. To what extent are they conflicting or complementary? Do companies pursue some particular strategy for participating in one rather than the other? How likely is technical know-how to flow between the two? Interviews suggest that participating companies view ESPRIT and Alvey as both necessary and therefore not duplicative or conflicting. There are obviously areas of technical overlap, but they are perceived as reinforcing each other. Because of the close timetable of events in launching both programs, plans for participation have reportedly been constrained from following a detailed formal strategy. Involvement is obviously founded on the expectation that participation will yield benefits that strengthen a firm's technical base and its competitiveness in product development. As an example, a firm may choose to pursue co-operative microelectronics research under Alvey when some basis for collaboration may already exist, and pursue software technology under ESPRIT when there are important implications for standards. Other firms may choose different approaches based on company needs and objectives. The formal relationship of Alvey to ESPRIT is also interesting: the director of the Alvey Program is also the British government representative to ESPRIT. Because British companies, universities, and research institutes participate in both programs, there is a considerable flow of technical exchanges between the two, at least in the opinion of the Alvey directorate.[27]

[27] Interview at the Alvey Program Directorate, Office of Trade and Industry, UK, January 1985.

It is, of course, too early to evaluate the success of ESPRIT in any concrete terms. One interesting opinion, often voiced by government officials and industry participants, is that the indirect effects of ESPRIT may ultimately prove more important than its direct effects on technical progress. The establishment of a workable model for co-operation among research partners who had previously competed on a product and national basis may be even more important than the achievement of specified technical objectives. Most European companies have not pursued research or technology co-operation across national boundaries in their own region to any great extent. Thus, ESPRIT might serve as an important catalyst in that process. Another potential effect of the program is the adoption of European-wide operating standards and protocols. ESPRIT partners have already agreed to some standards for "open systems interface" for office and data networks.

United States: The VHSIC Program

The three programs discussed above – the Japanese 5G Project, the British Alvey Program, and ESPRIT – share several characteristics and anticipated effects in common. All are designed with a commercial orientation; all are designed to push frontiers and applications in common technical areas; all seek to reduce time, cost, and risk by pooling resources; and all seek to facilitate technology transfer among participating research performers, with the 5G Project having perhaps the smallest circle of participants and ESPRIT the largest. And, finally, the ultimate objective for all three is to solidify a competitive position in one or more areas of IT.

By contrast, the American VHSIC program has substantially different features and intended effects. VHSIC is the first industrial co-operative research venture for semiconductors in the United States. It is thus a mechanism for research collaboration by industry. But this is where the similarity ends. Although VHSIC may ultimately have behind it a vision of American technical virtuosity eclipsed by that of Japan, the program is not explicitly designed to broaden or strengthen the nation's base of electronics advances. It is also not designed to facilitate the formation of industry or university–industry consortia for research co-operation in areas of commercial applications. Rather, the VHSIC program is a $900-million, ten-year effort (1980–9) to meet military needs for highly specialized silicon-based[28] digital IC technologies that can be inserted into defense systems. The specific goal is the development of thirty-six varieties of highly specialized chips that perform

[28] VHSIC is focused solely on silicon. Research in GaAs within the Department of Defense is being conducted by the Defense Advanced Research Projects Agency.

according to rigid specifications. The interest in competitiveness in this program relates to political adversaries and not trade rivals and thus is focused on national security and not on markets.

The VHSIC program has three main phases, including a Phase Zero that consisted in defining the program. The other two phases have specific objectives. The objective of the first is "the creation of chips with 'clock rates,' the speed at which they process data, of 25 million hertz, or cycles per second. The second is aimed at clock rates of 100 million hertz." Although speed is the program's principal development objective, increased chip density is a byproduct. VHSIC has already achieved feature sizes of 1.25 microns, while the next phase aims at half a micron. The Defense Department anticipates a number of military applications for the resulting high-speed chips, including: "'smart' flying bombs, sonar buoys that detect enemy submarines, jamming pods for electronic warfare, radars, electronic packages for fighter aircraft, sonar-guided torpedoes, surface-to-air missiles, and tank weapon-control systems."[29]

The number of prime contractors decreases in each phase. Phase Zero, launched in 1980, involved program definition by the nine contractors listed in Figure 7. A point to note is that although the focus of the program is the development of specialized chips, eight of the nine main contractors are systems houses and not semiconductor producers. This reflects the general trend of convergence of components and systems, but more particularly the familiarity of military systems suppliers with the required specifications and functions of the chips to be developed.

Phase One, which involved the design and fabrication of the 1.25-micron chip-sets, began in 1981. This included the design and fabrication of a viable prototype defense sub-system or brassboard, using Phase One chips. Six of the original nine contractors participated in this phase: Honeywell, Hughes Aircraft/Signetics, IBM,

General Electric/Intersil *
Honeywell
Hughes Aircraft/Signetics *
IBM
Raytheon/Fairchild Semiconductor *
Rockwell
Texas Instruments
TRW/Motorola *
Westinghouse/National Semiconductor *

Note: * Merchant semiconductor partner

Source: Haklisch (1986)

Figure 7 *VHSIC Phase One Participants*

29 "First of the 'Superchips' Arrive," *The New York Times*, 23 July, 1985, Section C.

Texas Instruments, TRW/Motorola, and Westinghouse/National Semiconductor.

In addition to fulfilling performance criteria demonstrated in functional brassboards, Phase One also included economic criteria to enhance the spread of applications in defense systems. This effort was focused on boosting yields through improved manufacturing technology. The Pentagon awarded an additional $15 million yield-enhancement contract to each of the Phase One contractors to develop more advanced fabrication processes so that there would be an improved yield of about 10 per cent. To augment this activity, the three military services are also spending about $100 million over the next three years to upgrade semiconductor-manufacturing technology for use by contractors in the VHSIC program.[30]

Phase Two, announced in late 1984, is devoted to developing chips with feature sizes of half a micron. It is being conducted by the three Phase One contractors who were the first to deliver functional chips: (1) IBM, who will focus on CMOS chips; (2) TRW and Motorola, who will focus on CMOS and bipolar chips; and (3) Honeywell and Motorola,[31] who will focus on bipolar chips.

As a defense-supported research project for military needs, VHSIC involves technology-transfer practices that differ markedly from those of national programs with commercial objectives. Information sharing is restricted to qualified defense users. However, within this circle, mechanisms have been established to disseminate technical data both among the VHSIC contractors and between VHSIC contractors and other defense contractors. All VHSIC technical reports are contained in the Defense Technical Information System; workshops are regularly scheduled with system designers to spark an interest in the use of the chips; and semiannual conferences are held to report on progress.[32] A measure of success for this system is that about 50 per cent of the so-called technology-insertion contracts were awarded to companies that did not participate in the VHSIC Phase One.

Given the program's focus on national security, however, unwarranted diffusion of VHSIC technology is a major concern. Thus, control mechanisms are in place to prevent dissemination outside the circle of specified participants. This control system involves several dimensions. The Defense Department lacks the authority to classify *all* the technology in the program since the technology *per se* was not developed under VHSIC. The use of control

[30] Julian (1985, p. 54)

[31] Motorola's participation involves two separate divisions of the firm.

[32] Interview, VHSIC program, Washington, D.C., 11 April, 1985.

mechanisms is thus limited primarily to two circumstances: the use of VHSIC parts in weapons systems, where the control comes under the International Traffic in Arms Regulations (ITAR), and "recipe" technology developed specifically for VHSIC parts which are controlled through classification. The classification mechanism is used most often for ROMs and cryptography. It would not be used, for example, for a given mask unless the mask were specific to a weapon system.[33] However, restrictions of technical data also apply. VHSIC contractors may not discuss performance characteristics or chip architectures in unclassified meetings. Discussion of software details related to either the CAD or fabrication process are prohibited in open symposia.[34]

A key aspect of technology transfer in the VHSIC program is the potential commercial spillover. Unlike other national programs, this is neither an objective of VHSIC nor a direct concern. Regulations, in fact, restrict the sale of certain commercial products with VHSIC-type advances. Nevertheless, some contractors may be able to sell some VHSIC-like products on the open market, for example, certain RAMs or signal-processing chips. More widespread and significant are the learning benefits in design and fabrication – particularly experience in managing the design of a complex system on a chip and improved lithographic processes. The Defense Department and VHSIC contractors are discussing plans for greater commercial use of the technologies that emerge from VHSIC. A prime incentive for commercialization is the small military market for the program's chips. For example, all military devices account for only about 7 per cent of the total semiconductor market. Moreover, the firms are concerned that Japan will gain a commercial edge if the best American technology is restricted to military chips. Another indication of potential commercial adaptation is the fact that VHSIC participants have supplemented government R&D with some $300 million of their own money, as well as with some of their best design engineers and managers.[35]

France: La Filière Electronique

The Filière Electronique is a broad national plan to strengthen the competitiveness of the French electronics industry. In contrast with other national programs of coordinated research, it is "a global

33 Interview, VHSIC program, Washington, D.C., 11 April, 1985.

34 Julian (1985, p. 57).

35 Julian (1985). For an argument that the spillover benefits of VHSIC will be greatly counterbalanced by the "crowding out" of scientists, engineers, and other technical resources from the commercial sector, see Brueckner and Borrus (1984). For a general discussion of the history and issues surrounding military–civilian spillovers, see Rosenberg (1986).

revitalization strategy"[36] that includes a research program. This breadth is perhaps its principal distinguishing feature: "filière" describes all activity related to a given good or technology. Filière électronique thus includes everything where electronics is or becomes the main technology, including: components, consumer electronics, office equipment, computers, professional electronics, telecommunications, instrumentation, medical electronics, aerospace electronics, and software. The plan is therefore designed to integrate all electronics-related activities under a common industrial policy.

The Filière électronique was initiated in 1982 as a five-year effort with projected public and private investments (including those of foreign firms such as IBM, Texas Instruments and Motorola) of \$20 billion.[37] The aim of this financial infusion is to increase the production of information technology products by 3 to 9 per cent a year, create a surplus trade balance in IT products and generate 80,000 new jobs per year. The program calls for a formidable coordination of national resources to link private and nationalized firms, labor, user communities, government research centers and institutes, and universities. The plan also calls for a substantial upgrading of manufacturing technology through subsidies, government-sponsored market-promotion efforts, and an expanded program of education and training of more scientists and engineers.

Funding for all R&D activities in the Filière over the five years of the program is likely to be in the order of \$5 billion or about FF35 billion. Table 34 provides a summary of funding for the period.

Most of the support for the Filière is coming from the Ministry of Defense, which is consistent with funding practices in the past.[38] See Table 35. The role of the Ministry of Defense in project selection, direction, and co-ordination is a primary one.

A critical dimension of the Filière électronique is its context, the extensive nationalization that took place under Mitterrand's Socialist government, resulting in the restructuring of the French electronics industry. For example, the government nationalized CGE, St. Gobain, Rhône-Poulenc, and Thomson. The government also acquired a majority interest in Matra and a 75 per cent interest in CII-Honeywell Bull, now called Bull. In addition, the government increased capital expenditures in key nationalized companies to offset a perceived trend of under-capitalization. With these changes, the overall profile of companies in the Filière is approxi-

[36] Farnoux (1983).

[37] This was the figure widely cited in the press at that time.

[38] Office of Technology Assessment (1983).

Table 34 *Five-Year R&D Funding Forecasts for Filière électronique*

Year	1982	1983	1984	1985	1986
Total Gov't Funding (FF Billions)	4.0	6.7	7.6	8.0(est)	N/A

Source: Ministere de l'Industrie el de la Recherche, lLa Politique Industielle de la Filiere Electronique,ž November 1983. The figures for 1984 and 1985 were obtained from interviews.

Table 35 *Sources of 1983 Funding for Filière électronique*

Source	Level of Funding (FF Billion)
Min. de la Defense	3.3
Min. des Telecommunications	1.7
Min. de l'Industrie (Direction des industries electroniques et de l'Informatique)	1.5
Min. de la Recherche et de la Technologie (Fond de la Recherche et de la Technologie)	0.2
ANVAR (government agency for innovation)	NA *
TOTAL	6.7

Note: * Less than 0.1

Source: Ministere de l'Industrie el de la Recherche, "La Politique Industrielle de la Filiere Electronique," November 1983, p. 6.

mately the following: 50 per cent controlled by the government; 20 per cent private companies; and 30 per cent subsidiaries of foreign companies.

Among government companies, boundaries were redrawn to consolidate resources and establish a leader for each technical area. St. Gobain was forced out of the Filière; it sold its share of Olivetti back to Olivetti, withdrew its capital in Bull, and sold its 50 per cent share of Eurotechnique to Thomson. One of the most pronounced changes in technical territory was the agreement signed between Thomson and CGE, dubbed the "Yalta of Electronics." CGE exchanged its consumer and components division for Thomson's telecommunications division. In addition, CGE and Thomson sold their subsidiaries involved in computers to Bull, and Thomson acquired the remaining 50 per cent of Eurotechnique from National Semiconductor (US) as well as EFICS from CEA. Figure 8

Field	Leader
components	Thomson Matra-Harris
consumer electronics	Thomson
professional electronics	Thomson
telecommunications	CGE (CIT-Alcatel)
computers	Bull
office equipment	Bull

Source: Haklisch (1986)

Figure 8 *Company Specialization in the Filière électronique*

provides an overview of the industry structure that emerged at the end of 1983.

Since the election of Jacques Chirac as Prime Minister in Spring 1986, there has been considerable talk of denationalizing some of the nationalized companies. At the time of writing, none of the specific proposals has yet touched the companies involved in the Filière.[39] Moreover, the role of government funding and control in French microelectronics is unlikely to change immediately.

The research emphasis of Filière électronique is concentrated in six national projects chosen by the French government from a plan of fourteen projects originally recommended. The selected projects are:

- large scientific and industrial computers;
- computer-aided design, engineering, and production;
- computer-aided design for VLSI;
- display;
- computer-assisted instruction; and
- computer-aided translation.

This program of six projects is the aspect of the Filière électronique that corresponds most closely to the other national research efforts discussed in this chapter.

R&D funding for the six projects is estimated to be FF1.5 billion or $215 million over a four-year period (1984–87). This sum will come from government sources and participating companies (50/50) as a joint funding of the projects. Details of the specific efforts within each of the six projects are evolving. However, the

[39] Apart from the proposed merger of the semiconductor operations of Thomson and the Italian firm SGS, which may be an indirect repercussion of the denationalization program.

general intent is to link government research centers, where the bulk of France's basic research occurs, with industry. This is intended to reinforce and complement technology-transfer practices already in place, such as the ongoing collaboration and exchange between Thomson and Laboratoire d'Etudes des Technologies Informatiques (LETI), a laboratory specializing in components, and between Matra and the Centre National d'Etude des Télécommunications (CNET).[40]

Under the Mitterrand government, Thomson and Matra were the firms singled out to provide the core thrust in microelectronics and thus will likely be the beneficiaries receiving the most advantages in the Filière électronique. Unlike the earlier Plan Composants, in which international joint ventures were an explicit objective, the Filière électronique has a primary objective of reinforcing and advancing independent French capabilities and only a secondary objective of encouraging co-operation. The relationships established under the Plan Composants to ally Thomson with Motorola and Matra with Harris are continuing as significant links for co-operation and technology transfer. At the same time, Matra maintains a connection with Intel and Thomson with National Semiconductor. In addition, Thomson acquired Mostek in November 1985.

The Filière électronique is similar to other national efforts in its program of six projects to coordinate resources and establish linkages between research performers engaged in generating and applying advances in microelectronics and IT. It differs from its predecessor, the Plan Composants, which looked to international linkages as the principal mechanism for enhancing French technical strength in electronics. Moreover, it differs significantly from the Japanese, British, and EEC programs in its vast intent simultaneously to restructure the industry and to integrate comprehensively all key factors involved in the entire field. Nevertheless, despite the pronounced role of government intervention and a grand plan, the Filière does not show the same level of detail in synchronization and coordination as the British, Japanese, and EEC approaches.

The Origins of Today's Policies

Government policies toward microelectronics in the United States, Japan, and Europe have recognizable roots in earlier national policies. It is useful briefly to review the evolution of policies in these three regions.

[40] Interviews at Thomson-CSF and Matra.

From the beginning, American policies in support of microelectronics and connected industries have been closely tied to defense objectives and, in particular, to military and space procurement. Of course, the American government had little to do with the work that led to the initial transistor, which was conducted at Bell Laboratories and motivated by perceptions of the value of such a device for the telephone system. However, once the transistor had been invented, the Department of Defense very quickly understood the potentials of the new technology for military hardware. The military was especially explicit about its interest in highly reliable miniature circuitry. It financed a considerable amount of research pursuing this objective, but – more importantly as things turned out – it indirectly induced private companies to invest their own monies.

The key breakthroughs at Texas Instruments and Fairchild were financed largely by private funds. But the decision to base the guidance and control systems of the Minute Man missile on integrated circuits, along with a parallel decision about project Apollo, presented the American microelectronics industry with an enormous market for state-of-the-art products. [41] These potential markets for future military procurement, along with considerable R&D funding from the Department of Defense, kept technology advancing rapidly during the 1960s, with American firms far out in front of the pack. There is no hint that anybody in government had in mind that they were helping to create an industry that would be a major economic asset. But of course the evolving semiconductor technologies had increasingly widespread civilian, as well as military, uses.

Computer technology and microelectronics technology have been closely intertwined for the last quarter century. In contrast with the microelectronics case, the American government played a central role in the birth of the modern computer. Virtually all of the exploratory R&D that led to the early electronic computers was financed by the armed forces. The government was almost the sole market for the early operational computers, and it continued to be the dominant market until the early 1960s. By the mid-1960s, of course, a vast civilian market for computers began to open up. As was the case with transistors and integrated circuits, the strong early government market provided American companies with experience and technology that foreign companies could not match. Again, however, building a commercially formidable computer industry was a byproduct, not a goal, of the government programs.

Knowledgeable observers have stated that, by the middle 1960s,

[41] For a discussion of the effect of military procurement on the early evolution of microelectronics technology, see Levin (1982a).

or the early 1970s at the latest, government procurement and R&D support were playing a relatively minor role in the evolution of microelectronics and computer technologies.[42] The key demands pulling technical advance were civilian demands for faster and more powerful computers. In turn, this fed back to pull integrated circuit technology. American firms in the forefront of computer technology and American firms in the forefront of microelectronics technology tended mutually to support each other.

The Japanese story is, of course, very different. In the first place, throughout the period in question Japanese military R&D and procurement has been on a tight leash, and government programs have had the express purpose of enhancing the commercial capabilities of the Japanese industries. In the second place, Japanese traditions and ideology regarding the role of government in guiding the economy are very different from the American. MITI and associated contemporary Japanese government agencies have grown out of an involvement of the Japanese government in economic planning and commercial entrepreneurship that dates back to the late nineteenth century.

Many Americans tend to date the rise of the Japanese microelectronics industry as from the middle 1970s and focus on the VLSI program as the beginnings of active governmental policies in support of the industry. In fact, by the late 1950s the Japanese electronics industry already was demonstrating its prowess by taking over the transistor radio and hearing aid markets and moving aggressively into black-and-white television. In the late 1960s, the Japanese began to take over the color television market. MITI support dates to that time. The Japanese surge in color television was based at least in part on a MITI-funded co-operative research program that enabled Japanese companies to get ahead of American ones in exploiting the opportunities afforded by integrated circuits.

Too much has been written about the VLSI program to warrant any detailed discussion of that program here. Suffice it to say that it marked the beginning of a commitment of MITI, and the Japanese government in general, to the notion that the future of Japanese industry depended on its strengths in microelectronics and connected industries such as computers. Also, the VLSI program was important not only in its own right but as the source and testing ground of ideas and strategies that have now become very familiar. The MITI-sponsored part of the VLSI program was about what was called "precompetitive research." The argument, or the rationale, was put forth that it was highly appropriate, and perhaps even

42 Levin (1982a, pp. 65–66); Rosenberg (1986, p. 26).

necessary, for the firms to band together to do precompetitive research co-operatively and then to go on to do proprietary process and product design separately and in competition with each other. These ideas now are part of the mind-set in the United States and Europe, as well as in Japan.

Policies in Europe have been much less consistent than policies in the United States and Japan. Unlike those in the latter two countries, policies in the European countries quite often have involved a mixing of military and commercial objectives; and the result, arguably, has not been happy. Also in contrast with the United States and Japan, where perceptions have tended to be that prevailing policies were on track, the European countries have suffered for a long time from a malaise and a feeling that existing policies were not working well. As a result, the European countries have tended to shift from one policy to another in a frustrating search for something that would work.

Rather than spread the discussion too widely, we will concentrate here on France. From its beginnings, French policies in support of microelectronics and computers have aimed for both military-design capabilities and for the commercial prowess of French companies. However, French military R&D spending and procurement have been very limited compared with the United States programs. Relatedly, it seems clear that the French military programs have neither been so ambitious about making state-of-the-art advances in particular procurement efforts, nor have they supported as wide a range of generic research aimed to open up new technologies, as have the American military programs. As a result, the French have felt themselves lagging in these areas, and have been concerned with the effect of this on their ability to produce first-class military equipment.

Indeed, modern French programs in support of semiconductors and computers have recognizable origins in French frustration at the refusal of the American government some twenty years ago to let the French buy a large computer needed for its nuclear programs from an American company. As a result of this experience and subsequent ones, the French government committed itself to the establishment of a French computer design and production capability that would, among other things, enable France to meet its military needs. By this time the commercial market, with both private and governmental customers, was large and growing. It was natural to think of government support for the French industry as furthering commercial capabilities as well as the particular ones judged essential by the French military. A similar dependency upon American companies for integrated circuits for military equipment and for computers led the French government to a similar commitment toward a French semiconductor industry.

Both French tradition and the centrality of procurement interests related to national security made it natural to proceed by identifying, or establishing, particular firms as "national champions" with the responsibility both to meet procurement needs and to develop a commercial capability. French military demands were judged not to be large enough to warrant the maintenance of several competing firms, and in any case the French faith in competition has always been much less strong than the American. Note, however, that by bundling its promotion program with its procurement program, the French government implicitly picked one company to carry its commercial banners as well as to develop and preserve the relevant military procurement capabilities. The French in effect blocked themselves off from the road followed by the Japanese of providing support and encouragement to a number of companies.

At the same time, this strategy broke down what otherwise would have been barriers to involvement by French government officials in the commercially oriented R&D strategies of its chosen French firms. Various writers have remarked that, while often allegedly for commercial purposes, government-pushed projects were seldom directed toward plausible markets, and that projects proposed by companies have been judged on the basis of how they fit national, not necessarily commercial, objectives.[43] Thus the French companies could not hunt for commercial niches that would be developed into areas of major commercial strength.

We will deal with British and German policies much more briefly. Like France, Britain has invested nontrivial amounts of public funds in procurement-related R&D in computers and semiconductors over the post-war period, and also has funded some R&D with the express objective of boosting commercial competence in these industries. However, until Alvey, it is fair to say that Britain has had no consistent and sustained policy regarding its microelectronics industry. Until recently, the same could also be said about West Germany. Unlike Britain and France, and like Japan, German military R&D and production has been quite limited. And German civilian-oriented programs in electronics have been kept relatively separate from the military-oriented ones. Over the last decade, German civilian-oriented programs have been operated largely under the auspices of the Ministry for Research and Technology (BMFT). This is an interesting institu-

[43] See, for example, Zysman (1977).

tion, quite different from anything found in the United States or Japan. The BMFT solicits proposals from industry and provides partial funding (generally less than one half) for the projects it accepts. In recent years, BMFT funding in microelectronics has been quite substantial. Overall, the West German government policy in microelectronics has leaned toward support for areas of strength and opportunity identified largely by industry. This contrasts sharply with France.

It is time to pull some strands together, and to consider what is similar, and what is different, about the various country programs. An important similarity is that they have been strongly nationalistic. Countries with significant military-procurement programs have felt it essential to have competent national firms in microelectronics so that they could meet defense-procurement needs without having to go abroad. The countries without major military-procurement programs, principally Japan and West Germany, also have been concerned that their national microelectronics industry be strong. There is an intensely held belief in all of these countries that national strength in microelectronics is a requirement for healthy national economic growth.

Both the United States and Japan have aimed to support a relatively wide-based semiconductor and computer industry consisting of a number of competitive firms. An express objective in both cases has been to keep as many firms as possible up to the generic technological frontiers. Japan did this through its co-operative precompetitive research programs. In the United States, the Department of Defense did something similar through a variety of mechanisms for sharing generic technological knowledge among defense contractors. The French experience and strategy has been quite different. In contrast with the United States and Japan, the French have tried to narrow down their key industries so that only one, or at most two, firms remained in the policy picture.

Despite the fact that their R&D-support programs clearly helped their industries gain a competitive advantage, in neither the United States nor Japan did policy makers try to influence the commercial bets laid down by firms. Again, France is different in that government officials have been concerned in many cases with the details of commercial strategy.

The Contemporary Scene

Current national programs clearly show their heritage in past ones. The current VHSIC program, as well as the Strategic Defense

Initiative (SDI), resemble their American antecedents. Similarly, the Fifth Generation Computer Program is well within the now relatively long-established Japanese policy traditions. The Filière électronique is archetypically French, and represents a natural extension and elaboration of earlier programs in support of computers and semiconductors. While we did not describe contemporary German policies, these too can be recognized as growing from German programs in the 1970s involving the BMFT. Alvey represents something new on the British scene. This is really the first coherent policy the British had ever been able to mount. ESPRIT is new in a more fundamental sense. It is a policy that aims to support a European-wide industry as contrasted with the industries of particular countries.

What is noteworthy about the new departures or about the context in which they will operate? There are several things.

First, governments seem much taken with the idea that R&D co-operation among firms is a good idea. In the case of Japan's 5G and related programs, this represents a continuation of past government policies and attitudes. It should be recognized, however, that the earlier VLSI program was advertised in terms of bringing a group of Japanese companies up to the frontier together. One can question whether the same format will prove as effective when the objective is to advance the frontier.

What is going on in the United States represents a clear, if subtle, change in belief about the appropriateness and efficacy of co-operative R&D arrangements. While the Department of Defense in earlier programs occasionally got groups of companies to work together, VHSIC bent strongly in this direction. There is no question that officials in the Pentagon had been influenced by Japanese programs. The change in governmental attitudes toward private co-operative arrangements in R&D is even more striking. Explicit new antitrust legislation was put into place setting out quite liberal guidelines under which co-operative R&D arrangements among firms in the same line of business would not be challenged. By contrast, It would have been unthinkable five years ago for the Antitrust Division of the Justice Department to accept an arrangement like MCC. The National Science Foundation has helped to establish several university-based microelectronics centers and has encouraged industry to participate in these. There are state-based centers, like the North Carolina microelectronics center, aiming to link university research and industry. A large group of companies has gotten together to finance a Center for Integrated Systems at Stanford, and the Semiconductor Research Corporation draws funds from a long list of companies to finance university-based research at several different locations.

The interesting question is whether this new zeal for co-operative R&D will in fact bear the fruits its advocates say it will, or whether R&D co-operation has been oversold. There are real questions about whether companies will continue to contribute to co-operative R&D arrangements when the financial going gets tough. Federal and state funding of microelectronic centers may, or may not, prove fruitful.

In Europe, the new programs in support of R&D co-operation are in part mimicry of Japanese programs and in part represent beliefs that only through R&D co-operation can even the large European firms match the resources of the larger American ones. In the case of ESPRIT, there is the additional purpose of breaking down intra-European national barriers. The latter has long been an objective of many European statesmen and corporate leaders, and co-operative R&D arrangements may turn out to be a fruitful beginning to its achievement. Alvey does seem to have provided British policy in microelectronics with an articulated strategy, which it has lacked in the past. However, again, one can wonder whether R&D co-operation will prove as fruitful and durable as its advocates say, or whether it will turn out to be a fad.

A second important and significant difference about the current situation is that a number of people inside, as well as outside, the Pentagon are talking about expected positive effects on commercial competence of programs funded by the Department of Defense. For many years the Europeans and the Japanese have argued that the American defense and space programs were American industrial policies in disguise and that they were so intended. As we noted earlier, while there is no doubt that, until the late 1960s at least, defense programs greatly enhanced the commercial competence of American companies, there is no evidence that anybody of importance in designing those programs gave much weight to that objective. But in its early days VHSIC was expressly advertised by some officials in the Pentagon as a program that would enhance commercial competence as well as military design capabilities. There has been a backing off from that line in recent years, and in fact Pentagon rules and procedures may make spillovers difficult to achieve even if the potential is there. But the Europeans took the earlier statements as confirming what they thought they had known all along.

There is indeed something new about the context in which VHSIC (and now SDI) was launched that is going to make it extremely difficult to avoid entangling military and commercial objectives. What is new is that over the last decade a good share of the frontier-breaking advances in microelectronics have come from projects aimed at commercial markets, and the military has in a number of instances piggybacked on these. Moreover, it is not just American firms that have been at the frontier in recent years. Japanese firms are there as well, and in some areas at least are ahead of American firms. In a sense, the Pentagon has lost control over the sources of new military-relevant technology and cannot even rest assured that these sources will be American. There is little question that VHSIC was motivated, in part at least, by the belief that Japanese firms might be getting ahead of American firms in certain areas of possibly high military relevance. Pentagon support of work on computers and in programming also reflects, at least partially, concerns that in the absence of such support American competence may drop behind that of the Japanese.

Put another way, we now seem to be in an era in which American military programs can be triggered by perceptions of technological advances that might be achieved first by foreign firms pursuing purely commercial objectives. And the situation is going to be confused, not clarified, by DOD policies aimed to restrict the civilian use of technologies the development of which they have funded.

All of these problems are beginning to take shape in the discussion about SDI. It is sometimes advertised that SDI will have large commercial fallout as well as military value. Many of the European governments seem to believe this is the case, and Americans are not discouraging such thinking. On the other hand, it seems clear that, as the work gets close to actual devices, use of the technology will be restricted through classification and export control.

A third aspect that is different about the current context is that the microelectronics industry is to a much greater extent international than it was earlier. The 1960s marked the beginnings of internationalization as American companies became increasingly multinational, establishing plants in Europe and elsewhere. The 1970s saw European, and later Japanese, companies begin to build or buy out companies in the United States. The last five years have seen a surge of co-operative R&D agreements and technology sharing among companies. We spent a good deal of time on these in Chapter 5. Much of this development has been at the initiative of the companies themselves. But such programs as ESPRIT have actively encouraged this development, at least among European companies. A consequence of this is that new technology is increasingly going to be truly impossible to keep contained within the borders of the country in which it originates. Another difficulty, at least for those who believe that supporting their national industry is important, is that it is already becoming extremely difficult to define clearly what one means by a national firm when compared with a foreign one.

Rocks in the Path Ahead

It is not unlikely that the present policy paths being taken by governments, in conjunction with those being taken by the companies, will lead to some very frustrating and unfortunate situations. Governments may be trying to accomplish things that they cannot achieve, although they can spend a lot of energy and money trying. Companies may absorb some of that money, but the costs to them of the overall programs may be high. We are concerned, once again, with two related but separable arenas. The first is that of policies aimed to help a nation's economy. The other involves military technology.

At the present time, countries are reacting strongly to the policies of other countries. The United States and European countries are trying to do themselves, in their own special way, the kind of things that they think the Japanese have been doing successfully. In turn, Europe and Japan are trying to mount policies that they believe will offset some of the advantages they see increased American military R&D as giving to American companies. Europe is acting a bit more like Europe and a tad less like a congeries of separate states; but nationalism still reigns strongly there. All three great regions see the others as rivals by whom it would be dangerous to be bested economically.

These highly nationalistic or regionalistic policies come about at the same time as the wave of cross-country, cross-region joint ventures and technical agreements. There are lots of reasons why companies in this industry are banding together for various activities, crossing national lines as never before. There is, however, clear evidence that in a number of cases an important objective of these private co-operative activities is to get around nationalistic policies. Joint ventures are one possible way to shed a politically untoward national taint.

A lot of contradictory things are going on. As a matter of policy, the Microelectronics and Computer Corporation excludes foreign members. At the same time, a large share of its American members have joint ventures and other arrangements with foreign companies. The North Carolina Microelectronics Center has a similar policy of keeping out the foreigners; but its members join up with them in other spheres.

In many of the joint arrangements in which they are engaged, the American partners are clearly trying to hold back much of their special competence from their foreign partner. But these ventures, by their nature as well as by their intent, augment technology sharing. Technology in the semiconductor industry today is cross-company – and cross-national – to a greater extent than ever before. Government-funded R&D, aside from that directed by the military, tends to go public relatively quickly. And public today means international. Thus a national policy may not help a nation's or a region's firms very much, in the sense of advancing their capabilities relative to those of their foreign competitors.

The R&D endeavors of individual companies, undertaken in their own laboratories and funded by themselves, are likely to lead to capabilities that diffuse away less rapidly than those ventures done co-operatively or publicly funded. Thus it is a good bet that, in the coming years, the strongest companies will be those that themselves fund and do the best work. What the strong companies get from R&D co-operation with other companies, or through participation in broadly defined public programs, may complement their own efforts; but is likely to be a minor part of the story. As a result, national policy may have very little influence on who the strong companies may be. If American or Japanese companies are going to be the technological leaders, there may be very little the policies of European governments can do about this.

One further implication is that the national "winners" in the race are likely to be satisfied with their government's R&D support programs, even though these may have had very little to do with success. On the other hand, the losers will be strongly tempted to push the government angle harder without accomplishing much in the effort.

Is the game worth the candle? All governments nowadays seem to believe that national strength in semiconductors is essential to national strength in high-technology industries more generally. Much of the focus is on the industries downstream from semiconductors, such as computers and telecommunications. There seems to be a belief that national computer companies do significantly better if there are strong national semiconductor industries, and that they are hindered if they have to rely on foreign suppliers. But given the way the semiconductor industry has been evolving, how valid is the concern? Most major semiconductor companies now have overseas plants and overseas laboratories. Money got from sales to a foreign company feeds the bottom line as well as money gained from sales to a domestic company, and overseas plants have leverage with headquarters just as do domestic plants. The joint ventures are part of the strategies of companies who see their markets as worldwide. Furthermore, the notion that companies that buy semiconductors ought to be served by strong national firms often leads to policies that tie those companies to national firms, even when they would do better buying their semiconductors from someone else.

In sum, a strong case can be made that, in this day and age, national policies aimed to support a national semiconductor industry with the objective of reaping economic gains make little sense. And the policies are likely to be expensive, and the experience frustrating and fractious for all but the "winners," who would have won in any case.

The bog into which concerns about national security are taking us may be even more treacherous. As noted, in the early days of the semiconductor industry, military technology led civilian technology, and spillover was dominantly from the former to the latter. Sometime during the late 1960s or early 1970s that evened up – or turned around. The spillover increasingly was from civilian-oriented research and development, and the resulting civilian technology, to the military. As this happened, the military lost control of the development of military-relevant semiconductor technology. Export controls of computers and other electronic equipment developed with private monies for a civilian market came under discussion, and later into implementation, to keep these technologies out of the hands of adversaries that might make military use of them, directly or indirectly. The integrated circuits contained in these devices usually had been developed totally with private funds, and aimed for a non-military market. But the United States could not block the flow of products designed and produced in Japan or Europe.

The record is clear that VHSIC, while pointed directly at technological advances desired by the military, was motivated in good part by the perception that Japanese companies, aiming for a civilian market, were creating semiconductor and related technologies that were nearly as advanced as the American, and that they threatened in the future actually to get ahead. Many have perceived the 5G project in Japan as posing just such a threat, and the Defense Advanced Research Projects Agency (DARPA) has responded by funding projects along similar lines out of Department of Defense monies. When the Department of Defense launches a major project because a commercially oriented industry in another country threatens to get in the forefront of a militarily relevant technology, that poses a problem.

Also, in the United States there is now much more explicit

recognition of spillovers. Commercial benefits from military R&D are, for some, an explicit rationale for certain DOD programs. For others, this is at least a sales pitch. But the spillover issue is obviously a thorny one. Can one at once encourage spillovers and try to guard against the technology getting into the hands of a potential enemy?

When the DOD funds are spent in a company, will that company be encouraged to exploit spillovers or will the fact that the Department of Defense funds significant R&D in an area it considers militarily important lead to restrictions on scientists working in the area but funded privately? Will it lead to export controls and other restrictions on privately developed products?

By raising these questions we do not pretend to know the answers. But there are rocks on the route ahead, and it is important to be aware of that fact.

8

Interdependence and Competition: What Does it All Mean?

The foregoing chapters have attempted a comprehensive look at the worldwide microelectronics industry. They have examined the industry from a multiplicity of perspectives: technology; market structure and foreign trade; patterns of technical alliances; corporate strategy; and government policy. Part of the objective has been purely informative: to present data about the industry – much of it not available elsewhere – in order to paint as accurate a portrait as possible. But we have also tried to offer more than raw data, to go beyond isolated congeries of facts.

All the chapters in this book have been linked and animated by a central theme: the growing technological and strategic interdependence of firms within the microelectronics industry. Both the fact of interdependence itself and the form that interdependence is taking have important implications for the conduct of corporate strategy and of government policy.

At the risk of oversimplification, we can analyze these implications under three distinct but overlapping headings.

- The tension between the growing international interdependence within the microelectronics industry and the quest by national governments for a "national" competitive advantage.
- The important difference between attempting to catch up to the technological frontier and attempting to operate at, and extend, that frontier.
- The significance for international competitiveness of the different industrial structures and strategic choices of microelectronics firms in the United States, Japan, and Europe.

Before taking on these issues, however, it might be useful to re-examine in starker lines the portrait of the microelectronics industry we have painted in this volume.

An Industry in Transition

That microelectronics is a dynamic and fast-growing, albeit somewhat cyclical, industry is an observation bordering on cliché. We do not quarrel with this commonplace. But we have attempted here to present a somewhat more complicated – more qualitative – story of dynamic growth. As the industry has grown, it has become more complex, more interdependent, more international. We have tried to document the fact of this complexity and to understand its implications. What follows is a broad-brush sketch of the pattern that emerged.

Technology

The technology of semiconductor production is one of the most complex in all manufacturing. Of course, a complex technology does not by itself imply that the industry employing it will be complex in structure. But when we examine the process of semiconductor production in more detail, we can in fact begin to see some of the reasons the industry is developing the way it is.

As we saw in Chapter 2, the production of semiconductor chips takes place in stages. Many of these stages, notably the middle stages involving the etching of successive layers of circuit-elements, must be closely integrated and are generally performed in a single production line. Indeed, it is to this part of the production process that the phenomenon of experience or learning effects attaches. As experience with the production process increases, the yield of chips increases and the unit cost of the devices declines. The principal source of these economies is typically incremental engineering improvements in the production process itself. An interesting feature of these learning economies is that they are extremely plant-specific, that is, they are difficult to transfer even among the various plants of a single firm let alone among different firms. One implication of learning economies is that the unit cost of standardized products that can be churned out in high volume will fall faster than those for custom or application-specific ICs produced in smaller amounts.

Not all stages of semiconductor fabrication require this level of co-ordination and physical proximity. Many stages are easily separated from the rest of the production process. As a result, these stages can be carried out elsewhere – even in a different country –

and can sometimes be delegated to independent suppliers or contractors. The principal examples here are the design stage at the front end and the assembly and packaging stages at the back end of production. Because these stages are easily separable, the location at which they are undertaken depends on factors other than proximity to adjacent stages. Design centers, for example, are often located so as to make best use of the crucial input to this stage: engineering design talent. These centers are typically in high-technology regions such as the San Francisco peninsula or the Boston area. Centers also spring up near potential buyers in order to facilitate communication with the users of the design. It is also common for a firm to have several design centers, often in different countries, all linked electronically to production facilities elsewhere. In the case of assembly and packaging, which do not partake of large economies of scale, location is often dictated by labor costs. This is the phenomenon of offshore assembly (discussed in Chapter 4), in which semifinished chips are shipped to low-wage countries for assembly before re-importation to the home country or export to third countries.

The fabrication of the production and testing equipment used in making semiconductors is also technologically separable from the production process itself. Indeed, most firms, especially American ones, rely heavily on outside equipment suppliers.

Market Structure and Foreign Trade

The technology of semiconductor fabrication suggests the possibilities for an intricate division of labor within the industry. By itself, however, technology does not determine the exact nature or extent of that division of labor. In fact, the organization of production differs considerably both across geographic regions and even within regions – especially in the United States.

The United States is not only the most diverse but also still the dominant producer of semiconductors. In 1986, for example, American production of integrated circuits amounted to almost $15 billion – almost 1.5 times Japanese production and more than five times European production in that year.[1] Both the Americans and the Japanese supply an overwhelming proportion of their own consumption of ICs from domestic sources. But the interpenetration of foreign markets is growing, and the increasing market share of Japanese firms has become a cause for concern – sometimes bordering on paranoia – on both sides of the Atlantic.

American firms have held a fairly constant share of the Japanese

[1] See Figure 6.

market – about 10 to 15 per cent overall and 16 per cent in ICs. Interestingly, and perhaps contrary to popular perceptions, the Japanese hold an even smaller share of the American market – about 9 per cent in 1986. The American market is larger in absolute size, of course, and the Japanese share is increasing rapidly. Moreover, the Japanese have for the past few years enjoyed a growing trade surplus with the United States in semiconductor products, a situation for which a strong dollar and its macroeconomic causes are not wholly to blame.

Until recently, American firms have dominated the European market, supplying more than half the region's semiconductors and more than 60 per cent of its ICs. Here too the Japanese share has been growing, first at the expense of European firms and now at the expense of the Americans.[2] (Several European firms have also bought American merchant producers, a point to which we return below.)

If we look behind the aggregate statistics of semiconductor trade, we see a clear, if shifting, international division of labor among types of products. The United States dominates the world market in all kinds of chips, and its strengths seem quite balanced across most of the basic areas. Japan has a relative strength in MOS ICs, an area in which it has lately been concentrating research and production efforts. The Europeans, by contrast, are comparatively weak in this area, especially in MOS microprocessors and memories. The European strength is in bipolar ICs, especially the linear variety useful in consumer applications. Indeed, compared with the United States, both Europe and Japan are strong in linear bipolar ICs; the American strength is in the digital bipolar chips useful in computers.

Within the area of MOS ICs, Japan's strength is in the production of memory chips. Indeed, it was Japan's strong and rapid penetration of the world memory market that largely galvanized American fears of Japanese competition. Starting with a tiny fraction of the merchant market for 1K and 4K DRAMs, Japanese firms seized more than 60 per cent of the 64K merchant market and threaten to capture the entire merchant market for the 256K and 1M DRAMs. (This ignores substantial in-house production of these devices by American captive manufacturers like IBM and AT&T.) By contrast, the American forte has lain in microprocessors. Japanese production of these devices has been confined until recently to second-source replication of American designs, sometimes involving a translation from bipolar to MOS technology. This pattern reflects an underlying Japanese strength in process technology

[2] See Figure 14.

(about which we will have a good deal more to say shortly) and an American strength in circuit design. Lately, the Japanese have begun producing microprocessor designs of their own: the American firm Zilog, for example, has become a second source for the NEC V-series microprocessor.[3] This development has already called forth the fear that Japanese firms will soon penetrate the microprocessor market the way they did the memory market.[4] We will return to this issue below.

Structure and Strategy

If we look even deeper behind the statistics, we see a quite complex pattern of industrial structure and corporate strategy. The American semiconductor industry stands out because of its enormous diversity along both structural and strategic dimensions. The industries of Japan, Europe, and – we must now add – Korea, are less diverse, but they differ markedly from one another and from that of the United States.

Semiconductor production in the United States is dominated by the merchant industry, that is, by firms who produce principally for sale on the open market rather than for internal consumption. There are some fifty-five such firms, not counting the fringe of minor suppliers. Some of these firms – such as Intel or National Semiconductor – are focused almost exclusively on and derive most of their revenues from the production of semiconductors. Others – like Texas Instruments or Motorola – are more diversified but still concentrate heavily on semiconductor production. Yet other merchants are divisions of highly diversified firms – like RCA (now owned by GE) or Harris – and account for only a small part of the parent's sales.

Diverse as merchant firms are, however, they are only part of the story. For a large fraction of American production takes place not in merchant firms but within the "captive" production facilities of large systems firms such as IBM, AT&T, and the Delco division of GM. Indeed, in 1986, captive production accounted for 35 per cent of American production of ICs.[5] Moreover, one of these captive producers – IBM – is responsible for the lion's share of American captive production. In 1985, IBM represented nearly two-thirds of American captive production of ICs and a fifth of all American production.[6]

[3] The NEC design, one should note, is sufficiently close to that of the Intel family of microprocessors that Intel sued NEC for copyright infringement.

[4] Ferguson (1985, pp. 63–68).

[5] See Figure 7. Production here is measured in terms of dollar value.

[6] Compare Figures 6 and 16.

In contrast with the structure of the American industry, the Japanese microelectronics industry is comparatively homogeneous in structure. Ten firms account for over 90 per cent of Japanese semiconductor production.[7] These firms are all large, diversified systems producers. In all of these firms, semiconductors account for a relatively small proportion (less than one quarter) of total company sales. All of these firms are substantial exporters, and the largest six, all members of *keiretsu*, are extensively multinational in their operations.

One factor behind the size and relative homogeneity of the Japanese firms is doubtlessly the much-discussed influence of Japanese government policies, particularly those of MITI and NTT. Yet this is surely not the whole story: there was, for example, much government guidance, R&D funding, and structured procurement in the early days of the American industry, most of it coming from the Department of Defense. An equally important explanation lies in differences in the American and Japanese capital markets. The American institutional structure – including tax and banking laws along with other factors – is far more conducive to the formation of venture capital than is the Japanese. Thus growth in the American industry was slanted toward entrepreneurial start-up ventures. By contrast, Japanese banking laws, unlike their American counterparts, do not prohibit banks from taking a large and active role in financing corporations; this, coupled with the close association of electronics firms and banks within the *keiretsu* structure, encouraged the growth of Japanese microelectronics within the boundaries of existing firms.[8] There is also another point to consider: organizational patterns often depend heavily on timing and the accidents of history. It may be that much of the difference between the American and Japanese industrial structures lies in the pioneering quality of the American contribution and its technological head-start over the Japanese. These are all issues to which we will return.

Whatever its causes, the structural differences between the American and Japanese microelectronics industries are reflected in differences in the typical corporate strategies employed on opposite sides of the Pacific. If we examine the two industries in terms of the notion of strategic groups – one of the central concepts in present-day discussions of competitive strategy – we see on the American side a wide diversity of approaches and on the Japanese side a comparative homogeneity of approach. American firms cover a wide range. Some firms offer a relatively complete line of

[7] Borrus, Millstein, and Zysman (1983).

[8] Flaherty and Itami (1984).

products, while others focus narrowly on a specific niche; some firms press for technological leadership and emphasize major innovation, while others rely on incremental, adaptive, and imitative advances. If there is any unifying strategic theme among American producers, it is the quest for some kind of uniqueness in product or market as a source of competitive advantage. By contrast, Japanese firms fall much more neatly into two strategic groups. One group undertakes a broad product line anchored by substantial production of MOS memory ICs. The other group concentrates on more specific ICs for consumer applications. The first group is quite large, and there is a noticeable trend of firms shifting from the consumer applications group to this broad product-line group. In general, the Japanese firms are far more comfortable with high-volume production of standardized products than are their American counterparts – and less inclined to look for unique product or market advantages. The competition between American and Japanese semiconductor firms thus shapes up as one between groups with fundamentally different characteristics. We discussed some of the implications of this in Chapter 6, and we will return to these issues below.

The structure of the European semiconductor industry is similar to that of the Japanese in its dominance by large vertically integrated systems firms and its comparative lack of entrepreneurial start-up ventures. Unlike the Japanese, however, the growth of semiconductor production within these firms has been relatively slow. In fact, several of the largest producers of semiconductors in Europe – such as Philips and Thomson-CSF – have acquired American merchant firms (Signetics and Mostek, respectively) and produce much of their semiconductor output in the USA. Europe is also more diverse than Japan in strategic terms. In addition to the large systems firms like Philips, Siemens, and Thomson, there are some relatively aggressive niche players such as Matra Harris and Plessey, along with some smaller, narrowly focused firms.

South Korean firms are beginning to come on the horizon as potentially strong competitors. The four major Korean players are vertically integrated systems houses. All are focusing on standardized products, especially memories. They are thus attacking markets where the Japanese are strong, using an imitative strategy that is reminiscent of the Japanese – or, at any rate, reminiscent of the Japanese when they first entered the market. The Koreans are licensing American technology and using American expertise, even to the point of producing first in the United States before moving production to Korea.

The Web of Interdependence

The technological. structural, and strategic characteristics of the worldwide microelectronics that we have so far highlighted are an important part of the overall picture of that industry. But they are by no means the whole picture. Indeed, in comparing the industries of the United States, Japan, and Europe, we have stressed the dissimilarities among them, leaving perhaps the impression of a textbook market of distinct and autonomous firms vying each from its home shores for a share of the semiconductor market. Although not entirely incorrect, such an impression would be misleadingly incomplete in this case. For an important – and relatively neglected – aspect of the story of the worldwide microelectronics industry is the extent of international interpenetration and interfirm connection.

FOREIGN DIRECT INVESTMENT AND ACQUISITION

The classic model of international trade is one in which firms produce goods at home and export them to other countries. In fact, of course, there are many other options open to firms in the international marketplace; in particular, they can produce the goods not at home but in the countries to which they wish to sell, either by building factories from scratch (so-called *de novo* investment) or by acquiring the existing facilities or organization of indigenous producers. Moreover, firms need not undertake all aspects of production in the host country: they can set up some activities – such as design or marketing – overseas, and retain some – such as production – at home. Firms can also establish operations in a host country for reimport home or export to a third country (as in offshore assembly). The microelectronics industry makes use of all these options and their permutations.

Once again we find the greatest diversity in the United States. American-based semiconductor firms engage in a significant amount of FDI; and there is substantial investment by foreign microelectronics firms in the United States, both *de novo* investment and acquisition.

American firms have pursued almost exclusively a strategy of *de novo* investment overseas. This should not be entirely surprising, since American firms pioneered semiconductor technology and have remained at the leading edge. American firms have been setting up shop in Europe since the 1950s, with the extent of investment growing throughout the 1960s and 1970s and continuing today. This investment often started with design and sales activities but progressed quickly into full-scale production. Europe has been by far the main focus of American FDI; but, despite barriers thrown up by the Japanese government, several American firms, including IBM, Texas Instruments, and Motorola, have major operations in Japan. Indeed, TI produces some 80 per cent of all its 64K DRAMs at its Japanese facility in Miho. American firms also tend far more than their Japanese and European counterparts to engage in offshore assembly in low-wage countries; the trend, however, seems to be away from this practice.

Both Japanese and European firms have invested heavily in facilities in the United States. The Japanese have favored *de novo* investment. Until recently, only Toshiba had attempted an acquisition of any significance, and that was at best a mixed success. In October, 1986, however, Fujitsu announced plans to acquire 80 per cent of the American merchant firm Fairchild from Schlumberger. At the time, many saw this deal as the harbinger of increased Japanese acquisition of American merchant firms. The price-fixing agreement signed by the American and Japanese governments in July of 1986 created an incentive for Japanese firms to develop more production facilities in the United States, where prices are not controlled. This, coupled with the increasing value of the yen and the depressed stock prices of many American firms, made acquisition an attractive alternative. But the July 1986 agreement did not work out as its proponents hoped. Semiconductor prices stabilized, but did not rise above levels prevailing at the time of the agreement. This result stemmed in part from a "gray market" for Japanese chips. Dissatisfaction with the agreement among some American producers and politicians helped precipitate a wave of protectionist sentiment that moved the American administration to impose sanctions against Japan in the form of tariffs on certain Japanese electronics items.[9] The Fujitsu–Fairchild deal also came quickly under attack from American business and government circles, creating a controversy that led Fujitsu to back out in March 1987. The entire saga has not yet played itself out. But what seems clear is that, despite American hostility to Japanese acquistion of American merchant firms, there remain strong incentives – stemming both from the value of the yen and the American protectionist climate – for the Japanese to produce in the United States. This may imply a trend to greater *de novo* investment.

In contrast to the Japanese, European firms have always largely favored acquisition of American firms over *de novo* investment. This no doubt reflects in part the fact that American technology has been more advanced than European, and acquisition is one way to plug into that technology. In all the major cases, the Europeans

[9] For a discussion of these recent moves in the context of international trade theory, see Erdilek (1987).

seem to have chosen ailing American firms for acquisition, and they have not shown a strong track record in turning these units around. Schlumberger recently attempted to divest itself of most of Fairchild; and Thomson's acquisition of Mostek, while quite sensible in view of the low price paid, nonetheless remains something of a gamble.[10]

Overall, Japanese firms have been cautious about FDI. They seem to prefer export to production overseas, partly for reasons of quality control. They have also favored licensing as a method of technology transfer, and have acquired few foreign firms. The Japanese have some production facilities in Europe as well as in the United States. Foreign investment into Japan has been limited by government policy. With few exceptions, foreign investors were restricted to minority ownership of joint ventures with Japanese concerns. Even before the July 1986 trade agreement, these restrictions seemed to be loosening; and foreign firms – mainly American – are increasing investment in Japan through expansion of existing facilities, construction of new facilities, and joint ventures.[11]

In contrast with Japan, Europe has encouraged FDI. This encouragement has come less in the way of conscious government policy than as a byproduct of protectionist EEC tariff policy, which makes production in Europe an attractive alternative to exporting there. Some European governments, including Britain and Ireland, have also used tax policy and/or subsidies to attract FDI; other governments, notably France, have been comparatively cool to FDI.

MARKET INTERDEPENDENCE

A less publicized, but perhaps more important, aspect of international interdependence is the web of connections among firms that take place through the marketplace, particularly the marketplace for components and intermediate goods. These interdependencies are harder to document than FDI or technical agreements, but they are no less real.

No microelectronics firm – even IBM – is completely vertically integrated in the sense that it produces or controls all aspects of the making of semiconductor products. All firms depend to a greater or lesser extent on other firms – including firms in other countries – for materials, components, and capital equipment. This dependence is

[10] "Why Thomson is Hungry for UTC's Lemon," *Business Week*, 11 November, 1985, pp. 35–36.

[11] Stephen Kreider Yoder, "Computer Chip Makers Head for Japan," *The Wall Street Journal* 1 August, 1986, p. 6.

probably less in semiconductors than it is at the level of systems, particularly computer systems. But there are still a number of key area in microelectronics in which production is dominated by specialized suppliers.

One of these areas is the production of the raw silicon wafers that are the basic building-blocks of integrated circuits. The process of growing, cutting, and polishing silicon crystals is one that partakes of significant economies of scale; moreover, it requires machinery, techniques, and skills somewhat different from those required for the later phases of chip fabrication. For these reasons, wafer production is typically carried out by specialized producers, often chemical companies. Here, as in other areas, there is a fear that the Japanese will come to dominate. For example, two small American wafer suppliers, NBK and Siltec, were recently acquired by Kawasaki Steel and Mitsubishi Metals.[12] But at least two large chemical companies, Monsanto in the United States and Wacker Chemie in West Germany, remain major forces in the field.

Another area dominated, in both the United States and Japan, by specialized producers is the manufacture of the process and test equipment used in making semiconductors. Many of these equipment suppliers are small firms such as GCA near Boston, the leading maker of steppers, the optical devices used in photolithography. GCA's major competitor is Nikon of Japan, a much larger company but also not a manufacturer of semiconductors. Nikon has been gaining ground on GCA, and the American company has been in the red during the recent industry downturn. This has led, once again, to fears of Japanese dominance.[13] There is a similar story to be told in the areas of automatic test equipment, lithography equipment, mask-making, and numerous other areas.[14] The dominance of the equipment market by small, specialized firms is not entirely complete: IBM, for example, produces most of its own capital equipment (which it does not sell on the market) and at least one semiconductor merchant (Fairchild) sells some capital equipment. Moreover, unlike their American counterparts, specialized Japanese equipment suppliers are often – though not always – subsidiaries of the major vertically

[12] Andrew Pollack, "Mitsubishi to Acquire Siltec," *The New York Times*, 9 September, 1986, p. D5.

[13] William Bulkeley, "GCA's Crisis Could Hurt the Industry," *The Wall Street Journal*, 7 January, 1986, p. 6.

[14] Arthur L. Robinson, "U. S. Electronics Needs a New Strategy," *Science* 232: 1496–7, 20 June 1986. For a particularly gloomy portrait, see also Ferguson (1985, p. 80–83).

integrated semiconductor manufacturers. The organizational structure of this part of the industry is an important issue to which we will return below.

Another kind of market interdependence is that between semiconductor manufacturers as suppliers and systems manufacturers as customers. Such relationships sometimes involve an equity stake by the customer (as in the Intel–IBM link) or an exclusive contract (as in the Fujitsu–ICL agreement); in other cases, the mechanisms of co-ordination are less formal. In all cases, however, such agreements are a kind of half-way house between complete vertical integration and ordinary spot purchasing. In an important sense, then, such agreements are a partial substitute for vertical integration, allowing at least some degree of explicit co-ordination and exchange of information. An industry that engages in such agreements may thus be less fragmented in terms of ability to co-ordinate and adapt than its decentralized ownership structure would indicate.

INTERFIRM TECHNICAL AGREEMENTS

Customer–supplier relationships are not the only kind of agreement one typically finds among firms in the worldwide microelectronics industry. Another category of relationships comes under the broad heading of technology sharing.

The most common kind of technology-sharing agreement is second-sourcing. This is a practice whose roots trace to Defense Department procurement policies that mandated, as a kind of insurance policy, at least two suppliers of certain critical components. The practice has a similar logic in the private sector. A firm marketing a popular proprietary item has the choice of either expanding production to make the device entirely in-house or licensing the technology (for a fee) to other manufacturers. The licensing alternative is attractive for a number of reasons. On the one hand, it allows the licensor to profit from its design without putting at risk the sunk investment of major additional capacity; and, on the other hand, it effectively increases the overall demand for the item by helping insure customers against supply disruptions and a potentially disadvantageous bargaining position.

In practice, second-source agreements are a more complicated strategic affair. For one thing, they are a potent source of technology transfer: in order to license another firm to produce a technology one has at the same time to provide that firm with the necessary technical competence – in complementary areas as well as in the licensed technology itself. Moreover, the licensee frequently advances or changes the licensed technology, and is thus sometimes able to use the license as a stepping-stone from which to leapfrog the licensor in the next generation.[15]

In the microelectronics industry, microprocessors are the most frequent subject of second-source agreements. Unlike memories, these devices are highly proprietary; moreover, as the centerpieces of computers and other sophisticated devices, microprocessor designs constitute a standard to which peripherals and the design of the overall system must be adapted. Manufacturers thus have an incentive to second-source in order to expand the market quickly and thereby capture to their standard as large a customer-base as possible. It is not surprising that American firms engage heavily in this sort of agreement, as American firms remain dominant in microprocessor design. Second sources include both other American firms as well as Japanese and European ones. Some Japanese firms began producing American microprocessor designs without a license, but this practice is diminishing. NEC, a second source (originally unlicensed) for Intel's 8086 microprocessor, is marketing a microprocessor called the V-series that is essentially a modified and improved version of the Intel device. The American firm Zilog has become a second source for the V-series. Intel views this design as infringing its copyright, and has so far prevailed in litigation that is not yet completely resolved. One extremely interesting aspect of the competition between Intel and NEC is that the litigation – and the rivalry between the products of the two companies – has not prevented them from simultaneously linking together in a number of second-sourcing, cross-licensing, and technology-exchange agreements.

A typical practice is for an American firm to license a Japanese firm to produce in CMOS what the American is already producing in bipolar form. The Japanese firm may sometimes transfer back the CMOS technology. Such an arrangement is one kind of second-source agreement; but one may also view it is a technology-swap arrangement. Examples include the 1981 agreement in which Hitachi gave Motorola access to its high-performance CMOS process technology in exchange for Motorola's design for the 68000 microprocessor. Another example is the 1982 cross-licensing agreement between Zilog and Toshiba, in which Zilog obtained CMOS technology and CMOS versions of its designs in exchange for licensing those designs. The two firms are now second-sourcing each other's version. Several authors have been able to portray such exchanges as unambiguously disadvantageous to the competitive position of

[15] Many licenses call for the licensee to transfer any new knowledge back to the licensor. But such provisions are not always easy to enforce.

American firms.[16] The issues here are subtle ones to which we will return; but at the *prima facie* level, these exchanges are eminently well-balanced. The flow of technology is bilateral, and the technology exchanged is of comparable sophistication.

Customized or application-specific ICs is another focus of interfirm agreements. Here, the story is almost identical to that in microprocessors. The partners are largely American and Japanese firms, linked together by mutual second-sourcing or technology-swap agreements in which the American partner provides a design in bipolar form and the Japanese partner provides the CMOS version. Peripherals are another area of interest. Among the most active partners in this area is NEC, which has contracted with several American systems firms to develop the peripheral chips for its V-series microprocessor.

The pattern of agreements in memories is somewhat different. Since Japan has established a dominant position in this area, the flow of process technology is more unidirectional than in other areas – from Japan to the USA and Europe.[17] There is every reason to think that what the Japanese are licensing is somewhat less than their domestic state of the art. Another interesting feature of agreements in the area of memories is the role of Korean firms. Here the technology flow is also unidirectional – but from *the United States* to Korea. The Koreans are attempting to reach the frontier in memory technology, and their alliance with the Americans rather than the Japanese most likely signals a Korean push to compete with Japan.

Another major agreement in the memory area comes under the heading not of technology exchange but of joint development.[18] Philips of the Netherlands and Siemens of West Germany are engaging in a joint effort to develop SRAMs and DRAMs with capacities in excess of one megabit. The project, which will enjoy a 40 per cent subsidy from the Dutch and German governments, is an attempt to move the capabilities of those firms nearer the technological forefront in what is generally perceived to be a strategically important area of technology.

In sum, the web of agreements among firms is an immensely large and intricate one; this brief portrait has only suggested the outlines. And the existence and nature of such interfirm agree-

[16] Reich and Mankin (1986); Ferguson (1985).

[17] One exception is the agreement by Japanese startup NMB to license 256K CMOS technology from Inmos of Great Britain.

[18] The agreements mentioned earlier between NEC and the American systems firms would also come under this heading.

ments must be taken into account in assessing the issues of competitive strategy and government policy in microelectronics.

CO-OPERATIVE RESEARCH

Interfirm technical agreements, moreover, do not exhaust the mechanisms by which firms are connected together in the microelectronics industry. Firm-to-firm agreements are almost always aimed at relatively near-term strategic goals: strengthening existing capabilities; moving into a new but related area; taking advantage of complementary capabilities in other firms, etc. But firms also have longer-term goals. These frequently come under the heading of research, and are generally addressed in ways other than one-on-one agreements between firms. There are basically two ways in which firms collect together for research: through private co-operative arrangements and through government-sponsored efforts.

One private mechanism is the research corporation. There are two principal examples, one in Europe and one in the USA. The European Computer Research Center (ECRC) was established in Munich by the three large European mainframe manufacturers – ICL, Siemens, and Bull. The central focus of the effort is artificial intelligence, but this will include a good deal of research on semiconductors. The Microelectronics and Computer Corporation (MCC) in Austin, Texas enjoys both a much larger budget and the sponsorship of twenty-one American semiconductor and computer firms. Almost half of MCC's research is oriented to semiconductors.

Both ECRC and MCC have their own research laboratories. The lion's share of privately sponsored co-operative research takes place, however, under the *aegis* of universities. University–industry ties seem to be a predominantly American institution, although other countries are trying to encourage this practice. One form of multifirm research in the university setting is that directed by the Semiconductor Research Corporation (SRC). Unlike the MCC, the SRC has no labs of its own; rather, it sponsors and directs research at universities for the benefit of its thirty-one member companies. Increasingly, universities themselves are seeking corporate sponsors directly and are setting up "centers" for microelectronics research. The largest of these are the Center for Integrated Systems (CIS) at Stanford and the Microelectronics Center of North Carolina (MCNC), which actually receives most of its funding from the North Carolina state government. There are many others as well. Our survey of seventeen major centers found a total budget of some $93 million in 1985. Nine have budgets of more than $2 million a year, and six of those have the support of at least sixteen corporate sponsors each.

The type of research carried out in these corporations and centers is varied and difficult to characterize. But it is by and large basic or at least "generic" research, that is, research aimed at improving knowledge and capabilities with relatively wide application. An important issue here is the extent to which such research can be appropriated by particular companies or groups of companies – and thus the extent to which such research can convey any kind of competitive advantage to those companies.

Another set of mechanisms for co-operative research involves funding – and sometimes direction and management – by national governments. Chapter 7 surveyed in depth some of the major programs around the world: the 5G program in Japan; Alvey in Britain; VHSIC in the United States; the Filière électronique in France; and ESPRIT in the EEC. These programs differ markedly in detail, but they have in common the support of basic or generic research. Here the appropriability issue becomes somewhat different and slightly sharper: when can such programs boost a national industry relative to its competitors in a world in which knowledge – especially basic or generic knowledge – is not fully appropriable and in which firms are connected together internationally in a complex way?

This question warrants a closer look.

International Interdependence: The Implications

We have tried so far to demonstrate that the worldwide microelectronics industry is becoming increasingly interdependent along a number of dimensions: interdependent through market exchanges; through equity cross-investment; through licensing and technology-exchange agreements; through joint ventures and co-operative research arrangements. It is now time to examine the implications of this trend and its various manifestations.

Implications for Competition

The word "interdependence" conjures up a sense of co-operation and dependence – a notion very much at odds, it would seem, with the classical idea of competition in markets. The tension between interdependence and competition is more apparent than real, however, and falls away quickly once we look more closely at the many different facets of interdependence among firms.

For example, one aspect of interdependence – market interdependence – is in fact a *manifestation* of competition in the classic sense. As market size increases, the division of labor among firms also increases; each is less self-sufficient, more dependent on other firms, for raw materials, components, capital equipment, distribution channels, etc. Add to this the classical notion of comparative advantage and the interdependence becomes international. A firm in the classically competitive world may be dependent on scores of firms across the globe, each of which has specialized in a particular part of the process of production and distribution.

Of course, no industry – microelectronics included – is quite as fragmented and interdependent as this picture suggests. But the basic insight remains that, in its impetus for increasing efficiency, competition frequently leads to reliance on others. This reliance often takes the form of market exchange. In all cases, however, it involves contractual arrangements linking one firm with other firms possessing complementary capabilities. Far from being in tension with interdependence, competition is as a general rule a source of and spur to interdependence among firms.

Interdependence in the sense of market exchange has long enjoyed the sanction of conventional economic theory and antitrust practice. By contrast, interdependence in the sense of "linking up" among firms has long been seen with suspicion if not downright hostility. This is fundamentally because the traditional theory sets up an idealized kind of fragmented, atomistic competition as a benchmark; any market structure or behavior that differs from this standard can only reflect "monopoly power," and that is, *ipso facto*, bad. The basic idea is that the linked partners can more easily collude to raise prices above efficient levels.

Given impetus in part by the growing internationalization of the American economy and the rise of foreign competition, many economists have begun rethinking this view. As a result, both theory and policy today are somewhat more ready to concede that agreements, joint ventures, and even mergers may have efficiency advantages – not collusion – as their principal motivation. This is particularly visible in the area of research joint ventures, where both Congress and the Antitrust Division of the Justice Department have sought to reduce legal obstacles to this form of agreement.[19] In 1984, Congress passed the National Cooperative Research Act, which weakened the brunt of antitrust law when applied to research joint ventures[20] and allowed prospective joint-

[19] White (1985).

[20] Specifically, the law weakened potential claims to actual damages rather than the treble damages allowed in other antitrust judgments; specified a rule-of-reason requirement rather than a *per se* rule, thus forcing courts to take into account the

venture partners to register in advance with the Justice Department and the Federal Trade Commission. This policy is consistent with what is arguably the mainstream view among antitrust economists today: research joint ventures can sometimes be "anticompetitive" vehicles of collusion, but are probably beneficial – or at least not positively harmful – most of the time.[21] From the point of view of industry, however, this position appears rather wishy-washy, and the policy changes seem neither to have allayed industry fears of antitrust action nor in fact to have lessened the level of scrutiny to which research joint ventures are subject.[22]

Much of the current policy debate about international competitiveness is, however, informed by a perspective quite opposite to that of traditional economic theory and antitrust policy. Far from seeing an atomistic, fragmented industry as some kind of ideal, many view market interdependence as undesirable and even dangerous, touting instead various kinds of agreements, co-operative ventures, and consolidations as the key to international competitiveness.

One version of this position arrives from the angle of national defense. If American computer firms are dependent on foreign (read: Japanese) firms for certain kinds of chips (DRAMs, for example) because American semiconductor firms have abandoned those markets, national defense – which relies heavily on computers and other semiconductor-using equipment – will no longer be fully under the control of the American government. If Japan becomes hostile or otherwise withholds the chips its firms produce, American security will be compromised.[23] This is a hoary argument, and the issues it presents are complex. For example, to what extent does market interdependence among countries *reduce* hostilities by, as it were, holding one another's national industries hostage?

There is also a deeper – or, at any rate, slightly different – line of argument attached to the national defense issue. Technological leadership is in a certain sense a traditional element of American defense strategy: modern weaponry, using state-of-the-art technology not available to potential adversaries, can help offset any

---

efficiency benefits of the venture; and required unsuccessful plaintiffs to pay court costs if the court declared their suit against a research joint venture to have been "frivolous, unreasonable, without foundation, or in bad faith." (White, 1985, pp. 43–44.)

[21] White (1985); Ordover and Willig (1985); Grossman and Shapiro (1986).

[22] Grossman and Shapiro (1986, p. 319).

[23] Andrew Pollack, "U.S. Sees Peril in Chip Drop," *The New York Times*, 30 September, 1986, p. D1.

numerical advantages those adversaries may possess. If the USA becomes less competitive, the logic goes, it will sink behind the technological frontier and thus destroy one pillar of defense strategy. Needless to say, the microelectronics industry is a principal area of concern. "Defense has a big stake in maintenance of broad technological competitiveness in the semiconductor industry," is the view of one member of the Defense Science Board.[24] What is interesting is that this second argument is also seen as calling for less market interdependence and more co-operative arrangements – especially research arrangements – among American firms. This does not necessarily follow, of course. Absent concern about trading with potential adversaries or quasi-adversaries, traditional theory would argue that, in large measure at least, the competitiveness of domestic industry is *enhanced* by the international division of labor that comparative advantage dictates. To hold the contrary requires additional argument.

Issues of national defense aside, it is an increasingly popular view today that competitiveness requires explicit collaboration among firms – co-operative research, joint development, technology exchange, perhaps even consolidation and vertical integration. Like all arguments in the public arena, the bases for this position come in several shapes, sizes, and degrees of sophistication. Some version of "the Japanese model" informs almost all variants, and a fuzzy form of the model constitutes almost the whole of the argument in the less sophisticated variants. At its most naive, this model holds that Japanese firms are succeeding because they collaborate with one another to a greater degree than do American and European firms; this collaboration takes the form of co-operative research (such as the VLSI project) as well as subtler forms of collusion orchestrated by MITI.

This picture is not wholly fanciful, of course. The VLSI project did help raise Japanese capabilities; and government policies, especially procurement by NTT and import control, did strongly shape Japanese development. But what is routinely overlooked is that self-reliance among Japanese firms is perhaps a more important factor in their success than is collaboration. The Japanese market contains at least ten major players of comparable size and ability – players who are strongly competitive among themselves as well as with foreign rivals. Moreover, the Japanese predilection for vertical integration and a full-product-line strategy makes those firms far more independent than the typical American or European

[24] Dr. Robert M. Burger, quoted in Pollack, *op. cit.* Dr. Burger is vice president of the Semiconductor Research Corporation.

firm.[25] And private funding of R&D is on the rise in Japan relative to government funding.

However one reads this blurry picture, it remains less interesting than the more sophisticated version of the model. Here, it is precisely the self-reliance of Japanese firms that is central. To oversimplify a bit, the vertically integrated structure of Japanese firms gives them a survival value lacking in the fragmented American merchant market, where firms rely heavily on market transactions for key elements of the production process. Might co-operation and joint ventures of various sorts emulate some of the virtues of vertical integration that Japan enjoys? The issues this line of argument raises are complex ones that will occupy us for much of the remainder of this chapter.

Implications for Government Policy

Before assessing the merits and implications of this argument we need to address a prior issue.

Throughout this chapter, we have depicted a web of overlapping international connections among firms in the microelectronics industry. At the same time, we have talked rather casually about the nationality of specific firms, frequently worrying about the competitive position of "American" as against "Japanese" or "European" firms. But as Chapter 7 hinted, growing international interdependence makes the issue of nationality a much more complicated one than casual usage suggests. This is especially true from the point of view of governments seeking policies to boost their national industries.

The first issue is: what counts as a national industry? Clearly, we can at some level associate each firm with a country. All firms are incorporated somewhere. But when the firms are large multinationals for whom microelectronics is only part – sometimes a small part – of the business, the site of the company's main headquarters is not always the most relevant detail. ITT, an American company, conducts most of its semiconductor business in Europe. And what about American-bred merchant firms such as Mostek and Signetics, now controlled by the the French and the Dutch, respectively? This is not entirely a matter of definition. Would a subsidy to ITT help Europe more than the USA? Should we not view Fairchild – built and run by Americans in the United States – as a component of American strength in microelectronics?

[25] For example, Egelhoff (1986, p. 24) found Japanese firms to be significantly less willing to engage in joint ventures than American or (especially) European firms.

Are the Japanese operations of IBM and Texas Instruments a credit to the USA or to Japan?

Moreover, the problem does not vanish even if we ignore these complexities and somehow identify a core of firms in each region whose nationality is clear. Policies aimed at firms in one country can sometimes ramify through the network of agreements to benefit firms elsewhere as much or even more. As we saw in Chapter 7, this may be especially true in the case of co-operative research in basic or generic areas. The knowledge generated in such activities is not inherently very appropriable, and it may easily find its way through various channels to competitors supposedly excluded.

None of this is to say that we cannot talk meaningfully about international competitiveness or that government policy does not matter. But we do have to be clear about an important distinction, that is, the distinction between competitiveness from the point of view of the individual firm and competitiveness from the point of view of the nation-state. For even if we can decide which firms belong to each country, it is still not the case that the competitiveness or technical capability – let alone the welfare – of the nation is identical with that of the national companies taken as a whole. A country with no indigenous firms but many divisions of overseas companies may have a healthier microelectronics industry than some of the countries in which the corporate headquarters are located. And a country in which existing firms routinely go out of business, but in which innovative new entry occurs readily, may have a more robust industry, and may do better in the long run, than a country whose existing firms always manage to survive.

In what follows we will begin by concerning ourselves with the somewhat better-defined, if not therefore simpler, matter of the competitiveness of individual firms. In doing this we will inevitably talk about the nationality of the firms, thus putting aside the issues just raised. But these issues cannot be ignored completely, and they should remain in the forefront of any discussion of national policy.

Catching Up or Getting Ahead?

If there is a single over-arching issue confronting the worldwide microelectronics industry, it is, of course, that of international competitiveness. A concern with this issue has lain behind most of our discussion, and it is now time to confront it directly.

For most firms in the semiconductor industry, the recent slump has been a severe test; for some, it has been a threat to survival. But the issue of international competitiveness is a longer-term concern. In the United States and Europe, there is widespread fear that industry leadership may be passing decisively into the hands of Japanese firms and that few firms elsewhere will be able to catch up or keep up. As we noted in Chapter 3, Japan's market share in most semiconductor areas is increasing at the expense of American and European firms; if one extrapolates the trend, Japanese production will outstrip American in a matter of years. In certain products, notably standardized memories, Japan has already captured an overwhelming share of the merchant market. Most significantly, Japanese technology in many key areas – including most aspects of process technology – is now considered either on a par with or superior to American technology.

What are the reasons for the Japanese success? What kind of a threat does this success pose to the American and European industries?

The answers to these questions will not likely be identical for the United States and Europe. But in both cases, diminished competitiveness flows from two kinds of sources: macroeconomic and microeconomic. The first has to do with causes not directly in the hands of the firms themselves, the second with causes located in the structure and strategy of the firms themselves.

In the case of the United States, macroeconomic policy probably has much to answer for. Economists are divided about the relative contribution of macroeconomic effects to the decline of American competitiveness; but almost all would assign them some role. Until recently, the American dollar had been extremely strong against other currencies, including the yen. A strong dollar raises the price of American semiconductors in terms of foreign currencies and lowers the dollar-price of Japanese semiconductors; this confers a cost advantage on Japanese imports even if the cost of production (in terms of real resources) is identical on both sides of the Pacific.

What caused the dollar to be strong? And why is it weakening now? The answers are complicated, or at any rate somewhat controversial. But the basic picture looks like this. The accession of Paul Volker to chairmanship of the Federal Reserve Board ushered in a period of reduced inflation in the United States (as much the result, perhaps, of lowered expectations of inflation as of reduced growth in the money supply). Low inflation is a boon to savers, and American investments became more attractive to investors, including foreign investors. At roughly the same time, the Reagan Administration embarked on a program of increased spending on defense, without fully compensating reductions in other programs and while lowering taxes. The result was a massive and growing budget deficit, financed by borrowing in private markets. This increased the supply of securities available to investors, including foreign investors. Not surprisingly, foreign investors quickly responded by pouring money into the United States.

What has this to do with the strong dollar? The strength of a currency depends not on the balance of trade in goods and services only but on the total balance of monetary payments. In this case, the surplus of currency flowing in for investment more than counterbalanced the trade deficit in goods and services. Thus the maddening paradox of a strong dollar and a large trade deficit. The budget deficit may not be wholly at fault. Some of the capital inflow may simply reflect a healthy American economy with many investment opportunities, along with a reduction of American bank loans abroad. But it seems clear that American macropolicy – including the budget deficit – must shoulder some of the blame for the problems of American export industries, including microelectronics.

There is more to the story. Quite apart from the issue of a budget deficit, there is also the issue of the absolute size of the budget itself. However one pays for government expenditures – whether it be with taxes, by borrowing in the credit markets, or via "monetizing" the debt through inflation – those expenditures remain withdrawals of resources from the private sector. A country that withdraws more resources imposes greater costs on its private industries. Now, one may argue that the government expenditures are justified and provide more social welfare than the resources would have yielded if left in the private sector. But such an argument would be cold consolation to an industry competing with a country – Japan – that withdraws almost no resources for purposes of national defense. The issue may be particularly acute for an industry such as microelectronics if, as is surely the case, defense expenditures compete directly for the same kind of resources (engineering talent, for instance).

The dollar has been weakening steadily against the yen and other currencies since its peak in early 1985. This is likely eventually to reduce some of the pressure on American semiconductor manufacturers. But the effects of an adverse exchange rate are not all instantly reversible. Some firms may have left the industry, and the skills and capabilities they had may not always be easily recreated. And even the survivors are likely to have reduced capabilities to the extent that stunted sales translated into foregone learning-by-doing effects.

It remains to be seen, then, how much the fall in the value of the dollar will moderate the increasing market-share of Japanese semiconductors in the United States and around the world. A continued low value for the dollar[26] is likely to dampen some of the more extreme predictions of doom for the American industry. But there will likely remain serious problems of competitiveness whose solutions do not lie at the macroeconomic level.

We have not said much so far about Europe. Here macropolicy is a factor in a number of respects. But European currencies did not typically appreciate against the yen as much as did the dollar, suggesting that the difficulties of European competitiveness in microelectronics are largely to be traced elsewhere.

In both Europe and the United States, there are a number of factors affecting competitiveness that are not within the control of firms but are also not strictly macroeconomic in the traditional sense of that term. One example we have discussed – and will discuss again – is government industrial policy. Another set of factors can be called economic institutions. Some of these, such as banking and capital-market institutions, are within the purview of government; others, like the society's propensity to save or the "cultural factors" that inevitably crop up in discussions of Japan, are somewhat less so. All of them are important; but we will largely treat them indirectly. Instead, we will focus in on issues of competitiveness that are "microeconomic" in a stricter sense – issues of industrial structure and of firm organization and strategy. In what follows, we will concentrate on the American case, though some of what we have to say will also be applicable to Europe.

The most widely discussed microeconomic sources of lagging competitiveness fall into two main categories: management short-sightedness and industrial fragmentation. As we will see, the two are not entirely unrelated.

In its broadest sense, the short-sightedness argument holds that American management has preferred harvesting quick-term profits to building capabilities for the longer term. One manifestation of this is a tendency to back out of markets when the going gets tough rather than hanging in and fighting it out. Another manifestation is the tendency to license forefront technology to competing nations (again, read Japan) in order to garner a fast payoff – but thereby helping those competitors to steal away one's business in the longer term.[27]

The fragmentation argument holds that, in part at least,

[26] We should also note that an extremely weak dollar may also have adverse macroeconomic consequences – including renewed inflation – whose specific effects on the microelectronics industry would be hard to predict.

[27] Reich and Mankin (1986), for example, describe this practice as "giving away our future."

management short-sightedness of this sort is not so much a cause of flagging competitiveness as it is a manifestation of deeper structural problems. The American semiconductor industry has at its core a group of relatively small merchant firms which are not systematically integrated either within semiconductor production or into systems manufacture. This is in sharp contrast to the Japanese structure of relatively large, similarly sized, vertically integrated producers. As a result, the argument goes, the Japanese firms are better able to co-ordinate strategy for the longer run and are better able to weather downturns. Coupled with the lower turnover rates for engineers and managers in Japan, this also means that Japanese firms are better able to appropriate the technical knowledge they generate or acquire.

Both of these arguments merit serious consideration. Indeed, our study does in fact support some aspects of them. In order properly to assess these claims, however, we first need to disentangle two issues – two sets of phenomena – that are inevitably confused in discussions of American–Japanese competition.

It used to be popular among American historians to discuss something called the "frontier thesis" – the notion that American economic and cultural history was shaped in large part by the existence of a vast western frontier. There is also a kind of "frontier thesis" in the history of post-war economic growth and technological development.[28] The "frontier" in this version is a technological one, and the tenor of the argument is entirely different. But one basic idea is analogous: a country's industrial development has to be understood in light of the existence of a technological frontier and, in particular, in terms of that country's proximity to the frontier.

There is one central fact that distinguishes life on the frontier from life further back: uncertainty.[29] This is not to say merely that high-technology is a risky business; rather, it means primarily that the road ahead is foggy at best. No one knows for sure which technological path will yield success, which new device will find a market, which approaches will fly. By contrast, firms which are not technological leaders have a much better idea what success will look like. The path has already been cleared, if not necessarily paved. And the successes of the leaders serve as guiding beacons.

The implication is a simple and important one. What is appropriate in getting to the frontier may be wholly inappropriate for staying there or for advancing the frontier. Market structures, organizational forms, corporate strategies, and government poli-

[28] See especially Rosenberg (1982, Chapter 12).

[29] For an elaboration of this point see Nelson and Winter (1977).

cies desirable in one regime may be entirely dysfunctional in the other. This is a crucial consideration; yet it is routinely forgotten in discussions of competitiveness. In order to make sense of the American (or European) competitive position, we have to ask the following distinct questions. Which aspects of Japanese structure, strategy, and government policies are responsible for the phenomenal feat of catch-up those firms have performed? And which aspects make them formidable competitors now that they have caught up? The answers may be quite different.

To begin addressing these questions, we need to look back at history. Japan and Europe were devastated by World War II in a way that left the United States the undisputed economic and technological leader for more than two decades. The transistor was invented at Bell Labs at a time when rubble was still being cleared from Tokyo and Berlin. Chapter 2 tells the subsequent story in more detail: semiconductor technology developed, and the semiconductor industry sprang up, almost entirely in the United States. Government policy, especially defense procurement, played an important role in the early days; but the chips were being laid (if one will pardon the expression) by a diversity of private firms, often small and entrepreneurial.[30] There is reason to think that this combination – a diverse, flexible set of firms and a light-handed government – is an effective one for advancing the technological frontier, especially when the technology involved is radically new and potentially powerful.

The task for Europe and Japan was one of rebuilding. Highly industrialized before the war, these countries found themselves without much physical capital but with a good deal of human capital intact in workers and managers.[31] The low starting point and the high potential for reindustrialization led to high rates of growth in both regions. Not surprisingly, the flow of technology was largely unidirectional: from the United States to Europe and Japan. The catch-up countries could take advantage of what the United States was learning by a painful trial-and-error process – but without having to make the same mistakes themselves. Not surprisingly,

[30] As Egelhoff (1986, p. 36) notes, however, the continuing influence of defense-related support on the American industry has favored a concentration on product rather than process technology. (This is because the Defense Department provided a willing market for innovative devices in which cost is of decidedly secondary importance.) By contrast, government support in Japan, which was entirely commercial in orientation, led to a greater emphasis on process technology. Thus government policy is also part of the explanation for the different structural and strategic paths taken in the two regions.

[31] And, if Mancur Olson (1982) is right, these countries also benefited from the destruction of moribund institutions and reactionary pressure groups.

then, for this and other reasons we do not find in either Europe or Japan a decentralized structure of small, entrepreneurial firms. Instead, we find the development of microelectronics in the hands of larger, more vertically integrated units. Just as the American structure makes sense for a regime of rapid trial-and-error learning, so the Japanese structure arguably makes sense for a regime of consolidation and catch-up.

How are we to account for the greater success of Japan relative to Europe under similar circumstances? This is too complex a question to be answered in passing.[32] Perhaps the much-discussed "cultural factors" are to blame. Or perhaps the remnants of the *zaibatsu* structure, inherited from the time of the Meiji Restoration, gave Japan a more solid base on which to build. Most likely, however, the answer lies in differences in government policy, both industrial policy in particular and economic policy in general. We discussed some of the differences in Chapter 7. European industrial policies were often conflicting and sometimes – as in the case of France – downright destructive of the ability of indigenous firms to achieve commercial success. Despite the superficial similarities of Japanese and European policy – both appearing interventionist and protectionist – the Japanese policies worked better. This may have been because the Japanese were more skillful in designing and carrying out the policies; or it may have been merely that MITI permitted or encouraged the development of a large cadre of aggressive, competitive firms – firms that would ultimately have succeeded whatever the policies of government.

In any event, the contrast between the United States and Japan remains sharp. The structure and strategy of Japanese industry was well adapted to imitating and borrowing from the United States. How did this borrowing take place?[33] Contrary to the now-fashionable argument, licenses from American firms were a quite small part of the story. It is certainly true that Japanese government policy restricted FDI into Japan and discouraged imports through tariffs and less-explicit controls. This left licensing as the principal avenue for American firms to sell their forefront know-how to Japan. And the Japanese government acted as a gatekeeper, helping to screen licensors and to negotiate favorable terms for its firms. But the licenses themselves were neither short-sighted nor the primary vehicle by which the Japanese built their capabilities. The Americans never licensed technology crucial to their competitive positions, and always held back from the forefront. Moreover, the licenses were largely for legal purposes – to ward off lawsuits or,

[32] But for a detailed discussion of this issue, see Malerba (1985).

[33] This paragraph draws on Finan (1982).

more importantly, American government reaction to massive patent infringement. The licenses themselves involved little direct transfer of technologies that the Japanese had not already acquired through other means. Apart from Western Electric, which allowed liberal visiting privileges to licensees,[34] there was little contact between licensor and licensee. It seems quite clear that the Japanese caught up by developing their own R&D capabilities and by taking advantage of what was available in the public domain in the USA. Indeed, if licensing had anything to do with the Japanese success, it was in a way quite different from what is normally supposed; by charging royalties, which the Japanese firms found increasingly onerous, the American firms encouraged the development of an indigenous R&D capability in Japan.

It is also clear that, as Japanese technology developed, the one-way licensing became a two-way flow. Licenses for royalties gave way to mutual cross-licensing. Now, one hears it said that even today the Japanese are getting essentially all the benefits of technology flow from the USA and are giving up little in return.[35] But this is not the picture that emerges from our study of technology-sharing agreements. Most of the flow of technology between the United States and Japan is now fully bi-directional. American firms typically license product designs (which are easily reverse-engineered in any case) or sometimes design software; in return, the Japanese license production technology. Neither partner is likely to be giving up its most competitive, forefront technology. In a sense, the Japanese are in principle giving up more – since, as we saw in Chapter 6 and will see again, process technology is a crucial element of any strategy in microelectronics. What makes the Japanese appear to be gaining disproportionately from these agreements is not that the agreements are one-sided but that the Japanese are able to make more visible use of what they receive. Because the Japanese are strong in process technology, gaining access to a new product puts a Japanese firm in a position to compete with its American licensor in that market. By contrast, gaining access to Japanese production technology helps keep the American partner nearer the leading edge in that area, but it does not open up an obvious new front on which to compete with the Japanese. We will return to these issues in a moment.

[34] For various reasons, notably the 1956 Consent Decree by the Antitrust Division of the Justice Department, AT&T maintained from the very beginning an open policy not only toward cross-licensing but toward technology-sharing in general. Japan took advantage of this, and maintained a close relationship with Bell Laboratories.

[35] Ferguson (1985, pp. 100–103); Reich and Mankin (1986, pp. 81–83).

Now that Japan has undeniably reached the technological frontier, many – but not all – of the features characteristic of Japanese firms in their catch-up years are disappearing. What is most significant about this is that the features disappearing from Japan at the frontier are precisely those that come up in discussions of how the United States ought to emulate Japan. One example is government-funded co-operative research. The VLSI project was extremely helpful to firms seeking to catch up – and eventually surpass – the Americans in process technology. Since the American competition was already relatively advanced in VLSI research and technology, the Japanese research partners did not have to fear that those competitors would reap large spillover benefits from what the VLSI project developed. By contrast, firms engaging in co-operative research to extend the frontier have far greater reason to worry about competitors free-riding on their work. Not surprisingly, then, we see today far less emphasis on government-sponsored co-operative research in Japan and greater emphasis on appropriable in-house work. The 5G computer project is a successor to the VLSI project in that it seeks to raise Japanese capabilities up to (and, again, perhaps beyond) American levels in a technological area – computers – where American firms still clearly set the pace.

Another area of change in Japan as it reaches the frontier is a slow liberalization of restrictive trade policies. Restrictions are slowly coming down in such areas as imports, foreign investment, and credit-market controls. Moreover, whatever MITI's role in helping to shape a young semiconductor industry, it is increasingly a dog being wagged by its own corporate tail.

It is more than a little ironic, then, that the most widely discussed proposals in the United States include government-financed co-operative research, restrictive trade policies of various sorts, and the creation of an American ministry of trade. Such proposals arguably fall victim of the "Japanese model" at its most misleading, confusing institutions useful in achieving the frontier with structures and policies adapted to competing at the leading edge.

Life at the Frontier

Seeing Japanese competition in historical perspective should have a cautionary effect. But it need not lead to complacency. A strong trend of increased Japanese competitive power may only reflect a quite natural catching-up phase in which Japanese firms will share the frontier with American (and European) firms. As Japanese firms achieve the frontier, as indeed they have in many if not most areas, we should expect to see a slowing in the rate of increase of Japanese market share and a convergence to a more stable (or more slowly changing) world market. But history suggests another scenario as well. When American manufacturing overtook the then-dominant British industry in the nineteenth century (based, like the Japanese success, on techniques of low-cost mass-production), British firms were unable to respond, dooming British manufacturing to a decline from which it has yet to emerge. It is, of course, this second model on which American (and European) fears are based.

The macroeconomic factors mentioned above make it difficult at this point to disentangle the two scenarios. But there remains much we can say at the microeconomic level about the factors that will influence the path of competition to come.

One manifestation of Japanese accession to the frontier, we argued, is the evolution of a number of Japanese institutions in the direction of their American counterparts. History is not easily undone, however, and there remain many other aspects of Japanese industry that remain different from those in the United States. How many of these are accidents of history – holdovers from the Japanese period of catch-up that have no important competitive value now? And how many reflect institutions, organizational structures, and corporate strategies that convey, and will continue to convey, a genuine competitive advantage at the frontier? This is the question we now have to answer.

Let us begin by taking stock. One legacy of history, we saw, is that the Japanese microelectronics industry consists of ten or more similarly sized firms. These firms are vertically integrated both within the semiconductor business and "downstream" into systems. The strategies of these firms are quite similar, at least relative to those of American firms. Japanese microelectronics firms fall into two main groups: those emphasizing a full line of semiconductor products and those focusing on a smaller line of (usually) consumer-related products. In both cases, however, the firms tend to concentrate strongly on manufacturing competence and low-cost production – not unique product or market advantages – as the source of their competitive advantage. Egelhoff (1986) found that even firms in the second group (those not offering a full line) normally look to low-cost production first, and often follow what he calls an "enhanced" niche strategy that involves producing at least some standardized products (such as DRAMs). As a result of this market structure and this strategic similarity, Japanese firms are intensely competitive among themselves; moreover, since these firms compete not by trying different strategies but by striving to implement a common strategy more successfully, they appear as particularly fierce competitors outside Japan, where firms are more diverse in both structure and strategy. Contrary to the perception that Japanese firms "co-operate" more with one another than do Western firms, the vertically integrated full-line structure makes Japanese microelectronics firms in fact more self-sufficient than most of their American or European counterparts. This allows them to appropriate to themselves and to retain more completely the benefits of any technological capabilities they develop. And, despite similarities in strategy, Japanese firms are far more diverse in their corporate organizational structures than are American or European firms.[36] This reflects a lower degree of communication among Japanese firms (via worker turnover, etc.) as well as the diminished influence of Western business-school dicta. One similarity, though, is that Japanese firms tend to be organized more along "functional" lines than along product lines.[37] This means that the organization is geared to concentrate on functions – especially the manufacturing function – rather than on seeking out and developing new products or markets.

History has left a different pattern in the United States. The American semiconductor industry consists of a large, diverse set of firms. These firms are diverse not only in size – ranging from the behemoth of IBM to small start-up firms – but also in structure. Some firms are captive divisions of systems houses; others are merchant divisions of larger firms; others are stand-alone merchants. The firms are diverse also in strategy. Some have a strategy of wholly captive production; others are merchants with a relatively full line of products; others attack niches that they know will soon turn into competitive battlegrounds; and still others seek out stable niches of a more familiar sort. What unites all these strategies – and what distinguishes the American strategy from Japanese – is that the American firms are oriented more to development of unique products or market advantages than to competing on price and quality in undifferentiated markets.[38] To put it another way, American firms tend to compete by finding better strategies rather than by trying to implement a common strategy more successfully. This bias is enshrined in American corporate organization charts, which show a much greater product orientation and a much lower "functional" organization. As a consequence, American capabili-

[36] Egelhoff (1986, p. 50).
[37] Egelhoff (1986, p. 52).
[38] The captive producers, especially IBM, do not fit neatly into this pigeonhole and should be considered separately.

ties are greatest in product design, new-product innovation, and customer relations – and are relatively weaker in process technology. This product orientation is a legacy of America's early adaptation to life alone on the frontier, helped along by the incentives of Defense Department procurement and R&D support.

European firms are a mixture of the Japanese and American models. Like the Japanese – and for many of the same historical reasons – European microelectronics firms are by and large vertically integrated systems houses, although the degree and consistency of integration is usually not as great as in Japan. There are few small start-up firms or stand-alone merchants in Europe. But unlike the Japanese – and like the Americans – European firms are more oriented to developing products than to competing on cost in high-volume standardized markets. In view of the poor performance of European firms relative to Japanese and American competition, one might argue that the European compromise is the worst of both worlds – lacking both the manufacturing efficiency of Japan and the product flexibility of the USA. Of course, this does not mean that European firms will not be able to adapt or that changing conditions in the market may not turn some disadvantages to advantages.

This is indeed the question: which of these structures is likely to prove most successful in the near future? The answer will depend on two factors: (1) the evolution of the semiconductor market and (2) the ability of firms in each region to adapt to changing conditions. Let us consider these in turn.

As the industry has developed in the last few years, the Japanese package appears unbeatable. Overall, the Japanese have taken a "fast second" approach. They have targeted market niches pioneered by American firms and, using superior production efficiency, have systematically gained market share. This strategy works well if one can maintain the forefront in low-cost production and if the niches one attacks are potentially wide enough to benefit from large-scale production. This was eminently true of the market for mass memories, and it is also proving true (to perhaps a lesser extent) of the market for standardized microprocessors.

By contrast, the American picture looks considerably bleaker under these conditions. American firms must rely on leadership in product development and marketing. Such a strategy has the tragic flaw of making one a victim of one's own success. Carving out a successful niche often attracts the attention of copycats with superior manufacturing ability, a problem that becomes more serious the more successful the carving. This leaves American firms with the choice of finding a more permanent (but therefore most likely smaller) niche or of hopping from innovation to innovation, one step ahead of the Japanese.

Why do American firms not roll up their sleeves and fight it out with their Japanese competition rather than leaving the market behind when the going gets tough? Some of this may have to do with what managers believe, including what they have learned in business schools. The idea that one should jettison unprofitable divisions or product areas makes sense only if there are no significant interdependencies between those areas and other, more profitable, ones. In microelectronics, it is widely believed that process technology is the key to success in other areas. And significant experience in high-volume production of standardized devices – even though unprofitable on its merits – is an important way to gain the necessary experience and maintain the forefront. To abandon DRAMs, for example, may be a mistake even in a glutted market in which one has no hope of being the cost leader.[39] But management attitudes are probably only part of the story. It may also be that the corporate organization of American firms, geared as it is to product and away from process considerations, makes it difficult for firms to fight battles on cost. Furthermore, and perhaps most significantly, it may be that the fragmented, decentralized nature of the American merchant industry encourages withdrawal because it lacks the Japanese mechanisms of strategic cross-subsidization within a vertically integrated structure.[40]

European firms have been perhaps even more vulnerable to the Japanese fast-second strategy than have the American, largely because they were seldom first to begin with. European firms have American as well as Japanese interlopers to contend with, and they have not so far shown themselves as nimble as the Americans in seeking out new niches to inhabit when the old ones are stolen. To varying degrees, the European microelectronics industry has hidden behind EEC protection and sometimes outright government subsidy. The one bright spot for Europe is that its structure of large, vertically integrated firms eliminates the difficulties some smaller American firms would have in implementing a policy of strategic cross-subsidization or of otherwise mimicking the Japanese. The joint development effort for submicron process tech-

[39] This is evidently the rationale behind the "enhanced" niche strategy described by Egelhoff (1986): participation in some commodity markets makes sense for a niche player if the spillover benefits to the niche technology are important. It is significant that most of the firms using this approach are Japanese and none (in the sample) is American.

[40] That is to say, a stand-alone merchant cannot finance a strategic loss in one market from revenues earned elsewhere with the same ease as can a larger, vertically integrated firm.

nology that Philips and Siemens are undertaking (with government subsidy) is at least some indication of a move in this direction.[41]

Nevertheless the issue remains: is the semiconductor market likely to continue to evolve in a way that favors the Japanese structures? Under one plausible scenario, the answer is yes. The microelectronics industry seems to be maturing, at least relative to what it looked like a few years ago. Capital set-up costs are escalating, as are the costs of R&D.[42] Perhaps a structure of flexible, entrepreneurial firms will never again have the value it once did. If we are entering an era of consolidation and incremental innovation, perhaps the Japanese model of vertical integration, large corporate resources, and manufacturing leadership cannot be beaten – and American industry will have to adopt this structure or fall by the wayside. This scenario is implicit in all the most dire of popular prognostications and in many of the recent policy proposals, including those by the Defense Science Board and the Semiconductor Industry Association,[43] that call for a massive federal program aimed at challenging Japanese firms in DRAM production.

This scenario may come to pass. But it is by no means the only possible one.

The fast-second approach, especially when buttressed by strength in high-volume production, requires a diet of fresh niches – and of sufficiently large niches – in order to produce continual growth. Under one plausible scenario, the market may not continue to offer up as tempting a menu as it so far has. It is certainly true that the trend in process technology has been to increased capital-intensity, favoring long production runs. But improvements in process technology are also having the opposite effect of lowering the unit cost of small production runs. If this trend continues, it will increase the market for – and the importance of – so-called application-specific ICs (or ASICs). As we saw in Chapter 2, there are several techniques for tailoring the design of a chip to specific uses. Such chips generally perform better in systems applications but are more costly than standardized ICs. If the relative cost of producing tailored ICs declines, then considerations of design and marketing become paramount and the payoffs to finely tuned

[41] Also, Egelhoff lists one European firm along with the several Japanese firms pursuing enhanced niche strategies.

[42] On which see Chapter 3.

[43] David E. Sanger, "A Pentagon Study Urges U.S. Aid for the Embattled Chip Industry," *The New York Times*, 13 February, 1987, p. A1; Peter Waldman and Brenton R. Schlender, "Is a Big Federal Role the Way to Revitalize Semiconductor Firms?" *The Wall Street Journal*, 17 February, 1987, p. 1. See also, Sumney and Burger (1987).

manufacture decline rapidly. Of course, the Japanese may continue to invade the niches carved out around these application-specific chips. But, as the designs become increasingly specific, the Japanese strength in high-volume production will give them no advantage. To compete, Japanese firms will have to adapt by imitating American capabilities in product innovation, design, and customer relations. The Japanese may well do this, but such a feat would represent a kind of threat distinctly different from the one against which current policy proposals are trying to gird American industry. Moreover, as Egelhoff (1986, p. 101 and *passim*) hints, this kind of reorientation would probably be as difficult for the Japanese as the analogous adaptation to Japanese structure and strategy would be for American firms.

A related aspect of the ASIC scenario – and one that is widely believed in the industry – is that semiconductor production will become much more closely integrated with systems manufacture (especially computer manufacture). Computer makers can gain competitive performance advantages by using specially designed chips. Such customized chips replicate in hardware what would require complicated software if standardized chips were used – but they do so in a way that is much more difficult for competitors to copy. In a sense, then, the niche advantages of ASICs are likely increasingly to be translated "downstream." Will the Japanese computer industry gain more from this situation than the American?[44] Despite claims that an advantage to the Japanese is obvious,[45] it is not at all clear who will benefit most from this development. It is almost certainly the case that some captive production by computer and other systems firms will become increasingly important. Several of the largest American firms – AT&T, DEC, and HP in addition to IBM – already have substantial captive capabilities. The remainder are more dependent on the merchant market. A nimble and innovative American merchant market, however, geared to ASICs and to close customer relations, may be a distinct advantage to these smaller American computer firms.

We can also ask these same kinds of questions from a broader perspective. Is the microelectronics industry really becoming more "mature"? As we saw, there is some reason to think that it is. On the other hand, it is always far too easy to underestimate the possibilities for novelty and for radical transformation in any industry – we all have an inevitable cognitive bias toward patterns and trends already familiar. If the microelectronics industry does

[44] A detailed discussion of the computer industry is beyond the scope of this report, but it is an obvious and important area for follow-on research.

[45] Ferguson (1985, pp. 113–116).

have some radical changes left up its sleeve, a decentralized, entrepreneurial industry is probably the most effective structure for initiating these changes and taking best early advantage of them.

And this raises an often-overlooked point. The future shape of the semiconductor market is not necessarily an inevitability, something that corporate or government policy can only try to forecast and adapt passively to. In many respects, the future is shaped by conscious choice, including both corporate and political choices. If this is so, the fear of a mature market perfectly adapted to Japanese capabilities could actually become a self-fulfilling nightmare. By attempting to reshape American industry in the (perceived) Japanese image, American policy may actually bring about a less-innovative, production-oriented market in which the Japanese have the advantage. In contrast, policies that emphasize and enhance existing American strengths in ASICs, product design, innovation, and close customer links may help shift the competitive battle more firmly on to fields American firms are comfortable in.

These scenarios are neither exclusive nor exhaustive, of course. Rather than attempting to predict the future, we can turn the question around and ask: which sets of institutions and corporate structures are likely to respond most flexibly to the future, whatever it brings? There are two ways that a population of firms can respond to changed conditions. Either the existing firms can change their structures and behavior to keep up with changing conditions, or the composition of the population as a whole can change, winnowing out the ill-adapted firms and rewarding the well-adapted ones. In relatively homogeneous populations like those of Japan or Europe, one might expect adaptation, to the extent it occurs, to take place in the first way – by changes in the existing firms. The large, vertically integrated firms in both regions certainly have the resources and potential to adapt, if not necessarily to set the pace of change. By contrast, the highly diverse American structure may well adapt to the future in the second – and perhaps more painful – way. A population of entrepreneurial merchant firms is, as we argued, a population geared for rapid trial-and-error learning. Even at its most successful, such an industry will produce a steady stream of casualties along with a few big winners. Indeed, bankruptcies can often be as much a sign of rapid progress as of decline. A structural shift away from rapid and toward incremental change, especially a shift based on mass-manufacturing capability, will certainly wreak havoc in the American industry, probably forcing considerable consolidation and destroying many smaller, stand-alone firms. The positive side, however, is that a diverse population is normally quite resistant to extinction. Consolidation and shake-out is likely to bring to the surface a few strong American firms – and this will probably hold whatever the nature of the changes the future brings. By contrast, a more homogeneous population unable to change its ways is in greater danger of permanent decline.

Bibliography

Anonymous (1984). "Reshaping the Computer Industry: for Companies Big and Small, Collaboration is the Key to Survival," *Business Week*, 16 July, p. 84.

Bloom, Justin (1984). "Japan's MITI As a Policy Instrument in the Development of Information Technology" (Harvard University: Center for Information Policy Research), Report P-84-6, p. 73.

Borrus, Michael, Millstein, James E. and Zysman, John (1983). "Trade and Development in the Semiconductor Industry: Japanese Challenge and American Response," in John Zysman and Laura Tyson (eds) *American Industry in International Competition: Government Policies and Corporate Strategies*. (Ithaca: Cornell University Press).

Braun, E. and Macdonald, S. (1978). *Revolution in Miniature* (Cambridge: Cambridge University Press).

Brueckner, Leslie with Borrus, Michael (1984). "Assessing the Commercial Impact of the VHSIC Program," Working Paper (Berkeley Roundtable on the International Economy, University of California, Berkeley).

Chang, Y. S. (1971). *Transfer of Technology: Economics of Offshore Assembly, The Case of the Semiconductor Industry* (UNITAR Research Report No. 11. New York: United Nations Institute for Training and Research).

Charles River Associates (1979). "International Technological Competitiveness: Television Receivers and Semiconductors". (Unpublished).

Dickson, David (1983). "Britain Rises to Japan's Computer Challenge," *Science*, vol. 220, 20 May, p. 799.

Dickson, David (1984). "Europe Seeks Joint Computer Research Effort," *Science*, vol. 223, 6 January, p. 28.

Egelhoff, William G. (1986). "Business Strategies and Competition in the Semiconductor Industry – A Comparative Study across U.S., Japanese, and European Firms," Center for Science and Technology Policy, School of Management, Rensselaer Polytechnic Institute.

English, Maurice and Watson Brown, Adam (1984). "Japanese National Actions in I.T.," Commission of the European Communities, Information Technology Task Force, Draft Eight.

Erdilek, Asim (1987). "Strategic Trade Policy in the Globalization of Imperfect and Dynamic Competition: the Case of the Semiconductor Industry." (Draft manuscript, Case Western Reserve University).

Ernst, Dieter (1981). *Restructuring World Industry in a Period of Crisis – The Role of Innovation* (Vienna: United Nations Industrial Development Organization).

Farnoux, Abel (1983). "Mission Filière électronique" (Rapport de synthèse. Paris: Ministère de la recherche et de la technologie).

Ferguson, Charles H. (1985). "American Microelectronics in Decline: Evidence, Analysis, and Alternatives," VLSI Memo No. 85–284 (Microsystems Research Center, Massachusetts Institute of Technology).

Finan, W. F (1975). "International Transfer of Semiconductor Technology Through U.S. Based Firms" (New York: National Bureau of Economic Research Working Paper no. 118), December.

Finan, W. F. (1982). "The Exchange of Semiconductor Technology between Japan and the United States," in C. Uyehara (ed.), *U.S.–Japan Technological Exchange Symposium* (Washington: University Press of America).

Flaherty, M. Therese (1983). "Market Share, Technology Leadership, and Competition in International Semiconductor Markets," in Richard S. Rosenbloom (ed.), *Research on Technological Innovation, Management and Policy*, vol. 1 (Greenwich, Conn.: JAI Press).

Flaherty, M. Therese (1984a). "Field Research on the Link Between Technological Innovation and Growth: Evidence from the International Semiconductor Industry," *American Economic Review*, May, pp. 67–72.

Flaherty, M. Therese (1984b). "Determinants of Market Share in International Semiconductor Markets," in *Race for a New Frontier* (New York: Simon and Schuster).

Flaherty, M. Therese, and Itami, Hiroyuki (1984). "Finance," in Daniel I. Okimoto, Takuo Sugano and Franklin B. Weinstein (eds), *Competitive Edge: The Semiconductor Industry in the U.S. and Japan* (Stanford: Stanford University Press).

Fusfeld, H. I. (1986). *The Technical Enterprise* (Cambridge: Ballinger).

Fusfeld, H. I. and Haklisch, C. S. (1985). "Cooperative R&D for Competitors," *Harvard Business Review*, November/December, pp. 60–67.

Fusfeld, H. I. and Langlois, R. N. (eds) (1982). *Understanding R&D Productivity* (New York: Pergamon Press).

Gresser, J. (1980). *High Technology and Japanese Industrial Policy: A Strategy for U.S. Policymakers* (Subcommittee on Trade, Committee on Ways and Means, U.S. House of Representatives, October).

Grossman, Gene M., and Shapiro, Carl (1986). "Research Joint Ventures: An Antitrust Analysis," *Journal of Law, Economics, and Organization* vol. 2, no. 2, pp. 315–37.

Grunwald, Joseph, and Flamm, Kenneth (1985). *Global Factory: Foreign Assembly in International Trade* (Washington, D.C.: Brookings Institution).

Gutmanis, I. (1979). "Statement on Behalf of the Electronic Industries Association of Japan Before the U.S. International Trade Commission" (Washington, D.C.: Sterling Hobe Corporation), May.

Haklisch, Carmela S. (1986). "Technical Alliances in the Semiconductor Industry" (Center for Science and Technology Policy, School of Management, Rensselaer Polytechnic Institute), February.

Haklisch, C. S., Fusfeld, H. I. and Levenson, A. (1984). "Trends in Collective Industrial Research" (Center for Science and Technology Policy, Graduate School of Business Administration, New York University).

Hazewindus, Nico with Tooker, John (1982). *The U.S. Microelectronics Industry* (New York: Pergamon Press).

Hladik, Karen J. (1985). *International Joint Ventures: An Economic Analysis of U.S.–Foreign Business Partnerships* (Lexington, Mass.: D. C. Heath).

Imai, Ken-ichi, and Sakuma, Akimitsu (1983). "An Industrial Organization Analysis of the Semiconductor Industry: A U.S.–Japan Comparison" (Institute of Business Research, Hitotsubashi University, Discussion Paper no. 113), December.

Integrated Circuit Engineering Corporation (1980). *Status 1980* (Scottsdale, AZ: Integrated Circuit Engineering Corp.)

Integrated Circuit Engineering Corporation (1981). *Status 1981* (Scottsdale, AZ: Integrated Circuit Engineering Corp.)

Integrated Circuit Engineering Corporation (1982). *Status 1982* (Scottsdale, AZ: Integrated Circuit Engineering Corp.)

Integrated Circuit Engineering Corporation (1983). *Status 1983* (Scottsdale, AZ: Integrated Circuit Engineering Corp.)

Integrated Circuit Engineering Corporation (1984). *Status 1984* (Scottsdale, AZ: Integrated Circuit Engineering Corp.)

Integrated Circuit Engineering Corporation (1985). *Status 1985* (Scottsdale, AZ: Integrated Circuit Engineering Corp.)

Integrated Circuit Engineering Corporation (1986). *Status 1986* (Scottsdale, AZ: Integrated Circuit Engineering Corp.)

Integrated Circuit Engineering Corporation (1987). *Status 1987* (Scottsdale, AZ: Integrated Circuit Engineering Corp.)

Japan Electronic Industry Development Association (1980). *Future of the Japanese Electronic Industry* (Tokyo: Fuji Corporation).

Julian, Ken (1985). "Defense Program Pushes Microchip Frontiers," *High Technology*, May, p. 49.

Kimura, Yui (1986). *Competitive Strategies and Strategic Groups in the Japanese Semiconductor Industry* (Ph.D. dissertation, New York University, Graduate School of Business Administration).

Lake, Arthur (1976). "Transnational Activity and Market Entry in the Semiconductor Industry" (New York: National Bureau of Economic Research), Working Paper no. 126.

Levin, Richard C. (1982a). "Semiconductor Industry," in Richard R. Nelson (ed), *Government and Technical Progress: A Cross-Industry Analysis* (New York: Pergamon Press).

Levin, Richard C. (1982b). "R&D Productivity in the Semiconductor Industry: Is a Slowdown Imminent?" in H. I. Fusfeld and R. N. Langlois (eds), *Understanding R&D Productivity* (New York: Pergamon Press).

Little, Arthur D. (1980). *World Semiconductor Industry in Transition: 1978–83* (Cambridge, Mass.: Arthur D. Little Decision Resources), February.

MacKnight, Susan (1987). "U.S.–Japan Competition in Semiconductors: American Makers Rethink Strategies," *JEI Report*, no. 16A, April 24.

Malerba, Franco (1983). *Technological Change, Market Structure and Government Policy: The Evolution of the European Semiconductor Industry* (Ph.D. dissertation, Yale University).

Malerba, Franco (1985). *The Semiconductor Business: The Economics of Rapid Growth and Decline* (Madison: University of Wisconsin Press).

Ministère de l'Industrie et de la Recherche (1983). "La Politique Industrielle de la Filière Electronique" (Paris).

Moore, Gordon E. (1979). "VLSI: Some Fundamental Challenges," *IEEE Spectrum*, April, pp. 30–47.

Moxon, Richard W. (1974). "Offshore Production in the Less Developed Countries," *Bulletin*, New York University, Institute of Finance, no. 98–99.

Moxon, Richard W. (1980). "Effects of Offshore and Onshore Foreign Direct Investment in Electronics: A Survey" (Unpublished).

National Academy of Engineering and National Research Council (1984). *Competitive Status of the U.S. Electronics Industry* (Washington, D.C.: National Academy Press).

Nelson, Richard R. (ed.) (1982). *Government and Technical Progress: A Cross-Industry Analysis* (New York: Pergamon Press).

Nelson, Richard R. (1984). *High-Technology Policies: A Five-Nation Comparison* (Washington: American Enterprise Institute).

Nelson, Richard R. and Langlois, Richard N. (1983). "Industrial Innovation Policy: Lessons from American History," *Science*, vol. 219, 18 February, pp. 814–18.

Nelson, Richard R. and Winter, Sidney G. (1977). "In Search of Useful Theory of Innovation," *Research Policy* 6, pp. 36–76.

Office of Technology Assessment (1983). *International Competitiveness in Electronics* (Washington DC: Government Printing Office).

Okimoto, Daniel I., Sugano, Takuo and Weinstein, Franklin B. (eds) (1984). *Competitive Edge: The Semiconductor Industry in the U.S. and Japan* (Stanford: Stanford University Press).

Olson, Mancur (1982). *The Rise and Decline of Nations* (New Haven: Yale University Press).

Ordover, Janusz and Willig, Robert (1985). "Antitrust for High-Technology Industries: Assessing Research Joint Ventures and Mergers," *Journal of Law and Economics* vol 28, no. 2, pp. 311–334.

Organization for Economic Co-operation and Development (1984). *Trade in High Technology Products: The Semiconductor Industry* (Paris: Directorate for Science, Technology and Industry).

Organization for Economic Co-operation and Development (1985). *Semiconductor Industry: Trade Related Issues* (Paris: Directorate for Science, Technology and Industry).

Peters, Lois S. and Fusfeld, Herbert I. (1982). "Current U.S. University–Industry Research Connections," in *University–Industry Research Partnerships* (Washington: National Science Board).

Porter, Michael E (1980). *Competitive Strategy: Techniques for Analyzing Industries and Competitors* (New York: The Free Press).

Porter, Michael E. (1983). "Technological Dimension of Competitive Strategy," in Richard S. Rosenbloom (ed.). *Research on Technological Innovation, Management and Policy*, vol. 1 (Greenwich, Conn.: (JAI Press).

Porter, Michael E. (1985). *Competitive Advantage: Creating and Sustaining Superior Performance* (New York: The Free Press).

Pugel, Thomas, Kimura, Yui and Hawkins, Robert (1984). "Semiconductors and Computers: Emerging Competitive Battlegrounds in the Asia-Pacific Region," in R. Moxon, T. Roehl, and J. Truitt (eds). *International Business Strategies in the Asia-Pacific Region* (Greenwich, Conn.: JAI Press).

Reich, Robert B. and Mankin, Eric (1986). "Joint Ventures with Japan Give Away our Future," *Harvard Business Review*, March–April, pp. 78–86.

Rosenberg, Nathan (1982). *Inside the Black Box: Technology and Economics* (New York: Cambridge University Press).

Rosenberg, Nathan (1986). "Civilians 'Spillovers' from Military R&D Spending: the American Experience since World War II," paper presented at a Conference on Technical Co-operation and International Competitiveness, April 2–4, Il Ciocco Conference Center, Italy.

Sciberras, Edmond (1977). *Multinational Electronics Companies and National Economic Policies* (Greenwich, CT: JAI Press).

Sciberras, Edmond (1986). "Scientific and Technological Exchanges and Applied Collective Research among OECD Countries," paper prepared for the Directorate for Science, Technology, and Industry of the OECD (London: The Technical Change Centre), April.

Scott, Bruce R. (1984). "National Strategy for Stronger U.S Competitiveness," *Harvard Business Review*, March–April, pp. 77–91.

Semiconductor Industry Association (1979). *1979 Yearbook and Directory* (Cupertino, CA: Semiconductor Industry Association).

Semiconductor Industry Association (1980). *American Response to the Foreign Industrial Challenge in High Technology Industries* (Cupertino, CA: Semiconductor Industry Association).

Semiconductor Industry Association (1981). *International Microelectronic Challenge* (Cupertino, CA: Semiconductor Industry Association).

Semiconductor Industry Association (1983). *The Effects of Government Targeting on World Semiconductor Competition: A Case History of Japanese Industrial Strategy, and Its Costs for America* (Cupertino, CA: Semiconductor Industry Association). (Preliminary version.)

Sigurdson, Jon (1986). *Industry and State Partnership in Japan: the Very Large Scale Integrated Circuits (VLSI) Project* (Discussion Paper no. 168, Research Policy Institute, University of Lund, Sweden).

Sterling Hobe Corporation (1978). "International Transfer of Semiconductor Technology," prepared for the US Department of Labor, Bureau of International Labor Affairs.

Sumney, Larry W., and Burger, Robert (1987). "Revitalizing the U.S. Semiconductor Industry," *Issues in Science and Technology,* summer, pp. 32–41.

Takai, Toshio (1983). "Setting the Record Straight on Semiconductors," *Journal of Japanese Trade and Industry*, July/August, pp. 7–13.

Tilton, John E. (1971). *International Diffusion of Technology: The Case of Semiconductors* (Washington: Brookings Institution).

Tulder, Rob van and Empel, Eric van (1984). *European Multinationals in the Semiconductor Industry: A Pilot Study* (University of Amsterdam).

US Department of Commerce (1979). *Report on the U.S. Semiconductor Industry* (Washington, D.C.: Government Printing Office).

US Senate, Subcommittee on International Finance of the Committee on Banking, Housing, and Urban Affairs (1980). *Hearings on Trade and Technology in the Electronics Industry* (Washington, D.C.: Government Printing Office).

US Senate, Subcommittee on International Trade (1980). *Conference on U.S. Competitiveness: Can the United States Remain Competitive?* (Washington, D.C.: Government Printing Office).

Webbink, Douglas W (1977). *Semiconductor Industry: A Survey of Structure, Conduct, and Performance* (Washington, D.C.: Federal Trade Commission).

Wheeler, Jimmy, *et al.* (1982). *Japanese Industrial Development Policies in the 1980s: Implications for U.S. Trade and Investment* (New York: Hudson Institute, Research Report HI-3470-RR).

White, Lawrence J. (1985). "Clearing the Legal Path to Cooperative Research," *Technology Review* vol. 88, no. 5, pp. 39–44.

Wilson, Robert W., Ashton, Peter K. and Egan, Thomas P. (1980). *Innovation, Competition, and Government Policy in the Semiconductor Industry* (Lexington, Mass.: D. C. Heath).

Yano Economic Research Institute (1982). *Semiconductor/Microelectronic Industry in Japan* (Tokyo: Yano Economic Research Institute).

Yano Research Institute (1984). *Japanese Semiconductor and IC Industry* (Tokyo: Yano Research Institute).

Zysman, John (1977). *Political Strategies for Industrial Order: State, Market, and Industry in France* (Berkeley: University of California Press).

Zysman, John (1983). *Governments, Markets, and Growth: Financial Systems and the Politics of Industrial Change* (Ithaca: Cornell University Press).

Zysman, John, and Tyson, Laura (eds) (1983). *American Industry in International Competition: Government Policies and Corporate Strategies* (Ithaca: Cornell University Press).

Index